AMC'S **BEST DAY HIKES** IN

THE SHENANDOAH VALLEY

FOUR-SEASON GUIDE TO **50** OF THE BEST TRAILS
FROM HARPERS FERRY TO JEFFERSON NATIONAL FOREST

JENNIFER ADACH AND MICHAEL R. MARTIN

Appalachian Mountain Club Books
Boston, Massachusetts

AMC is a nonprofit organization, and sales of AMC Books fund our mission of protecting the Northeast outdoors. If you appreciate our efforts and would like to become a member or make a donation to AMC, visit outdoors.org, call 800-372-1758, or contact us at Appalachian Mountain Club, 10 City Square, Boston, MA 02129.

outdoors.org/books-maps

Distributed by National Book Network.

Front cover photograph © Michael R. Martin
Back cover photographs © Michael R. Martin (left), Jennifer Adach (right)
Interior photographs by © Jennifer Adach and Michael R. Martin, unless otherwise noted.
Maps by Ken Dumas © Appalachian Mountain Club
Cover design by Gia Giasullo/Studio eg
Interior design by Eric Edstam

Library of Congress Cataloging-in-Publication Data

Adach, Jennifer.
  AMC's best day hikes in the Shenandoah Valley : four-season guide to 50 of the best trails from Harpers Ferry to Jefferson National Forest / Jennifer Adach and Michael R. Martin.
     pages cm
  Includes index.
  ISBN 978-1-62842-017-3 (pbk.)—ISBN 1-62842-017-0 (pbk.) 1. Hiking—Virginia—Shenandoah National Park—Guidebooks. 2. Shenandoah National Park (Va.)—Guidebooks. I. Title.
  GV199.42.V82A33 2015
  796.520975.5'9
                    2015016803

The paper used in this publication meets the minimum requirements of the American National Standard for Information Sciences-Permanence of Paper for Printed Library Materials, ANSI Z39.48-1984. ∞

Outdoor recreation activities by their very nature are potentially hazardous. This book is not a substitute for good personal judgment and training in outdoor skills. Due to changes in conditions, use of the information in this book is at the sole risk of the user. The authors and the Appalachian Mountain Club assume no liability for accidents happening to, or injuries sustained by, readers who engage in the activities described in this book.

Interior pages and cover are printed on responsibly harvested paper stock certified by The Forest Stewardship Council®, an independent auditor of responsible forestry practices.
Printed in the United States of America, using vegetable-based inks.

5 4 3 2   19

In memory of Ernest Adach.

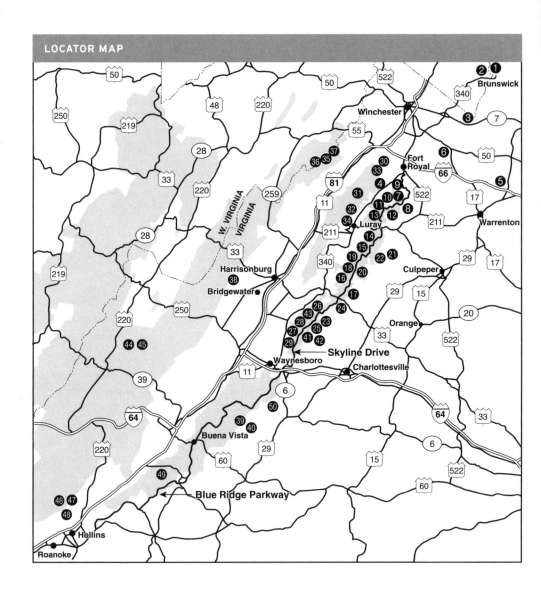

CONTENTS

SECTION 1: HARPERS FERRY AND NORTH VIRGINIA PIEDMONT

SECTION 2: NORTH SHENANDOAH NATIONAL PARK

SECTION 3: CENTRAL SHENANDOAH NATIONAL PARK

SECTION 4: SOUTH SHENANDOAH NATIONAL PARK

SECTION 5: MASSANUTTEN MOUNTAIN

SECTION 6: GREAT NORTH MOUNTAIN AND
THE RAMSEYS DRAFT WILDERNESS

SECTION 7: JEFFERSON NATIONAL FOREST AND THE BLUE RIDGE MOUNTAINS

ESSAYS

APPENDIX

AT-A-GLANCE
TRIP PLANNER

#	Trip	Page	Location (Town)	Rating	Distance and Elevation Gain
	HARPERS FERRY AND NORTH VIRGINIA PIEDMONT				
1	Maryland Heights	3	Harpers Ferry National Historical Park	Moderate	4.4 mi, 1,378 ft
2	Loudoun Heights	8	Harpers Ferry National Historical Park	Strenuous	7.8 mi, 2,278 ft
3	Raven Rocks	12	Bluemont, VA	Moderate	4.7 mi, 1,744 ft
4	Shenandoah River State Park	15	Bentonville, VA	Moderate	6.5 mi, 1,368 ft
5	Bull Run	19	Broad Run, VA	Easy	2.0 mi, 544 ft
6	Sky Meadows State Park	24	Delaplane, VA	Moderate	6.7 mi, 1,575 ft
	NORTH SHENANDOAH NATIONAL PARK				
7	Compton Gap	31	Shenandoah National Park	Easy	2.2 mi, 763 ft
8	Big Devils Stairs	36	Shenandoah National Park	Moderate	4.7 mi, 1,313 ft
9	Dickey Ridge	40	Shenandoah National Park	Easy-Moderate	4.9 mi, 1,130 ft
10	Elkwallow	44	Shenandoah National Park	Easy	3.8 mi, 1,049 ft
11	Overall Run	48	Shenandoah National Park	Strenuous	9.5 mi, 3,094 ft

Estimated Time	Fee	Good for Kids	Dogs Allowed	Waterfalls	Trip Highlights
2-3 hours	$		🐕		Historic landmarks; Civil War ruins
4-5 hours	$		🐕		Jefferson Rock; view over Harpers Ferry
2-3 hours			🐕		Rock hop to big views
3-4 hours	$				River walk over easy terrain
1 hour	$	🚶			Easy, historical walk
3-4 hours	$		🐕		Meadow rambles
1-2 hours	$		🐕		Views; regional geology
2-4 hours	$		🐕		Overlooks; hollows; rhododendron
2-3 hours	$				Park history; family farm ruins
2-3 hours	$	🚶	🐕		Easy walk with ice cream at the end
4-6 hours	$		🐕	〰	Spectacular 93-foot falls

Estimated Time	Fee	Good for Kids	Dogs Allowed	Waterfalls	Trip Highlights
3-5 hours	$		🐕	〰	Classic, wild VA climb
5-8 hours	$		🐕	〰	Wet, wild leg-stretcher
1-2 hours	$		🐕		360-degree views; rock scrambles
1-2 hours	$				Park's second-tallest peak; loop hike
1-2 hours	$		🐕		Waterfalls; Blackrock Cliffs
2-3 hours	$		🐕	〰	Wading in the falls
3-4 hours	$			〰	Two waterfalls; views; loop hike
1-2 hours	$		🐕		Park's highest peak
3-5 hours	$		🐕	〰	Historic presidential retreat
4-7 hours	$				Popular summit; lots of scrambling
3-6 hours	$		🐕	〰	Classic VA hike to an unforgettable waterfall
1 hour	$	🚶			Short, if steep, hike to great views
2-3 hours	$	🚶	🐕		Steady hike; scenic summit
3-5 hours	$		🐕	〰	Attractive waterfall walk
4-7 hours	$		🐕	〰	Pools and cascades deep in the park
5-6 hours	$		🐕		Ridge walk; big views

Estimated Time	Fee	Good for Kids	Dogs Allowed	Waterfalls	Trip Highlights
1–1.5 hours	$		🐕		Gentle hike to 360-degree views
5–6 hours	$		🐕	)))	Swimming holes; waterfalls; big views
4–6 hours			🐕		Knife-edge ridge
2–4 hours			🐕		Views of Fort Valley and more
2–3 hours			🐕		Scramble up to wide vistas
5–6 hours			🐕		Big, big views; varied terrain
5–6 hours			🐕		Rocky ridge walk
3–4 hours			🐕		Cliff-top views
2–4 hours			🐕		Scramble to vistas
4–6 hours			🐕		Big gains; eagle's eye views of the valley
4–7 hours			🐕	)))	Gentle miles; ridge walk; loop hike
1–2 hours			🐕		Rhododendron in the spring; steady climb on a fire road
1–2 hours	$		🐕	)))	Blue Ridge vistas after a steep climb; one of VA's prettiest waterfalls
2–4 hours			🐕		360-degree views of Blue Ridge, piedmont
2–4 hours			🐕		Demanding but quiet climb

#	Trip	Page	Location (Town)	Rating	Distance and Elevation Gain
43	Apple Orchard Falls	197	Glenwood & Pedlar Ranger Districts, George Washington and Jefferson National Forests	Moderate	6.7 mi, 2,438 ft
44	Cold Mountain	201	Glenwood & Pedlar Ranger Districts, George Washington and Jefferson National Forests	Moderate	6.1 mi, 1,586 ft
45	Mount Pleasant	205	Glenwood & Pedlar Ranger Districts, George Washington and Jefferson National Forests	Moderate	6.5 mi, 1,781 ft
46	Tinker Cliffs	209	Eastern Divide Ranger District, Jefferson National Forest	Strenuous	7.2 mi, 2,632 ft
47	McAfee Knob	213	Jefferson National Forest	Moderate	7.7 mi, 2,460 ft
48	Dragon's Tooth	217	Jefferson National Forest	Moderate	4.72 mi, 1,720 ft
49	Devil's Marbleyard	221	Glenwood & Pedlar Ranger Districts, George Washington and Jefferson National Forests	Moderate	3.2 mi, 1,073 ft
50	Three Ridges	225	Glenwood & Pedlar Ranger Districts, George Washington and Jefferson National Forests	Strenuous	13.2 mi, 4,914 ft

Estimated Time	Fee	Good for Kids	Dogs Allowed	Waterfalls	Trip Highlights
3–5 hours			🐕	〰	Popular hike to a 200-foot cascade
5–6 hours			🐕		Alpine meadows with abundant spring wildflowers
3–5 hours			🐕		Expansive views of the Blue Ridge Mountains
3–4 hours			🐕		Jewel of VA's "Triple Crown;" switchbacks and scrambles
3–4 hours			🐕		Jewel of VA's "Triple Crown;" perfect photo spot
3–4 hours			🐕		Jewel of VA's "Triple Crown;" scramble to a striking rock formation
2–3 hours			🐕		Giant marble boulders
6–7 hours				〰	An epic hike; great views and waterfalls

ACKNOWLEDGMENTS

THE OUTPOURING OF SUPPORT FROM OUR FRIENDS AND FAMILIES for this book was overwhelming. People shared their time, gamely posed for pictures, and kept checking in to see what they could do to help. Words fail to express the full extent of our appreciation. Special thank-yous go to Sandra and Paul Shaklan, who let Jen co-opt some of their monthly hikes for this book; Lora Polowczuk for being the wonderful sounding board that she is; Colin Babb for his thoughts on the history of the Shenandoah Valley; and Cynthia and Chuck Hildenbrand for being game to go and try any hike, especially ones that only went uphill.

To Gabi: Listen to your parents, and never lose your sense of wonder. It was a delight to go hiking with you.

The list could be endless. A deep thanks to everyone who joined us on hikes and otherwise provided support: Carrie Graff (BootyLess), Dana Mulhall (Roomie), Mark Anderson (Mountain Slayer), Kerry McGovern, Rob Keast, Haile and Megan McCarthy Gebregziabher, Kim Engle, Jude Hey, Molly Arndt, John Meagher, Jennifer Stern, Mike Hajjar, Amy Kehring, George Ivanov, Maureen Wingfield, Rachel Evans, Joe Matukonis, Douglas Boorstein, KC Yi, Krista Gates, Crystal FitzSimons, Madeleine Levin, Denise Odell, Alexandra Ashbrook, Heather Hartline-Grafton, Jimmy Jin (GQ), Ellen Teller, Etienne Melcher, Betsy Edwards, Stephanie Chan (Hawkeye),

Christy Sappenfield (Short Stick), Alison Benson (Covergirl), Misun Chang, Deb Tune, Mark Tune, Sharon Grant (MacGyver), Doug Wolfe, Ali Soylu (along with Charlie, aka Big Pimpin'), Marika Oliff, Genevieve Rose (Radiance), Kayla Hinrichs, Miles Barger (The Most Interesting Man in America), Jessica Horton (Burrito), MikeVW (Eeyore), Charles Wang, Jasmine Thailand, Michelle Aulson, Mollie Steinberg, Bruce Steinberg, Liza Johnson, BlueRiverDream, Bryan Abe, Joe Pranio, Barbara Southworth, Aileen Kroll, Joshua Orozco, and Carly O'Neill. Your support made all the difference. And some of you did wind up making good models.

To our fellow backpackers at DC UL Backpacking: Thanks for indulging our creative routing as we explored new trails for this book.

Thanks to the wonderful staff at the Appalachian Mountain Club, including Victoria Sandbrook Flynn for shepherding this book and Peter Tyson for giving us the opportunity to write about one of our favorite activities.

To our families: Carol and Katie Adach, who may think this is all a bit crazy but who have given unconditional support. And to Bob and Emile Martin, Michael's champions and buyers and distributors of many books. And also his parents. Thank you.

Finally, Ernest Adach, Jen's father, passed away just as this book was started. Little did he realize that teaching her as a little girl on Long Island to jump the waves would foster her sense of adventure. He was proud to see the beginning stages of this book, and he'd be even prouder to see the final product. This book is in memory of him.

INTRODUCTION

HOME TO PRESIDENTS, CRADLE OF COLONIAL AMERICA, battleground during the Civil War, and crucible for the United States' recovery from the Great Depression, Virginia's Shenandoah Valley is one of the iconic landscapes of the American outdoors. Stretching from Harpers Ferry in the north, where the Shenandoah and Potomac rivers meet, to the James River in the south, the peaks and ridges of the Blue Ridge march into the characteristic blue mists produced by the mountains' lush and deep foliage. Between these ridgelines lie the fruitful valleys of the Shenandoah River, divided into its north and south forks, home to prosperous agriculture, rich horse land, and, more recently, promising vineyards.

This mountainous and rugged land is also a haven for hikers, serving as the backdrop for the Shenandoah National Park, the George Washington and Jefferson National Forests, the Blue Ridge Parkway, and a multitude of state and local parks, wild areas, and national monuments and recreation areas. The great trails run through it as well. More than 300 miles of the Appalachian Trail (AT) pass through the Shenandoah Valley, from Dragon's Tooth (Trip 48) near Roanoke, Virginia, to Harpers Ferry, West Virginia, passing some of the AT's most iconic sights: Mary's Rock (Trip 14), Stony Man (Trip 15), Blackrock (28), and Tinker Cliffs (Trip 46). McAfee Knob (Trip 47) is perhaps the most photographed sight on the entire trail. And there are other trails to walk. The

Tuscarora Trail (Trip 11) begins its diversion from the AT toward Pennsylvania in the northern Shenandoah; the Massanutten Trail (Section 5) runs a long circuit along the flat and rocky ridgelines of Massanutten Mountain; the Wild Oak Trail (Trip 37) passes a rugged course on the eastern edge of the Alleghenies. And where these great trails go, there are side trails, link trails, and blue and yellow blazes. You could hike for years and not see everything.

The hikes in this book can help you start such a journey. They range across the entire region. In truth, we extend a little beyond the Shenandoah Valley proper, giving you a taste for hiking along the Allegheny Plateau (the western Shenandoah boundary) and including a few hikes in the James River area. They were too wonderful to pass up. Together, our hikes include a little of everything, from big airy views to rocky scrambling, from bountiful waterfall hikes to cooling swimming dips. Though there are a few challenging, longer hikes, we have kept most of them short. Many of our trips are easy or moderate, and they can be hiked in just a few hours. We've tried to focus on the real reason for doing a particular hike—what makes it distinct from other hikes—instead of adding miles just for exercise. Thus, our hikes facilitate, we hope, photography, bird-watching, fishing, or whatever interests you.

Hiking Virginia is also an opportunity to explore the history of the United States, and we have selected hikes that visit a goodly array of historical sites, including Rapidan Camp (President Hoover's retreat in the Shenandoah), some of the first Civilian Conservation Corps projects, and locations that played a role in the Civil War and, in a few cases, even the Revolutionary War. George Washington was, of course, a Virginian, and in his early life, surveyed land in the Shenandoah Valley. He knew this land better than most.

With a light pack and some rugged footwear, a bottle of water and a picnic lunch, hikers can explore this beautiful and storied land, finishing by exploring Virginia's wine country or touring rustic villages. The Shenandoah Valley is, truly, a garden and a superb destination for hikers of all levels of ability and of all inclinations.

HOW TO USE THIS BOOK

WITH 50 HIKES TO CHOOSE FROM, you may wonder how to decide where to go. The locator map at the front of this book will help you narrow down the trips by location, and the At-a-Glance Trip Planner that follows the Table of Contents will provide more information to guide you toward a decision. Once you settle on a destination and turn to a trip in this guide, you will find a series of icons that indicate whether there are fees, whether the hike is good for kids, and whether dogs are allowed.

(For those hikes with the "good for kids" icon, the authors suggest ages for children who would most likely enjoy the hike, but of course children can surprise you with their hiking skills; it's not uncommon to see young hikers even on the summit of Old Rag [Trip 21, the most technically challenging hike in this book]. We have used the designation conservatively, basing suggestions on hikes we feel are appropriate for children whose families hike together regularly. Some of the hikes designated for kids visit waterfalls or cliffy lookouts; these can be great rewards for kids' efforts to get there but can also be hazardous. Ultimately, to determine whether a hike is appropriate for your family, gauge your children's level of interest, motivation, and ability.)

Information on the basics follows: location, rating, distance, elevation gain, estimated time, and maps. The ratings are based on the authors' perception and are estimates of what the average hiker will experience. You may find them to be easier or more difficult than stated. The distance and estimated hiking time shown are for the whole trip, whether it's an out-and-back hike (with distance noted as "round-trip") or a loop. The estimated time is also based on the authors' perception. Consider your own pace when planning a trip. The elevation gain is calculated from measurements and information from U.S. Geological Survey (USGS) topographic maps, landowner maps, and Google Earth. Information is included about the relevant USGS maps, as well as where you can find trail maps.

The boldface summary that follows the list of basics provides an overview of what you will see on your hike. The directions explain how to reach the trailhead by car and include Global Positioning System (GPS) coordinates for parking lots. Whether or not you own a GPS device, it is wise to bring an atlas such as the *DeLorme Atlas & Gazetteer for Virginia*, which shows small roads and forest roads in detail. In the trail description, you will find instructions on where to hike, the trails on which to hike, and where to turn. You will also learn about the natural and human history along your hike, as well as about flora, fauna, and any landmarks or objects you will encounter. The trail maps that accompany each trip will help guide you along your hike, but it would be wise to take an official trail map with you as well. Official maps are often—but not always—available online, at the trailhead, or at the visitor center. Each hike description also lists the best available topographic map of the area. We highly recommend that frequent hikers purchase these maps.

Each trip ends with a More Information section that provides details about access times and fees, the property's rules and regulations, and contact information for the place where you will be hiking. The Nearby section offers suggestions for places to continue the experience when the hike is done and where to find the closest restaurants.

TRIP PLANNING AND SAFETY

PLANNING YOUR TRIP WELL is the first step to having a safe hike. Some of the trips in this book ascend to summits where winds and lower temperatures necessitate extra clothing. Other hikes visit clifftops or waterfalls or have rocky stretches where you'll need to use extra caution with children and dogs. Learn about the terrain you will travel through so you can pack the right gear and prepare for the experience. Allow extra time in case you get lost. You will be more likely to have an enjoyable, safe hike if you plan ahead and take proper precautions. Before heading out for your hike, consider the following:

- Select a hike that everyone in your group is comfortable taking. Match the hike to the abilities of the least capable person in the group. If anyone is uncomfortable with the weather or is tired, turn around and complete the hike another day.
- Plan to be back at the trailhead before dark. Before beginning your hike, determine a turnaround time. Don't diverge from it, even if you have not reached your intended destination.
- Check the weather and assume it will be cooler and windier on the mountain than at the base. If you are planning a ridge or summit hike, start early so that you will be off the exposed area before the afternoon hours, when thunderstorms most often strike, especially in summer. Weather

conditions can change quickly, and any changes are likely to be more severe the higher you are on the mountain.

- Bring a pack with the following items:
  - ✓ Water: Two quarts per person is usually adequate, depending on the weather and the length of the trip. On extended day hikes, consider carrying some method of water purification so you can refill your water bottles en route.
  - ✓ Food: Even if you are planning just an hour-long hike, bring some high-energy snacks such as nuts, dried fruit, or snack bars. Pack a lunch for longer trips.
  - ✓ Map and compass: Be sure you know how to use them. A handheld GPS device may also be helpful but it is not always reliable.
  - ✓ Headlamp or flashlight, with spare batteries.
  - ✓ Extra clothing: waterproof/breathable rain gear, synthetic fleece or wool jacket, hat, and mittens or gloves.
  - ✓ Sunscreen.
  - ✓ First-aid kit, including adhesive bandages, gauze, nonprescription painkillers, moleskin, and any necessary prescription medication in case you are on the trail longer than expected.
  - ✓ Pocketknife or multitool.
  - ✓ Waterproof matches and a lighter.
  - ✓ Trash bag.
  - ✓ Toilet paper and double plastic bag to pack it out.
  - ✓ Whistle.
  - ✓ Insect repellent.
  - ✓ Sunglasses.
  - ✓ Cell phone: Be aware that cell phone service is unreliable in rural areas. If you are receiving a signal, use the phone only for emergencies to avoid disturbing the backcountry experience for other hikers.
  - ✓ Trekking poles (optional).
  - ✓ Binoculars (optional).
  - ✓ Camera (optional).

- Wear appropriate footwear and clothing. Wool or synthetic hiking socks will keep your feet dry and help prevent blisters. Comfortable waterproof hiking boots or shoes will provide support and good traction. Avoid wearing cotton clothing, which absorbs sweat and rain and contributes to an unpleasant hiking experience. A synthetic or wool base layer (T-shirt, or underwear tops and bottoms) will wick moisture away from your body and keep you warm in wet or cold conditions. Synthetic zip-off pants that convert to shorts are popular. To help avoid bug bites, you may want to wear synthetic pants and a long-sleeve shirt.

- When you are ahead of the rest of your hiking group, wait at all trail junctions until the others catch up. This avoids confusion and keeps people from getting separated or lost.
- If you see downed wood that appears to be purposely covering a trail, it probably means the trail is closed due to overuse or hazardous conditions. If a trail is muddy, walk through the mud or on rocks, never on tree roots or plants. Water-resistant boots will keep your feet comfortable. Staying in the center of the trail will keep it from eroding into a wide hiking highway.
- Leave your itinerary and the time you expect to return with someone you trust. If you see a logbook at a trailhead, be sure to sign in when you arrive and sign out when you finish your hike.
- After you complete your hike, check for deer ticks, which carry the dangerous bacteria that causes Lyme disease.
- Poison ivy is always a threat when hiking. To identify the plant, look for clusters of three leaves that shine in the sun but are dull in the shade. If you do come into contact with poison ivy, wash the affected area with soap as soon as possible.
- Wear blaze-orange items in hunting season. In Virginia, hunting begins in September, with various seasons extending throughout winter and spring. Yearly information, regulations, and fees are available at www.dgif.virginia.gov/hunting/regulations.

Check on trail or road closures with land managers prior to heading out in any season, particularly in winter. Winter conditions can lead to full or partial closures of Shenandoah's Skyline Drive. To get the most current status of Skyline Drive, call 540-999-3500; the park's Facebook and Twitter feeds are also great ways to check on the status of the drive. Certain forest roads may also be closed in the winter months; check with the relevant park agency to get updated information on gaining access to certain trailheads.

Winter hiking can be an enjoyable way to experience the Shenandoah Valley, but it requires extra gear and planning. All winter hikers need to bring more food and warm layers than they would in summer, and exercise more caution; fewer daylight hours, colder temperatures, and slower travel times magnify any problems that may occur, like getting lost or twisting an ankle. Near-freezing temperatures freeze hoses on hydration systems. Consider using insulated water bottles and packing them as close as possible to your body heat to keep your water from freezing during the day. Small-mouthed water bottles tend to freeze faster. Traction devices—such as Microspikes—can help you navigate icy stretches. Prudent winter travelers do not go out alone and make sure at least one person in the group has a sleeping bag and a small camp stove in case of emergency. When properly prepared, hikers can safely and comfortably experience the deep quiet and spectacular beauty of the Shenandoah Valley in winter.

When the weather warms up, the bugs start to come out. Mosquitoes can be a nuisance in some places, depending on seasonal and daily conditions. West Nile virus and eastern equine encephalitis (EEE) virus can be transmitted to humans by infected mosquitoes and cause rare but serious diseases. More prevalent, however, are deer ticks, which can transmit Lyme disease. Reduce your risk of being bitten by using insect repellent and wearing long sleeves and pants. Check yourself carefully for ticks when you finish your hike. A variety of options are available for dealing with bugs, ranging from sprays that include the active ingredient DEET, which can potentially cause skin or eye irritation, to more skin-friendly products. Head nets, which often can be purchased more cheaply than a can of repellent, are useful during especially buggy conditions.

APPALACHIAN TRAIL CONSERVANCY

The Appalachian Trail Conservancy (ATC), headquartered in Harpers Ferry, West Virginia, preserves and manages the Appalachian Trail from its origins in Georgia to its terminus in Maine. The ATC works cooperatively with volunteers, trail clubs, and other agencies to develop policies of trail design, and to protect the landscapes and cultural and natural resources along the Appalachian Trail. Their Appalachian Trail Guides include excellent, AT-focused text and maps; for coverage of this area, refer to the Maryland/Northern Virginia, Shenandoah National Park, and Central Virginia guides. For more information, visit appalachiantrail.org.

POTOMAC APPALACHIAN TRAIL CLUB

The volunteer-based Potomac Appalachian Trail Club, headquartered in Vienna, Virginia, was founded in 1927. Now the club partners with the National Park Service, the Appalachian Trail Conservancy, and other trail clubs and maintains and monitors over 1,000 miles of hiking trails in the Mid-Atlantic region, as well as cabins, shelters, and hundreds of acres of conserved land. PATC also publishes indispensable resources for hiking in the region, including books and maps covering the Appalachian Trail, Massanutten Mountain, and Great North Mountain. For more information, visit PATC headquarters or patc.net.

SHENANDOAH NATIONAL PARK

Shenandoah National Park encompasses nearly 200,000 acres in Virginia. Almost 40 percent of the park is designated as Wilderness Areas, but its most well-known feature is Skyline Drive, which runs 105 miles through the length of the park and past 75 scenic overlooks. The park has approximately 500 miles of trails, including 101 miles of the Appalachian Trail. For more information, visit nps.gov/shen.

GEORGE WASHINGTON AND JEFFERSON NATIONAL FORESTS

Together, the George Washington and Jefferson National Forests form one of the largest areas of public land on the East Coast. Covering 1.8 million acres in Virginia, West Virginia, and Kentucky, the two forests are home to 2,000 miles of trails and 139,461 acres of designated Wilderness Areas. For more information, visit www.fs.usda.gov/gwj.

LEAVE NO TRACE

The Appalachian Mountain Club (AMC) is a national educational partner of Leave No Trace, a nonprofit organization dedicated to promoting and inspiring responsible outdoor recreation through education, research, and partnerships. The Leave No Trace program seeks to develop wildland ethics— ways in which people think and act in the outdoors to minimize their impact on the areas they visit and to protect our natural resources for future enjoyment. Leave No Trace unites four federal land management agencies—U.S. Forest Service, National Park Service, Bureau of Land Management, and U.S. Fish and Wildlife Service—with manufacturers, outdoor retailers, user groups, educators, organizations such as AMC, and individuals.

The Leave No Trace ethic is guided by the following seven principles:

1. **Plan Ahead and Prepare.** Know the terrain and any regulations applicable to the area you're planning to visit, and be prepared for extreme weather or other emergencies. This will enhance your enjoyment and ensure that you've chosen an appropriate destination. Small groups have less impact on resources and on the experiences of other backcountry visitors.

2. **Travel and Camp on Durable Surfaces.** Travel and camp on established trails and campsites, rock, gravel, dry grasses, or snow. Good campsites are found, not made. Camp at least 200 feet from lakes and streams, and focus activities on areas where vegetation is absent. In pristine areas, disperse use to prevent the creation of campsites and trails.

3. **Dispose of Waste Properly.** Pack it in, pack it out. Inspect your camp for trash or food scraps. Deposit solid human waste in catholes dug 6 to 8 inches deep, at least 200 feet from water, camps, and trails. Pack out toilet paper and hygiene products. To wash yourself or your dishes, carry water 200 feet from streams or lakes and use small amounts of biodegradable soap. Scatter strained dishwater.

4. **Leave What You Find.** Cultural or historical artifacts, as well as natural objects such as plants and rocks, should be left as found.

5. **Minimize Campfire Impacts.** Cook on a stove. Use established fire rings, fire pans, or mound fires. If you build a campfire, keep it small and use dead sticks found on the ground.

6. **Respect Wildlife.** Observe wildlife from a distance. Feeding animals alters their natural behavior. Protect wildlife from your food by storing rations and trash securely.

7. **Be Considerate of Other Visitors.** Be courteous, respect the quality of other visitors' backcountry experience, and let nature's sounds prevail.

AMC is a national provider of the Leave No Trace Master Educator course. AMC offers this five-day course, designed especially for outdoor professionals and land managers, as well as the shorter two-day Leave No Trace Trainer course, at locations throughout the Northeast.

For Leave No Trace information and materials, contact the Leave No Trace Center for Outdoor Ethics, P.O. Box 997, Boulder, CO 80306; 800-332-4100 or 302-442-8222; lnt.org. For a schedule of AMC Leave No Trace courses, see outdoors.org/education/lnt.

1

HARPERS FERRY AND NORTH VIRGINIA PIEDMONT

THE HISTORIC TOWN OF HARPERS FERRY lies at the confluence of the Potomac and Shenandoah rivers, on the borders of Maryland, West Virginia, and Virginia. Known as the "psychological halfway point" on the Appalachian Trail, the town was taken eight times during the Civil War and was the site of John Brown's famous raid—a bloody attempt to spark a slave revolt. A wealth of ruins and monuments on the area's trails commemorates these moments so important to the country's history. Harpers Ferry National Historic Park encompasses 4,000 acres of protected land and has about 20 miles of hiking trails crossing Civil War battlefields and mountains alike. The Appalachian Trail crosses through the park; the 184.5-mile C&O Canal Towpath can be reached from the park by a footbridge over the Potomac. Two hikes in this book pass over the two highest cliffs overlooking Harpers Ferry: Maryland Heights (Trip 1) and Loudoun Heights (Trip 2).

The rolling hills and ridges of the Piedmont region stretch between the Potomac, Rappahannock, and James rivers to the Blue Ridge Mountains and run north–south from North Carolina, through central Virginia, and into Maryland and Pennsylvania. From above, the Piedmont looks like a patchwork of secondary forests, pastures, and agricultural fields. Virginia pine and tulip trees are prevalent in the rather young forests here, which have begun to establish themselves after a history of repeated cutting and clearing. Mature forests in the area vary widely depending on topography and soil composition, supporting oak, hickory, beech, sycamore, silver maple, American elm, and eastern box elder. This section includes just a handful of the public lands in this region, focusing on landscapes that lead into the Shenandoah Valley itself, including the Raven Rocks (Trip 3), Shenandoah River State Park (Trip 4), the state's Bull Run Mountains Natural Area Preserve (Trip 5), and Sky Meadows State Park (Trip 6).

TRIP 1
MARYLAND HEIGHTS

Location: Harpers Ferry National Historical Park, WV
Rating: Moderate
Distance: 4.4 miles round-trip
Elevation Gain: 1,378 feet
Estimated Time: 2–3 hours
Maps: *Harpers Ferry, Maryland Heights Trail Map* (National Park Service)

Enjoy a trip through Harpers Ferry before heading up Maryland Heights for a great view of town.

DIRECTIONS

From I-270, Exit 32, take I-70 west for 1.0 mile to Exit 52 (US 340, Charles Town and Leesburg). Follow US 340 South/West for 22.0 miles into Harpers Ferry. Cross over the Potomac and Shenandoah rivers. Turn left into the main entrance of Harpers Ferry National Historical Park and proceed to park near the visitor center. (Parking fees apply.) Park-operated shuttle buses through Harpers Ferry run frequently; check with the park service for current hours and schedule. *GPS coordinates:* 39° 19.007′ N, 77° 45.381′ W.

TRAIL DESCRIPTION

A hike up Maryland Heights is a historical tour, starting and ending in Harpers Ferry and leading past several Civil War ruins. While there is parking in Harpers Ferry itself, it is hard to come by. The easiest way to reach the trailhead is to park at the Harpers Ferry Visitors Center and take the park-operated shuttle into town.

From the Shenandoah Street shuttle stop, turn right and follow the street past the restored shops. In the distance, the vista of Maryland Heights stretches above the town. Look for a white blaze on a signpost—the Appalachian Trail (AT) cuts through the town of Harpers Ferry, and this route follows its path for a short distance. At the end of the street, 0.2 mile from the shuttle stop, follow the wide gravel road, cross the railroad bridge, and descend the metal steps. These steps can be slippery when wet, and their open-grate surface can cause some pets to be concerned with the descent.

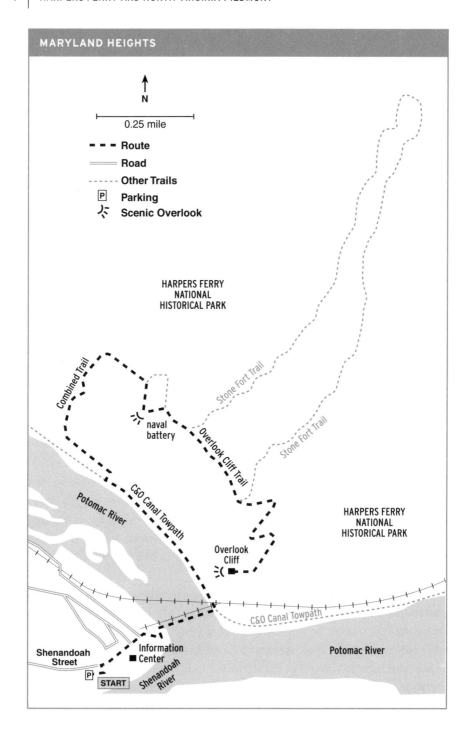

MARYLAND HEIGHTS

N

0.25 mile

- - - Route
══ Road
---- Other Trails
P Parking
⋋ Scenic Overlook

HARPERS FERRY
NATIONAL
HISTORICAL PARK

Combined Trail

Stone Fort Trail

naval
battery

Overlook Cliff Trail

Stone Fort Trail

Potomac River

C&O Canal Towpath

HARPERS FERRY
NATIONAL
HISTORICAL PARK

Overlook
Cliff

C&O Canal Towpath

Potomac River

Shenandoah
Street

Information
Center

P

START

Shenandoah River

Marking a psychological half-way point, Harpers Ferry is a major milestone for AT thru-hikers.

Turn left onto wide C&O Canal Towpath, which runs through the park here. A footbridge and the main trailhead for Maryland Heights come into view on the right. At 0.8 mile, cross the footbridge over the canal and then cross the road. Pass the gate and start heading uphill on green-blazed Combined Trail. Rather quickly, the trail ascends, giving views of the Potomac River to the left. The trail will swing to the right and enter the woods, still making its way uphill.

The trail will come to its first fork at 1.4 miles. Stay to the right to pass ruins of the Naval Battery, the first Union fortification built in Maryland Heights as protection against Stonewall Jackson's Valley Campaign. (Read War in the Shenandoah Valley to learn more.) After seeing the ruins, follow the path back up the hill to where it rejoins Combined Trail and take a right. (You may also take a left from the fork to stay on Combined Trail. Both options will lead you to the same point.)

The trail forks again at 1.6 miles. Blue-blazed Stone Fort Trail is to the left, but follow red-blazed Overlook Trail to the right. Overlook Trail continues the journey uphill. A final steep pitch leads to another intersection with Stone Fort Trail at 1.8 miles and the peak of the climb itself. Stay on Overlook Trail, which shortly turns to the right, and start the descent. At 2.2 miles, the trail reaches a view of the Potomac and Shenandoah rivers meeting, as well as the town below—specifically the street on which you started the hike; descend the rocky area carefully for nice spot to sit down.

After taking in the view, retrace your steps along the red- and green-blazed trails.

MORE INFORMATION

Harpers Ferry National Historical Park (nps.gov/hafe, 304-535-6029). A basic trail map is available online. The park is open year-round, with the exception of Thanksgiving Day, Christmas Day, and New Year's Day, from 9 A.M. to 5 P.M. Entrance fees are collected for visitors arriving by foot, bicycle, or vehicle.

NEARBY

The town of Harpers Ferry is full of restaurants, ice cream shops, and more—perfect for replacing all the calories you just burned. If you're looking for another chance to stretch your legs, consider adding to this route blue-blazed Stone Fort Trail, which loops into the woods from the endpoint and adds about 2 miles to the hike as well as some more climbing. The hike to nearby Loudoun Heights (Trip 2) is also accessible from Harpers Ferry.

HARPERS FERRY

Harpers Ferry stands at the northernmost point of the Shenandoah Valley. Most modern-day visitors will marvel at the picturesque town perched between the Shenandoah and Potomac rivers, but its position has made it a key strategic point throughout much of American history, particularly during the Civil War. The town's importance was only increased by the U.S. government's decision in the nineteenth century to build an armory there—one of only two federal armories in the country.

In 1859, the abolitionist John Brown attacked Harpers Ferry with a band of 21 men, hoping to seize the armory and escape to Virginia, where news of his actions would ignite a slave revolt. Brown and his followers were cornered in Harpers Ferry, however, after the surrounding townships were alerted. A force of marines under the command of Robert E. Lee and J.E.B. Stuart swiftly put down the revolt, and John Brown was hanged for treason on December 2, 1859. While Brown's actions thrust Harpers Ferry into national prominence, the meaning of his raid has always been hotly debated. Some saw Brown as a bloodthirsty vigilante; others regarded him as a martyr fallen to the cause of freedom. All will agree that his attack on the armory presaged the violence to come and was one of the crucial events leading up to the Civil War.

The beginning of the Civil War also spelled the end of prosperity for Harpers Ferry. The town changed hands no fewer than eight times during the battles that raged around the DC area. More recently, Harpers Ferry has been designated a National Historical Park and is known chiefly for tourism and outdoors activities. As it winds from Virginia to Maryland, the Appalachian Trail passes over the town's bridges and through its cobbled streets. Many thru-hikers pose for photos before the Appalachian Trail Conservancy Headquarters to indicate that they have completed half of the trail (though the true halfway point is in Pennsylvania). Other outdoors enthusiasts travel along the 184.5-mile Chesapeake & Ohio (C&O) Canal, which was built in the nineteenth century to enable trade from Washington, DC, to Cumberland, Maryland. Today, the flat canal towpath is popular with cyclists, hikers, and runners.

Even if you're not traveling long distances, Harpers Ferry is an attractive destination for day hikes. Trip 1 in this book takes you to Maryland Heights, where you can wander through Civil War ruins and peer down at the foundations of the old armory where John Brown made his last stand. Loudoun Heights, visited in Trip 2, also offers superb views of the town. If you visit in summer, be sure to enjoy a cooling float down the river!

TRIP 2
LOUDOUN HEIGHTS

Location: Harpers Ferry National Historical Park, WV
Rating: Strenuous
Distance: 7.8 miles round-trip
Elevation Gain: 2,278 feet
Estimated Time: 4–5 hours
Maps: PATC, *Map 7, Appalachian Trail in West Virginia and Northern Virginia, Potomac River & Harpers Ferry, WV to VA 7*, 2013.

Quieter than Maryland Heights, this hike rewards you with stunning views and fewer crowds. A ramble through the town of Harpers Ferry brings you past some of the history in the area.

DIRECTIONS
From 1-270, Exit 32, take I-70 west for 1.0 mile to Exit 52 (US 340, Charles Town and Leesburg). Follow US 340 South/West for 22.0 miles into Harpers Ferry. Cross over the Potomac and Shenandoah rivers. Turn left into the main entrance of Harpers Ferry National Historical Park and proceed to park near the visitor center. (Parking fees apply.) Park-operated shuttle buses through Harpers Ferry run frequently; check with the park service for current hours and schedule. *GPS coordinates:* 39° 19.007′ N, 77° 45.381′ W.

TRAIL DESCRIPTION
Thomas Jefferson famously marveled at the views encountered along this hike: "It is as placid and delightful as that is wild and tremendous. For the mountains being cloven asunder, she [nature] presents to your eye, through the cleft, a small catch of smooth blue horizon, at an infinite distance in that plain country, inviting you, as it were, from the riot and tumult roaring around to pass through the breach and participate in the calm below." Starting in Harpers Ferry, the trail takes you to an overlook of the town and the confluence of the Shenandoah and Potomac rivers. While there is parking in Harpers Ferry itself, it is hard to come by. The easiest way to reach the trailhead is to park at the Harpers Ferry Visitors Center and take the park-operated shuttle into town.

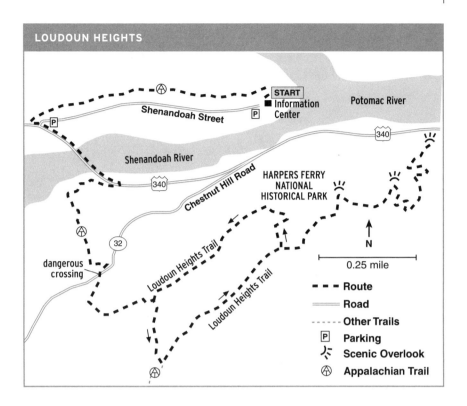

From the Shenandoah Street shuttle stop, turn left onto Potomac Street toward the railroad station. Turn up Hog Alley. At the top, make a left and then a quick right up hand-carved rock steps; look for the white blaze of the Appalachian Trail (AT). These steps lead past St. Peter's Roman Catholic Church—its steeple being perhaps one of the most visible sights when entering Harpers Ferry—and the ruins of St. John's Church. Here, the white blazes of the AT become more visible, and the trail leaves the town and becomes more of a wooded path.

In 0.3 mile from the shuttle stop, just past the ruins of St. John's Church, the trail reaches Jefferson Rock. Thomas Jefferson, who stood here on October 25, 1793, wrote that this "scene is worth a journey across the Atlantic." The rock now has pillars supporting it, but the view still stands. Hikers, however, are cautioned not to climb on the rock.

After taking in the views from Jefferson Rock, continue along the white-blazed AT. Side trails lead toward Harpers Cemetery and the Appalachian Trail Visitors Center, but continue to follow the white blazes. When the trail

For centuries visitors—including Thomas Jefferson—have marveled at the impressive views over Harpers Ferry.

splits, stay to the right. Just before the trail reaches US 340, it descends along a series of rock steps. A secondary parking lot is located nearby—parking here would shorten the hike but lose the sights of Harpers Ferry. Follow the trail to the left, and at 1.1 miles head over the US 340 bridge spanning the Shenandoah River. In warmer seasons, look for kayakers and rafters negotiating the rapids below.

At the end of the bridge, the trail descends down a staircase and back under the bridge, returning to a dirt path. Follow the white blazes as the trail climbs toward Loudoun Heights. The trail is easy to follow but does have occasional rocky patches. At 1.9 miles, cross Chestnut Hill Road and continue to ascend. Pass an orange-blazed path at 2.2 miles (your return route), and turn left onto blue-blazed Loudoun Heights Trail at 2.4 miles. After climbing for just over 2 miles, the trail reaches a stretch of level walking, passing an intersection with the orange-blazed trail, before it descends to and ends at the overlook.

From the overlook, gaze over Harpers Ferry and spot day-hikers enjoying the views across the river from Maryland Heights (Trip 1). To continue the hike, head back along the blue-blazed path and turn right onto the orange-blazed trail at 4.9 miles. A quick and steep descent leads to some level walking and good views to the right of the river and Harpers Ferry. Arrive at the intersection with the AT you passed earlier in the day at 5.6 miles. Turn right and follow the white blazes back down the mountain and into Harpers Ferry.

DID YOU KNOW?

The top slab of Jefferson Rock was so precariously balanced that hikers and tourists were able to move it with a gentle push. The pillars were placed under the slab between 1855 and 1860 to protect the town below.

MORE INFORMATION

Harpers Ferry National Historical Park (nps.gov/hafe, 304-535-6029). A basic trail map is available online. The park is open year-round, with the exception of Thanksgiving Day, Christmas Day, and New Year's Day, from 9 A.M. to 5 P.M. Entrance fees are collected for visitors arriving by foot, bicycle, or vehicle.

NEARBY

The town of Harpers Ferry is full of restaurants, ice cream shops, and more—perfect for replacing all the calories you just burned. The hike to nearby Maryland Heights (Trip 1) is also accessible from Harpers Ferry.

TRIP 3
RAVEN ROCKS

Location: Bluemont, VA
Rating: Moderate
Distance: 4.7 miles round-trip
Elevation Gain: 1,744 feet
Estimated Time: 2–3 hours
Maps: PATC, *Map 7, Appalachian Trail in West Virginia and Northern Virginia, Potomac River & Harpers Ferry, WV to VA 7*, 2013.

On this portion of the Appalachian Trail's famous Roller Coaster section, a few dips and climbs lead to an outcropping that has an impressive view of the valley.

DIRECTIONS
From VA 267, Exit 1A, merge onto US 15 South/VA 7 West/Leesburg Bypass toward Leesburg/Warrenton. Follow VA 7 West for 18 miles, then turn right onto Pine Grove Road (VA 679) and look immediately to the right for the small parking area and trailhead. Parking rules here are strictly enforced. Obey the No Parking signs or risk being towed. *GPS coordinates: 39° 6.999′ N, 77° 51.143′ W.*

TRAIL DESCRIPTION
This hike is rated moderate for its distance, but the rocky terrain could be a challenge for hikers unused to rock hopping. This short route on a segment of the Appalachian Trail (AT) climbs and dips its way up to the Raven Rocks overlook. The route to the overlook covers a short portion of a notorious 13.5-mile stretch of the AT known as the Roller Coaster, which can tire even the hardiest of hikers. This challenging section of trail rewards effort with big views.

From the parking lot, look for the white blazes and an information post to signal the start of the hike. Head up the trail for the first climb of the day before the trail switchbacks steeply down. Near the end of this descent, at 0.6 mile, look out for a modest sign signaling the 1,000-mile marker for northbound thru-hikers of the AT. From here, the trail jogs slightly uphill, a relatively easy stretch of hiking for a while.

The trail climbs again steeply, leading to a nice westerly view of the area, and then dips again at 1.9 miles to a rocky stream crossing. From here, the

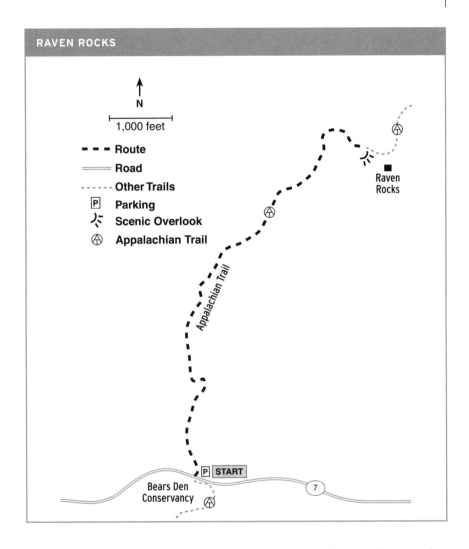

RAVEN ROCKS

N

1,000 feet

- - - **Route**
===== **Road**
- - - - - **Other Trails**
P **Parking**
Scenic Overlook
Appalachian Trail

Appalachian Trail

Appalachian Trail

Raven Rocks

P START

Bears Den Conservancy

7

trail starts its final climb to Raven Rocks. Compared with the rockier stretches before, this portion of the trail is easier to navigate—or it may be that many hikers are used to rock hopping by this point.

At 2.2 miles, the trail passes a marker for the Virginia–West Virginia border. This sign signals that the end of the climb is near: the trail opens up dramatically and leads straight to the Raven Rocks area at 2.4 miles. This outcropping is popular not only with hikers but with rock climbers as well—looking below, you may be able to spot a few making their way up the rock.

After enjoying the views, retrace your steps back down (and up) along the rocky path to the parking lot.

Impressive views reward hikers who endure the famous Roller Coaster section of the AT in Virginia.

DID YOU KNOW?

Experienced rock climbers flock to Raven Rocks—also known as Crescent Rocks—to take advantage of its nearly 30 climbs. Route names range from the ordinary (The Dish) to the fanciful (Litigiousness Psychosis), but all require experience and skill to get to the top safely.

MORE INFORMATION

Appalachian Trail Conservancy (appalachiantrail.org/hiking/trail-updates; 717-258-5771 (regional office); 304-535-6331 [incident reports]). Local information may be available at Bears Den (see below) during trail center hours.

NEARBY

You're not too far from civilization along this hike. Heading in either direction on VA 7 will lead you to Winchester and Leesburg, which have shops and restaurants for all budgets and tastes. The Appalachian Trail Conservancy's 66-acre Bears Den property (bearsdencenter.org, 540-554-8708) is across VA 7 from the trailhead and offers a variety of overnight accommodations, including a lodge, campground, cottage, and hiker hostel. The trail center is open from 8 A.M. to 9 P.M.; the lodge and store are open from 5 P.M. to 9 P.M. unless there is an event. There is a small fee for parking in the day-use lot.

TRIP 4
SHENANDOAH RIVER STATE PARK

Location: Bentonville, VA
Rating: Moderate
Distance: 6.5 miles
Elevation Gain: 1,368 feet
Estimated Time: 3–4 hours
Maps: Shenandoah River State Park Trail Map (www.dcr.virginia.gov/
state-parks/shenandoah-river.shtml)

**Not to be confused with its national park sibling, Shenandoah River
State Park has a little bit of everything for an outing: a river walk,
wide paths, woody climbs, and an overlook fit for a lunch break.**

DIRECTIONS

From I-66, Exit 6 (Front Royal), turn left (south) onto US 340 and follow it
through Front Royal. The park entrance is about 7.5 miles south of the junction of US 340 and VA 678. Turn right into the park (parking fees apply), and
follow Daughter of Stars Road to the Horsebarn Area. Park here for trailhead
access. *GPS coordinates: 38° 50.877′ N, 78° 18.352′ W.*

TRAIL DESCRIPTION

A hike perfect for those looking for easy terrain while still getting in some
miles, this lollipop route meanders along the Shenandoah River before heading up into the nearby woods.

Look for the information kiosk in the parking lot to find the trailhead; if
you're facing the horse barn, the trail starts to the left. The trail quickly splits,
heading in one direction toward Bear Bottom Loop and in another to Culler's
Trail. Follow the signs for Culler's Trail (orange blazes) and proceed along the
trail as it wraps behind the barn and leads you into the woods.

The trail crosses the road at 0.75 mile and changes from a woodsy walk
along a dirt trail to an open gravel path. Keep following this path and the signs
for Culler's Trail, which heads closer to the Shenandoah River. Birdhouses dot
the wooden fence that lines your path, and benches just off the trail invite sitting along the river. Pass the intersection for Tulip Poplar Trail just ahead of
the 1.5-mile point. At 1.6 miles, turn right on River Trail (dark-green blazes).

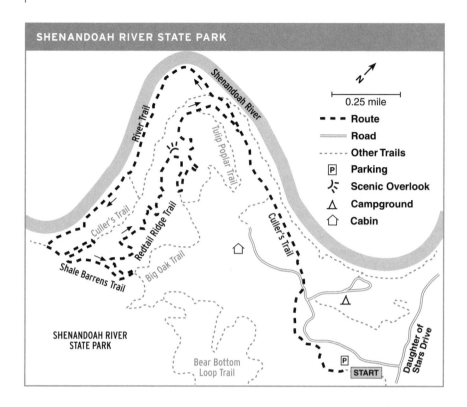

SHENANDOAH RIVER STATE PARK

This trail lives up to its name, drawing closer to the Shenandoah River and inviting even better views of the water and surrounding Massanutten Mountain. A connector trail comes in from the left, but stay alongside the river as long as possible.

At 2.8 miles, River Trail meets up with Culler's Trail again. At this junction, take a left onto Culler's. At 3.0 miles, take a right onto gray-blazed Shale Barrens Trail. The path heads back into the woods and starts the first (and only) steep climb of the day. The trail switchbacks up the hill and eventually leads to the top of the ridge. At 3.4 miles, turn left to follow Redtail Ridge Trail (red blazes). Good views of the river start to appear below, and the route mirrors the path you just took—although now from a higher vantage point. A short spur trail leads to a nice overlook at 4.2 miles, and a perfectly placed bench provides an excellent break spot.

At 4.5 miles, turn left onto Tulip Poplar Trail (pink blazes) and follow it as it meanders through the woods. Tulip Poplar Trail is a lollipop loop itself. Continue straight through an intersection for this loop at 5.5 miles to finish the hike and rejoin Culler's Trail at 5.2 miles, Turn right onto Culler's and retrace

Hikers enjoy a gentle ramble as the route parallels the Shenandoah River.

your path back along the gravel path, recross the road, and follow Culler's Trail back to your car.

DID YOU KNOW?

The Shenandoah River flows for 55.6 miles and has two forks—the north and the south—that each are 100 miles long. A tributary of the Potomac River, the Shenandoah starts northeast of Front Royal where the north and south forks meet and eventually joins the Potomac near Harpers Ferry. George Washington is credited by some with naming the river (and the valley) after Oskanondonha, an Oneida chief who provided help to Washington's troops during the Revolutionary War.

MORE INFORMATION

Shenandoah River State Park (www.dcr.virginia.gov/state-parks/shenandoah-river.shtml; 540-622-6840). The park is open 8 A.M. to dusk and is a trash-free facility. A campground, bunkhouses, cabins, and a lodge are available for overnight stays; for reservations, contact ReserveAmerica at reserveamerica.com or 800-933-7275.

NEARBY

En route from I-66, you will drive right past the entrance to Shenandoah National Park. Dickey Ridge (Trip 9) is just a short distance down Skyline Drive. Also nearby are Duncan Knob (Trip 32) and Buzzard Rock (Trip 29). Front Royal has a number of stores, shops, and restaurants to fit every budget and cuisine preference.

TRIP 5
BULL RUN

Location: Bull Run Mountains Natural Area Preserve, Broad Run, VA
Rating: Easy
Distance: 2.0 miles
Elevation Gain: 544 feet
Estimated Time: 1 hour
Maps: *Bull Run Mountains Natural Area Preserve Trail Map* (Bull Run Mountains Conservancy)

This easy ramble takes walkers on a tour of nineteenth-century Virginia history: an old mill, an icehouse, and a family cemetery.

DIRECTIONS

From I-66, Exit 40 (Haymarket, US 15S), turn left (south) onto US 15, and then turn right (west) onto VA 55. In 2.7 miles, turn right onto Turner Road and take the first left onto Beverly Mill Drive. Drive nearly a mile to the Bull Run Mountains Natural Area Preserve's welcome center, which will be on the left. *GPS coordinates: 38° 49.492′ N, 77° 42.382′ W.*

TRAIL DESCRIPTION

This popular hike is an easy drive from the Washington, DC, metro area and an easy outing for hikers seeking a day outside. Parking by the welcome center can be tight; arrive early to get a spot in the parking lot. Bull Run Mountains Natural Area Preserve offers countless options and loops, but navigation can be tricky as trails are blazed mostly by signpost. Make sure to grab a copy of the map before heading out on the trail, and pay careful attention to the signage.

The 2,500-acre preserve is owned by the Virginia Outdoors Foundation; 800 acres in the south of the preserve are managed by the Bull Run Mountains Conservancy, Inc., which partners with the Virginia Division of Natural Heritage, Environmental Studies on the Piedmont, George Mason University, and other organizations to offer public education programs, from day hikes to weeklong nature camps. The conservancy's ongoing research projects include geology, plant communities, riparian assessments, and more.

From the welcome center, cross the road, pass through a gate, and cross over the train tracks. Turn left onto Mountain Road Trail. At signpost 1, reached in

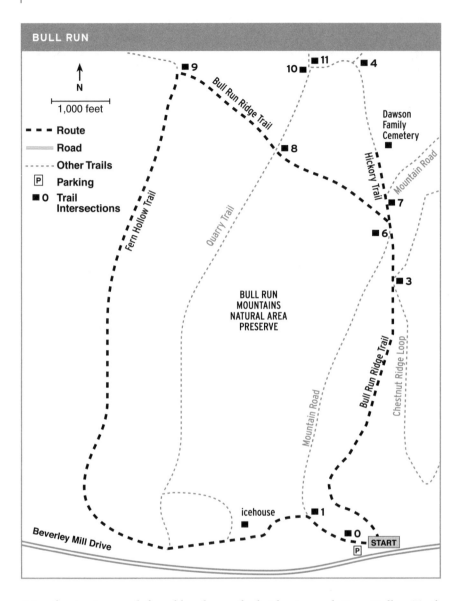

0.1 mile, stay to your left and head over the bridge to reach Fern Hollow Trail. (Mountain Road Trail turns to the right into the woods at the first signpost.)

Follow Fern Hollow Trail past signpost 2 at 0.25 mile. On the left are the remains of Meadowland, a house, and the Icehouse, a stone-lined pit that lies next to the trail. Meadowland was built by the Chapman family and destroyed by fire around 1880, and it's believed that the pit was used to store ice harvested from shallow ponds. The trail continues past the Icehouse, crosses a stream, and then

The stone-lined Icehouse gives curious history fans a glimpse back in time, one of the many sights you'll encounter along this hike.

swings to the right at 0.4 mile. Follow the trail into the woods, and look to the left to spy the remains of a mill, also built and run by the Chapman family. This mill was used by both Union and Confederate soldiers during the Civil War.

The trail takes a slight jog uphill, but most of it is relatively flat. Continue along Fern Hollow Trail, and arrive at signpost 9 at 0.9 mile. Turn right onto Bull Run Ridge Trail. (Turning left will take you uphill to an overlook, adding 3 miles to your hike.)

Follow Bull Run Ridge Trail, and pass signpost 8 at 1.1 miles. The intersection is a little tricky: Take the second trail to the right to stay on relatively flat Bull Run Ridge Trail. (Taking the first trail to the right would place on you on Quarry Trail, which heads uphill.)

Signpost 6 comes up quickly at 1.25 miles. For a short detour to see one of the cemeteries preserved in Bull Run, turn left at signpost 6 and then make another quick left at signpost 7 to head uphill along Hickory Trail. The side trail to the cemetery is not marked, but it is a distinct path lined by rocks and logs, which leaves at 1.4 miles. (If you start to head downhill, you've gone too far and missed the side trail.) Turn right onto this trail and follow it back to the Dawson Family Cemetery.

To continue the hike, return back down Hickory Trail and turn right at signpost 7. Pass signpost 6 and continue along Bull Run Ridge Trail. Rejoin the trail you started on, and proceed back over the train tracks to the welcome center.

DID YOU KNOW?

The Bull Run Mountains are the most easterly mountain chain in the Piedmont, an area characterized by rolling hills and ridges.

MORE INFORMATION

Bull Run Mountains Conservancy (brmconservancy.org, 703-753-2631). Trails are open from dawn until dusk. Review preserve usage guidelines at brmconservancy.org/guide.html. For more information on the Bull Run Mountains and the preserve in particular, visit virginiaoutdoorsfoundation .org/vof-special-project-areas.

NEARBY

The nearby towns of Marshall, Haymarket, and Gainesville offer a multitude of eating options. Bull Run is also nestled in the heart of Virginia's wine country, perfect for sipping and snacking after the hike.

WAR IN THE SHENANDOAH VALLEY

Gazing across the Shenandoah Valley, it is hard to imagine the bucolic scene dotted with troops moving en masse, the area devastated by war. Yet during the Civil War, the Shenandoah Valley was an area of strategic importance for the South and the site of two major campaigns.

Long before the war, the valley's bounty was integral to the lives and lore of its native people, and German and Scots-Irish immigrants were lured by the fertile soil. European settlers produced food in abundance and exported their surplus to cities in the East. In this, the Shenandoah Valley was unique. Much of the economy of the South depended on growing cotton, sugar, and tobacco—crops people couldn't eat. The Shenandoah Valley was the only major region in Virginia that had mixed agriculture, growing wheat and corn and raising livestock. "In terms of feeding the people of Virginia, and especially the South's most important army, the Army of Northern Virginia, it was vital," explains Colin Babb, a local historian.

Of equal importance was the pathway that the valley provided for the South as an invasion route to Maryland, Washington, DC, and Pennsylvania. The Valley Pike—now known as VA 11—was used to transport food, but also provided a quick route for troop and equipment movement. During the Valley Campaign in 1862, Confederate Major General Stonewall Jackson moved his troops up and down the valley, guarding the gaps with his "foot cavalry" and using the gaps—Thornton, Swift Run, and others with names familiar to hikers and park visitors—to surprise Union troops. The Union could only guess at the size of Jackson's forces and how fast they were moving. Jackson retained control of the valley for the first part of the war.

The Union didn't understand the importance of the Shenandoah Valley until later in the war. In 1864, Ulysses S. Grant was placed in charge of the Union Army. He and President Abraham Lincoln realized that the only way for the Union to defeat the Confederacy was to destroy the social and economic infrastructure of the South. Grant designed a plan to strike at the Confederacy from multiple directions, including the Shenandoah Valley.

In the Valley Campaigns of 1864, Grant designated a smaller army to parallel his movements south, but Confederate General Jubal Early frustrated his initial attempts by pushing the Union back up the valley, coming within striking distance of Washington, DC. Grant then placed General Philip Sheridan in charge. Sheridan had served with Grant and Major General William Tecumseh Sherman in the West, and understood the concept of total war. As Sheridan moved through the valley, his army laid waste and burned farms, a precursor of Sherman's infamous March to the Sea in Georgia. The valley was devastated, but not destroyed. While many residents left, others returned to rebuild on the fertile soil.

TRIP 6
SKY MEADOWS STATE PARK

Location: Delaplane, VA
Rating: Moderate
Distance: 6.7 miles
Elevation Gain: 1,575 feet
Estimated Time: 3–4 hours
Maps: *Sky Meadows State Park Trail Map* (Sky Meadows State Park)

Ramble through meadows on this moderate hike that gives grand views of the surrounding Virginia Piedmont area.

DIRECTIONS

From I-66, Exit 23 (US 17 North/VA 55 West), follow US 17 north for 6.4 miles. Turn left onto VA 710 to enter the park. (Parking fees apply.) Park in the main lot by the Mount Bleak House. *GPS coordinates:* 38° 59.478′ N, 77° 58.281′ W.

TRAIL DESCRIPTION

This moderate hike starts off with a climb to get your heart pumping; sweeping views open up during the latter half of the hike as the route wanders through woods and meadows. The 19 miles of hiking trails at Sky Meadows State Park meander through the woodlands and pastures of a historical farm. Designated trails are also available for bicycles and horses.

From the parking lot, look to the west to spot the start of the hike. Follow this gravel path past the wooden fence and then turn left onto graveled Boston Mill Road. Follow the road for 0.2 mile, passing through the intersection with Gap Run Trail to South Ridge Trail. Turn right and make a quick left to keep following South Ridge Trail. The climb starts here.

South Ridge Trail leads into the woods and past the ruins of the old Snowden homestead. The trail swings to the right, and the incline increases. At 1.0 mile, the path passes a bench and an overlook of the Piedmont.

While the route continues, steep climbs are behind you for the next mile or so. From the overlook, the trail heads to the right and back into the woods, all along a steady uphill grade. At 1.9 miles, the path intersects North Ridge Trail; turn left for the last big climb for the day. North Ridge Trail can be rocky at times and ends at the intersection with the Appalachian Trail (AT) at 2.5 miles. Turn right on the white-blazed Appalachian Trail for a short distance and then turn left onto purple-blazed Old Trail.

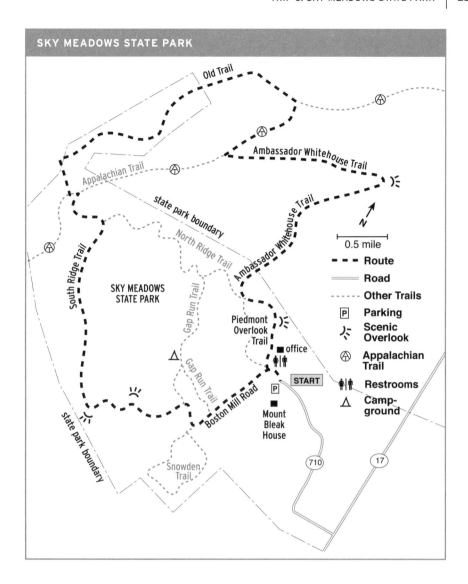

SKY MEADOWS STATE PARK

Old Trail

Ambassador Whitehouse Trail

Appalachian Trail

state park boundary

North Ridge Trail

South Ridge Trail

Ambassador Whitehouse Trail

SKY MEADOWS
STATE PARK

Gap Run Trail

Piedmont
Overlook
Trail

Gap Run Trail

office

START

Boston Mill Road

Mount
Bleak
House

state park boundary

Snowden
Trail

710

17

N

0.5 mile

- - - **Route**

=== **Road**

---- **Other Trails**

P **Parking**

)⁕(**Scenic
Overlook**

Ⓐ **Appalachian
Trail**

Restrooms

△ **Camp-
ground**

Old Trail is less maintained than the other trails in the park—keep an eye out for blowdowns and stretches where the path is a bit overgrown—but it leads through some lovely stretches of forest. The trail takes a sharp right turn and briefly opens up as it passes by a gas pipeline cut. Keep following the purple blazes. Eventually, the path pops briefly onto a fire road and then swings uphill to the right. Follow Old Trail until it reaches another intersection with the AT at 4.2 miles.

Turn right onto the AT, which mildly climbs through the woods and then enters an open meadow. At 4.8 miles, turn left onto Ambassador Whitehouse Trail and follow the wide, blue-blazed path through the meadow. The trail

Wide open meadows give hikers good opportunities to enjoy views of the Virginia Piedmont area.

reaches the sweeping views of Paris Overlook and its perfectly situated picnic table at 5.2 miles.

From the vista, Ambassador Whitehouse Trail swings to the right and makes its way back into the woods. The trail passes another gas pipeline along the downhill slope and eventually meets up with North Ridge Trail at 5.8 miles. Make a left at this intersection and then another quick left onto Piedmont Overlook Trail (red blazed). A short 0.1-mile climb leads to a stile. Climb over the stile and enter the meadow at 6.0 miles for sweeping views and a bench.

When ready, follow the path down the meadow. A word of caution: Cows sometimes graze this field and leave behind mementoes. Keep an eye on your footing. The trail swings close to a wooden fence; climb over another stile on the right at 6.4 miles before crossing a short bridge. To the left, Boston Mill Road—the gravel path from the start of the hike—is within sight. Head down the steps to regain Boston Mill. Turn left and follow the path back to your car.

(To shorten the hike slightly, skip the left turn onto Old Trail and stay on the AT through the intersection with Ambassador Whitehouse Trail, on which you'll turn right instead of left to rejoin the published route. This saves about 1 mile.)

DID YOU KNOW?

Sky Meadows is for the birds—bird-watching, that is. Bird watchers flock to the park to spot a wide variety of woodpeckers. Sky Meadows is known for its colony of red-headed woodpeckers, and bird watchers also can spy six other types of woodpeckers that are found in this part of Virginia: downy, hairy, red-bellied, and piliated woodpeckers; the northern flicker, and the yellow-bellied sapsucker.

MORE INFORMATION

For additional information, contact Sky Meadows State Park at 540-592-3556 or www.dcr.virginia.gov/state-parks/sky-meadows.shtml. The park is open daily, 8:30 A.M. to dusk. All pets must be kept on a leash no longer than six feet. Year-round primitive hike-in camping is available at the designated campground; for reservations, contact ReserveAmerica at reserveamerica.com or 800-933-7275.

NEARBY

Driving along VA 17 will bring you past a few of Virginia's many wineries, perfect for sipping and snacking after the hike.

2

NORTH SHENANDOAH NATIONAL PARK

ONE OF THE NATION'S MOST VISITED NATIONAL PARKS, Shenandoah National Park's 200,000 protected acres encompass eight counties, 105 miles of Skyline Drive, and 101 miles of the Appalachian Trail—all within 75 miles of Washington, DC. Despite the park's welcoming of more than 2 million visitors every year, 79,579 acres have been designated as Wilderness Areas. This designation is intended to preserve (as the 1964 Wilderness Act states) "the earth and its community of life" as "untrammeled by man, where man himself is a visitor who does not remain." Such Wilderness Areas also ensure that there are many wild places where hikers can escape the crowds just out for a scenic drive. (For a brief overview of park history, read the introduction to Section 3; for more on the park's ecology, read the introduction to Section 4.)

Shenandoah National Park's northern district encompasses 25,000 acres of designated Wilderness and stretches from Front Royal to Thornton Gap (from milepost 0 on Skyline Drive to just after milepost 31). Facilities in the area include the Dickey Ridge Visitor Center (between mileposts 4 and 5); 179 campsites of Mathews Arm Campground; and the Elkwallow Wayside (milepost 24). The Potomac Appalachian Trail Club maintains numerous cabins throughout the park, including Range View, which is located off the Appalachian Trail, just east of Elkwallow (visit patc.net to make reservations). Throughout the park there are several overnight shelters on or in the immediate vicinity of the

Appalachian Trail. Seventeen overlooks line Skyline Drive in this district; the highest peak in the northern section is Hogback Mountain (3,474 feet). The park's highest waterfall, at Overall Run (93 feet), is also here (Trip 11).

Several trips in this section begin at or pass through Elkwallow Wayside or Mathews Arm Campground, giving hikers direct access to concessions, carryout food, and camping supplies without leaving the park.

TRIP 7
COMPTON GAP

Location: North District, Shenandoah National Park, VA

Rating: Easy

Distance: 2.2 miles

Elevation Gain: 763 feet

Estimated Time: 1–2 hours

Maps: PATC, *Map 9, Appalachian Trail and other trails in Shenandoah National Park, North District,* 2009.

A short hike along the Appalachian Trail brings you to western views and a geology lesson.

DIRECTIONS

From I-66, Exit 6 (Front Royal), follow US 340 South for 2.1 miles. Turn left onto Skyline Drive (fee). The Compton Gap Parking is located between mileposts 10 and 11. *GPS coordinates: 38° 49.424′ N, 78° 10.233′ W.*

TRAIL DESCRIPTION

The trail up to Compton Gap is short, but the rocky path may demand a slower pace as you ascend nearly 500 feet to gain views of the surrounding area.

From the parking lot, cross Skyline Drive and start to follow the white-blazed Appalachian Trail (AT). The trail climbs steadily as it makes its way up to the peak. While it is a well-defined path, the trail can be rocky at times. Keep an eye out for a tricky left turn at just 0.5 mile.

The trail ascends up the ridge and eventually levels out as it closes in on the summit. In less than a mile from the start, the path reaches a concrete post that marks spur trails (blue blazes) to the east and west. Both spur trails are less than 0.2 mile in length, and both are worth exploring.

The rocky western spur trail (to the right) climbs to clear views of the park, Skyline Drive, and Massanutten Mountain.

Follow the eastern spur trail (to the left) for some geology. This trail dips down before arriving at a large boulder. Climb to the top of the boulder for some views, which are a bit obstructed. Pass the boulder on the blue-blazed path to a rock outcrop and a chance to see an example of a geologic phenomenon known as columnar jointing. This particular rock is part of the Catoctin Formation and is metamorphosed basalt formed around 700 million years

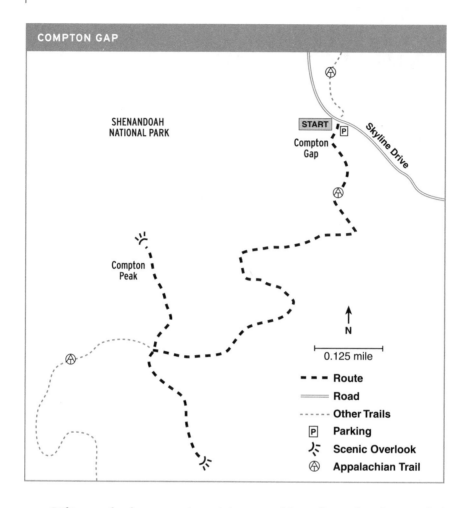

ago. Rifting and other tectonic activity caused lava flows that then cooled quickly when exposed. This quick cooling led to the rock forming in distinct columns, rather than blocks.

After exploring both spur trails, return to the concrete post and retrace your steps along the AT back to the parking lot and your car.

DID YOU KNOW?

The striking look of columnar jointing can be found across the world, and in much larger arenas. The most famous example is the Giant's Causeway in Northern Ireland, which was featured as part of the artwork on Led Zeppelin's *Houses of the Holy* album.

A young hiker—and her father—take a moment to enjoy the scenery.

MORE INFORMATION

Shenandoah National Park (nps.gov/shen, 540-999-3500, 800-732-0911 [for emergencies]). Park facilities are generally open from March through late November; a facilities schedule is online. In cases of inclement weather and at night in deer-hunting season (mid-November through early January), call the park to confirm whether Skyline Drive is open to vehicles. Overnight lodging in the park includes lodges, cabins, and campgrounds; visit nps.gov/shen/planyourvisit/lodging.htm or nps.gov/shen/planyourvisit/campgrounds.htm for more information.

NEARBY

The trails in this trip sit at the top of Skyline Drive, placing them close to Front Royal. This town has a number of stores, shops, and restaurants to fit every budget and cuisine preference.

When searching for a site for a national park in the East, many had their eyes on the Appalachian Mountains. They fit the bill: a park along their reach would be close enough to serve the then 40 million Americans living in cities on the East Coast, including Washington, DC.

It wasn't easy, however, to open a national park in the East. Unlike the western half of the United States, there were not many public lands left. Decades—if not centuries—of logging also were taking their toll. Fears of a "timber famine" were mounting as deforestation led to large swaths of cut-over trees. The disappearance of these forests was leading to wildfires, erosion, and flooding in nearby communities. The creation of the Forest Reserve Act in 1891 gave the president the authority to set aside public land to protect watersheds—lands that would eventually be known as national forests—but many felt that more needed to be done. Citizens formed groups such as the Appalachian National Park Association, begun in 1899, to urge the protection of natural resources. The group was renamed the Appalachian National Forest Reserve Association in 1903 and disbanded just two years later, but its mission to create a national park in the Appalachians was taken up by the American Forestry Association.

Congress again stepped in to help. The Weeks Act of 1911 paved the way for the creation of a national forest system in the East, allowing the U.S. Forest Service to start acquiring land. In the meantime, the idea of a national park in the Appalachian Mountains continued to gain steam. The U.S. Department of the Interior formed the Southern Appalachian National Park Committee in 1924 to study options for a national park. Concerns about deforestation brought them to the Blue Ridge Mountains, but fascination with the automobile led to the suggestion of a "sky-line drive" that would provide tourists with views of the surrounding valleys.

Two years later, in 1926, Congress enacted a bill to create two national parks in the Appalachian Mountains: Great Smoky Mountains National Park and Shenandoah National Park. Groundbreaking on Skyline Drive started in 1931, a project largely spurred by the Depression in an attempt to provide jobs and stimulate the economy (See Putting the Nation to Work).

The groundwork for building a national park in Shenandoah was set, but hundreds of people still lived within what would be its boundaries. Some of them sold their land willingly to the government; others had to be forcibly displaced. A very select few were allowed to live in the park for the remainder of their lives. Annie Lee Bradley Shenk was the last of such residents with life tenancy, and she passed away in 1979 at the age of 92. As families moved out of Shenandoah, the Civilian Conservation Corps (CCC) moved to eradicate any visible sign of their existence. Hikers with keen eyes, however, can still spot the remains of foundations and chimneys, but entire communities were removed to make way for the park. The park still encompasses at least 100 cemeteries—including the Bolen Cemetary along Little Devils Stairs (Trip 12).

Work on the park and Skyline Drive moved quickly. The section of Skyline Drive from Thornton Gap to Swift Run Gap opened to the public on September 15, 1934. In 1936, the section from Thorton Gap to Front Royal opened, and the remaining sections—Swift Run to Jarman Gap and Rockfish Gap—were opened in 1939. In total, Skyline Drive stretches 105 miles through Shenandoah National Park, with 75 overlooks and numerous hiking trails. Nearly 2 million people find themselves on Skyline Drive each year.

TRIP 8
BIG DEVILS STAIRS

Location: North District, Shenandoah National Park, VA
Rating: Moderate
Distance: 4.7 miles, round-trip
Elevation Gain: 1,313 feet gain
Estimated Time: 2–4 hours
Maps: PATC, *Map 9, Appalachian Trail and other trails in Shenandoah National Park, North District,* 2009.

From Skyline Drive descend into the steep canyon of Big Devils Stairs and peer into the hollow from the cliffs high above.

DIRECTIONS
From I-66, Exit 13, follow VA 55 West for about 5 miles through Front Royal, then turn left onto US 340 South. In about 0.5 mile, turn left onto Skyline Drive (fee). The Gravel Springs Gap parking lot is on the left past milepost 17. *GPS coordinates:* 38° 46.071′ N, 78° 14.013′ W.

TRAIL DESCRIPTION
This fairly straightforward out-and-back hike is complicated slightly by the web of trails that weaves around the Appalachian Trail (AT) and the Gravel Springs Hut, a first-come, first-served AT shelter; in summer, these shelters are more commonly used by AT thru-hikers. In the parking lot, orient yourself by noting that the AT crosses Skyline Drive in the gap. You will not be walking on the AT for this trip.

Instead, head south on an old, grassy, forest road. This road will bend sharply to your left in just over 0.1 mile. Keep an eye out to your left: At the next turn in the road at 0.3 mile, there is a post marking a footpath. Head straight into the woods and descend gently to the next intersection, where a trail on the right heads to the AT shelter. Yellow-blazed Bluff Trail, on the left (west) at 0.5 mile, continues toward Big Devils Stairs.

Heading west on yellow-blazed Bluff Trail, it is comparative smooth sailing. Over the next 1.4 miles, the path rolls some but generally stays fairly level. At 1.8, Bluff Trail intersects Big Devils Stairs Trail; turn right to follow the blue

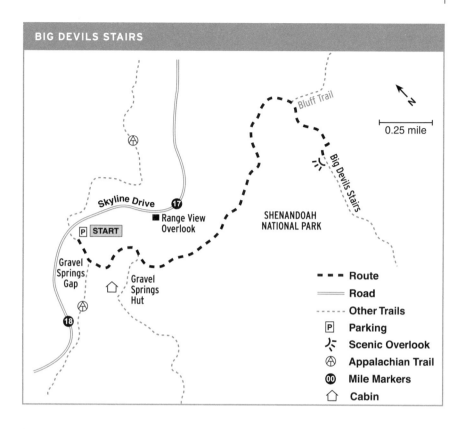

BIG DEVILS STAIRS

blazes. At first, Big Devils Stairs Trail is fairly flat as it passes a few attractive campsites tucked in among the rhododendron, but the trail begins to lose elevation quickly. As it dives about 500 feet to the cliffs, the echoing sound of rushing water greets you. The trail brings you to the first overlook, and a series of stone steps drop down to the best views. Explore a little farther down along the cliffs, however, as there are a few other vistas.

Big Devils Stairs Trail continues on past these overlooks, but there is no access from the base of the park and few views, so the trail becomes sketchy and rarely walked. If you're keen for some additional exercise, feel free to explore to the trail's end.

To return, climb Big Devils Stairs back to Bluff Trail and take a left. Back in the vicinity of the Gravel Springs Hut, two right-hand turns bring you back to the parking lot.

If by chance you end up at Gravel Springs Hut instead, just continue on until you reach the AT, then turn right to reach Skyline Drive and the parking lot.

Hikers study the cliffs above Big Devils Stairs.

DID YOU KNOW?

Big Devils Stairs Trail used to follow the course of the streambed, much like its cousin Little Devils Stairs (Trip 12). After the trail had been washed out repeatedly, however, the park service decided to relocate it to the cliffs overlooking the gorge. Remnants of the old trail are still there, but they have not been maintained in many years.

MORE INFORMATION

Shenandoah National Park (nps.gov/shen, 540-999-3500, 800-732-0911 [for emergencies]). Park facilities are generally open from March through late November; a facilities schedule is online. In cases of inclement weather and at night in deer-hunting season (mid-November through early January), call the park to confirm whether Skyline Drive is open to vehicles. Overnight lodging in the park includes lodges, cabins, and campgrounds; for more information, visit nps.gov/shen/planyourvisit/lodging.htm or nps.gov/shen/planyourvisit/campgrounds.htm.

NEARBY

There's plenty of additional hiking to be done in the northern Shenandoah. Consider hiking Little Devils Stairs (Trip 12), which offers quite a different experience, or branch out to hike Overall Run (Trip 11), Jeremy's Run (Trip 13), or Elkwallow Gap (Trip 10). A little additional driving will take you to the riches of the Central District as well.

After the hike, consider stopping in Front Royal, if you're leaving the park to the north, or Sperryville, if you're leaving from Thornton Gap.

TRIP 9
DICKEY RIDGE

Location: North District, Shenandoah National Park, VA
Rating: Easy–Moderate
Distance: 4.9 miles
Elevation Gain: 1,130 feet
Estimated Time: 2–3 hours
Maps: PATC, *Map 9, Appalachian Trail and other trails in Shenandoah National Park, North District*, 2009.

Located close to the park's northern entrance, this hike takes you on a tour of the park's history as you pass remnants of Shenandoah's family farms.

DIRECTIONS

From I-66, Exit 6 (Front Royal), follow US 340 south for 2.1 miles. Turn left onto Skyline Drive (fee). The Dickey Ridge Visitors Center is located between mileposts 4 and 5. *GPS coordinates:* 38° 52.263′ N, 78° 12.260′ W.

TRAIL DESCRIPTION

This easy-to-moderate hike keeps it simple, following a well-marked trail past ruins of the Fox family farm on the first loop and the Snead Farm on the second loop.

From the visitor center parking lot, cross Skyline Drive and head for the large sign to the trailhead. Follow the path to your left, which quickly intersects with blue-blazed Dickey Ridge Trail (marked by a concrete post). Head to your left and follow Dickey Ridge Trail for 0.3 mile to its intersection with Fox Hollow Trail, then take a right.

This unblazed trail follows a rather obvious path down through the remains of the Fox homestead, passing rockpiles and eventually the family cemetery. The trail will take a sharp right turn after the cemetery and start heading uphill. At 1.2 miles into the hike, Fox Hollow Trail returns to its previous intersection with Dickey Ridge Trail. Turn left to follow Dickey Ridge for the second loop of the hike.

A brief and pleasant walk along Dickey Ridge Trail leads to an intersection with Snead Farm Road, a wide fire road, at 1.7 miles. Turn left, and in a few short steps the road passes an intersection with a trail coming in from the

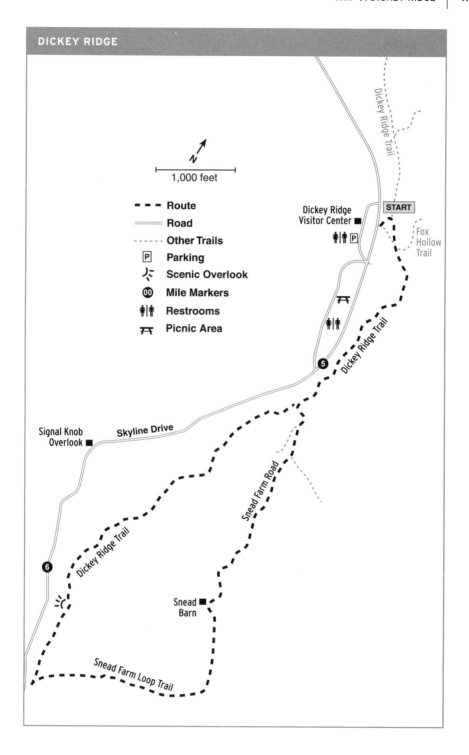

DICKEY RIDGE

N

1,000 feet

- - - Route
——— Road
- - - - Other Trails
P Parking
人 Scenic Overlook
00 Mile Markers
♦|♦ Restrooms
🎪 Picnic Area

START

Dickey Ridge Trail

Dickey Ridge
Visitor Center ■

♦|♦ P

Fox
Hollow
Trail

5

Dickey Ridge Trail

Signal Knob
Overlook ■

Skyline Drive

Snead Farm Road

6

Dickey Ridge Trail

Snead ■
Barn

Snead Farm Loop Trail

Young hikers may not be up for the entire 4.8-mile route, but a shorter 1.2-mile loop is family-friendly.

woods on the right (your return route). Continue along Snead Farm Road, which has two well-marked forks in quick succession. At the first fork in the trail, stay to your left and head downhill. The second fork is just a short distance after the first; here, follow the path to the right that leads up the hill. At 2.4 miles, this grassy path will lead you to the remains of Snead Farm, which was abandoned in the 1950s. The barn still stands—one of the last non–National Park Service structures in the park—and you can see the stone foundation of the house.

After exploring the ruins, look for a concrete post and follow Snead Barn Loop Trail (blue blazes) back into the woods. This path maintains a steady and mild uphill track, and eventually leads to Dickey Ridge Trail at 3.1 miles. Turn right and continue to climb on Dickey Ridge Trail. Good views of the valley open on the left. Keep a lookout for a short spur trail at 3.3 miles that leads to a nice open viewpoint where you can take in the valley, the south fork of the Shenandoah River, and Massanutten Mountain.

The trail continues uphill for a short distance before descending on an easier grade and then regains the fire road at 4.3 miles. Turn left onto the fire road, and then make a quick right to stay on Dickey Ridge Trail. Retrace your steps back along the blue-blazed trail. At the intersection marked with the concrete post (at 4.8 miles), turn left to complete the hike and to return to the visitor center.

Since this hike follows a figure-eight shape, you can choose to shorten it by taking just one of the two loops. The first loop is a hike of roughly 1.2 miles, while the second loop is 3.7 miles.

DID YOU KNOW?

Four generations of the Fox family lived in Shenandoah before being displaced to make room for the creation of the park. Thomas and Martha Fox settled in Fox Hollow in 1856; Lemuel Fox Jr. and his wife, Martha, left the Hollow in 1935.

MORE INFORMATION

Shenandoah National Park (nps.gov/shen, 540-999-3500, 800-732-0911 [for emergencies]). Pets are not permitted on Fox Hollow Trail. Park facilities are generally open from March through late November; a facilities schedule is online. In cases of inclement weather and at night in deer-hunting season (mid-November through early January), call the park to confirm whether Skyline Drive is open to vehicles. Overnight lodging in the park includes lodges, cabins, and campgrounds; visit nps.gov/shen/planyourvisit/lodging.htm or nps.gov/shen/planyourvisit/campgrounds.htm for more information.

NEARBY

The trails sit at the top of Skyline Drive, placing them close to Front Royal. This town has a number of stores, shops, and restaurants to fit every budget and cuisine preference.

TRIP 10
ELKWALLOW

Location: North District, Shenandoah National Park, VA
Rating: Easy
Distance: 3.8 miles round-trip
Elevation Gain: 1,049 feet gain
Estimated Time: 2–3 hours
Maps: PATC, *Map 9, Appalachian Trail and other trails in Shenandoah National Park, North District,* 2009.

For children, for the childlike at heart, or really for anyone with a hankering for ice cream (soft serve and blackberry!), the gentle hike from Mathews Arm down Elkwallow Trail will be a trip to remember.

DIRECTIONS

From I-66, Exit 43A, take US 29 South 13.2 miles to Warrenton. Turn right onto US 211 and drive for 34 miles. West of Sperryville, US 211 twists and turns to meet the park entrance at Thornton Gap (fee). Drive north (right) on Skyline Drive for about 9.0 miles, passing Elkwallow Wayside on your left. A little farther down the road, turn left onto Mathews Arm Road and park in the hikers' lot on your right, just shy of the Mathews Arm Campground gate. *GPS coordinates: 38° 45.599′ N, 78° 17.837′ W.*

TRAIL DESCRIPTION

Refreshment awaits at the end of this hike thanks to the conveniently placed Elkwallow Wayside facility. Carryout meals, groceries, gifts, and camping supplies are available. In spring, expect to see Appalachian Trail (AT) thru-hikers taking a break on the nearby picnic tables. It's always fun to chat with them about their journeys.

From the parking lot, look southward across Mathews Arm Road and spot the post marking Elkwallow Trail. The trail, which is blue blazed, climbs gently for a few feet, then descends about 200 feet. The sound of running water on your left greets you before you reach a creek, which is helpfully bridged, at 0.25 mile. From that point, the trail rolls slightly as it goes along, though there are no dramatic changes in elevation.

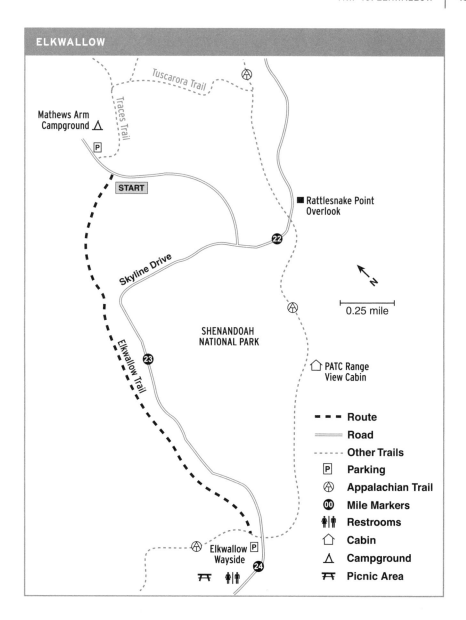

ELKWALLOW

Tuscarora Trail

Traces Trail

Mathews Arm
Campground △

P

START

■ Rattlesnake Point
Overlook

Skyline Drive

22

0.25 mile

SHENANDOAH
NATIONAL PARK

Elkwallow Trail

23

⌂ PATC Range
View Cabin

- - - **Route**

═══ **Road**

----- **Other Trails**

P **Parking**

Ⓐ **Appalachian Trail**

⓪⓪ **Mile Markers**

🚻 **Restrooms**

⌂ **Cabin**

△ **Campground**

🏕 **Picnic Area**

Elkwallow P
Wayside

24

The trail keeps Skyline Drive on its left throughout the hike, and the road will draw closer as you near Elkwallow Wayside; you may hear the occasional passing car. Just before you reach the AT at 1.8 miles, you should be able to spot Skyline Drive through the trees. Cross the AT—whites blazes to your left and your right—but continue following the blue blazes to the wayside at 1.9 miles.

The wayside at Elkwallow offers a number of scrumptious treats for the hungry hiker.

For very small children, consider starting at the Mathews Arm parking lot; have another adult in your party drive your vehicle to Elkwallow Wayside and walk north on the trail to meet the southbound party. This results in a one-way hike of 1.9 miles, with 383 feet of gain and 666 feet of loss—overall, it's nice, gentle downhill walking. And ice cream at the end.

If going out-and-back on Elkwallow Trail does not appeal, consider making a gentle loop by heading north on the AT from the Elkwallow Wayside. Return to the west side of Skyline Drive and take a left onto Tuscarora Trail, then another left on Traces Trail to return to your vehicle about 0.5 miles farther along (total distance for this loop is about 4.9 miles). Pets are not allowed on Traces Trail, but this loop is suitable for children.

DID YOU KNOW?

From the same parking lot, Traces Trail makes a gentle, 1.7-mile loop around Mathews Arm Campground that would be suitable for children.

MORE INFORMATION

Shenandoah National Park (nps.gov/shen, 540-999-3500, 800-732-0911 [for emergencies]). Elkwallow Wayside is open daily from 9 A.M. to 6 P.M. between April and early November; visit goshenandoah.com for additional concessioner information. Other park facilities are generally open from March through late November; a facilities schedule is online. In cases of inclement weather and at night in deer-hunting season (mid-November through early January), call the park to confirm whether Skyline Drive is open to vehicles. Overnight lodging in the park includes lodges, cabins, and campgrounds, including Mathews Arm Campground; visit nps.gov/shen/planyourvisit/lodging .htm or nps.gov/shen/planyourvisit/campgrounds.htm for more information.

NEARBY

Post–ice cream, you may hunger for some real food. If so, drive north on Skyline Drive to the north gate and the nearby town of Front Royal. Sperryville also offers several eateries and shops. A wider range of businesses can be found in Warrenton. Additional hikes in Shenandoah's north district include Jeremy's Run (Trip 13), Overall Run (Trip 11), and Little Devils Stair (Trip 12).

TRIP 11
OVERALL RUN

Location: North District, Shenandoah National Park, VA
Rating: Strenuous
Distance: 9.5 miles
Elevation Gain: 3,094 feet gain
Estimated Time: 4–6 hours
Maps: PATC, *Map 9, Appalachian Trail and other trails in Shenandoah National Park, North District*, 2009.

This ramble in Shenandoah's north district features one of the finest views in the area: the 93-foot falls at Overall Run, which can be especially spectacular in the spring.

DIRECTIONS
From I-66, Exit 43A, take US 29 South 13.2 miles to Warrenton. Turn right on US 211 and drive for 34 miles. West of Sperryville, US 211 twists and turns to meet the park entrance at Thornton Gap (fee). Drive north (right) on Skyline Drive for about 9.0 miles, passing Elkwallow Wayside on your left. A little farther down the road, turn left onto Mathews Arm Road, and park in the hikers' lot on your right, just shy of the Mathews Arm Campground gate. *GPS coordinates:* 38° 45.599′ N, 78° 17.837′ W.

TRAIL DESCRIPTION
When you're ready to begin hiking, walk on the pavement past the entrance to the campground—this is Mathews Arm Road. Beyond the entrance, bear left on Knob Mountain Road. Pass the hook-up station for RVs, walk around a gate, then continue downhill on a road that turns to gravel. Shortly thereafter, at 0.5 miles, you'll spot a post on the right indicating the Heiskell Hollow Trailhead—your route. On the left is a sign for Knob Mountain Trail.

Begin your descent of the western face of the Shenandoah by following the yellow blazes of Heiskell Hollow Trail, which drops 1,500 feet over the next 2.4 miles into the drainage of Compton Run. The trail turns sharply to the right, then reaches an intersection with Weddlewood Trail, also blazed yellow, at 1.25 miles. This trail cuts across the mountain's shoulder and reaches Overall Run from above. Your route turns sharply to the left, continuing to

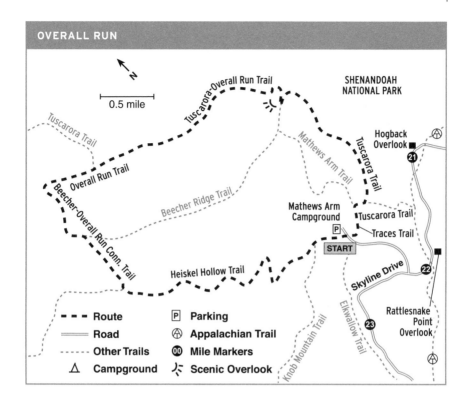

follow Heiskell Hollow Trail. As the descent continues, listen carefully for the sound of water on the left. Soon, the hollow flattens out, and the trail follows the stream before reaching an intersection on the right with Beecher Ridge Trail at 2.9 miles.

Take the right, cross the creek several times in the stream bottom, and follow the yellow blazes as Beecher Ridge Trail traverses the western face of the Shenandoah at its knees. The path climbs some; the footing becomes sandy and, in spring, the mountain laurel will bloom around you. At 3.9 miles, the climb tops out on Beecher Ridge, where the trail heads right to climb back toward Skyline Drive. Instead, stay left and follow the blue blazes of Beecher Ridge–Overall Run Connector Trail as it descends into Overall Run Valley at 4.6 miles.

After a few creek crossings, the path reaches the very base of Overall Run Trail, which is blazed blue. Turn right to follow this trail as it climbs back toward Mathews Arm—almost 2,500 feet and 4.4 miles away from this point. For the first section, the grade is fairly gentle as the trail follows the run, on the right. The route passes a trail leading off to the left at 5.25 miles, which is

A hiker enjoys the view west towards Massanutten Mountain from the viewpoint near Overall Run falls.

actually Tuscarora Trail headed out of the park. Continue straight onto what is now Overall Run–Tuscarora Trail. The footing becomes rocky and again crosses the run several times.

When the trail pulls away from the last creek crossing to the left at 6.25 miles, it gets serious about getting up the mountain, switchbacking very steeply for a section, then going straight uphill. Thankfully, this difficult climb ends at 6.8 miles, with a stunning view of Massanutten Mountain to the west, as well as of the valley out of which you've climbed. Take time to explore these outcroppings and a short spur trail farther down the path for opportunities to photograph and to get closer to the falls. The grade relents above this point, but the climbing continues.

Navigating the web of trails around Mathews Arm can be tricky, but never fear, as a serious error would be difficult to make. At 7.25 miles, your route reaches turnoffs to the left and the right, very near together, for Mathews Arm Trail. Ignore these and continue to follow Overall Run–Tuscarora Trail, which brings you to an intersection at 9.1 miles. At this intersection, bear right and then left to follow Traces Trail (unblazed, but very easy to follow) as it rounds the campground and brings you to your vehicle.

If you are looking to shorten this loop, consider descending Beecher Ridge Trail instead of Heiskell Hollow. A slightly longer variant could start from the AT parking lot near Hogback Overlook off Skyline Drive.

DID YOU KNOW?

As you're climbing Overall Run, for much of the distance, you'll be walking on the first few miles of Tuscarora Trail, a variant of the Appalachian Trail that starts in the Shenandoah and rejoins the AT just shy of Harrisburg, Pennsylvania (see The Tuscarora Trail). As Tuscarora Trail leaves the national park, it descends via Overall Run Valley to cross the Shenandoah River and then reach Massanutten Mountain.

MORE INFORMATION

Shenandoah National Park (nps.gov/shen, 540-999-3500, 800-732-0911 [for emergencies]). Pets are not allowed on Traces Trail. Park facilities are generally open from March through late November; a facilities schedule is online. In cases of inclement weather and at night in deer-hunting season (mid-November through early January), call the park to confirm whether Skyline Drive is open to vehicles. Overnight lodging in the park includes lodges, cabins, and campgrounds, including Mathews Arm Campground; visit nps.gov/shen/planyourvisit/lodging.htm or nps.gov/shen/planyourvisit/campgrounds.htm for more information.

NEARBY

There are a number of additional hikes in Shenandoah's northern district detailed in this book, including Jeremy's Run (Trip 13), Elkwallow (Trip 10), and Little Devils Stair (Trip 12).

Once you've hiked to your heart's content, consider stopping at Elkwallow Wayside or Mathews Arm for a picnic or a snack. The nearest good-sized town is Front Royal, but Sperryville offers several eateries and shops. A wider range of businesses can be found in Warrenton.

TRIP 12
LITTLE DEVILS STAIRS

Location: North District, Shenandoah National Park, VA
Rating: Moderate
Distance: 5.7 miles round-trip
Elevation Gain: 1,940 feet gain
Estimated Time: 3–5 hours
Maps: PATC, *Map 9, Appalachian Trail and other trails in Shenandoah National Park, North District,* 2009.

Winding its way between the steep cliffs of the gorge, Little Devils Stairs is a classic Virginia climb renowned for its wildness and it backcountry feel, though it is just steps away from the Appalachian Trail and Skyline Drive.

DIRECTIONS
From I-66, Exit 43A, take US 29 South 13.2 miles to Warrenton. Turn right onto US 211 and drive for 24.8 miles. Just shy of Sperryville, turn right onto VA 622/Gidbrown Hollow Road and proceed 1.9 miles. Turn left onto VA 614/Keyser Run Road and drive about 3.1 miles. The parking lot on the right can hold about a half dozen cars. *GPS coordinates:* 38° 43.836′ N, 78° 15.491′ W.

TRAIL DESCRIPTION
In its first 2.0 miles, Little Devils Stairs Trail takes you on one of the most picturesque climbs in the Shenandoah as it twists and turns past waterfalls, steep rock faces, rockfalls, and dark forests. And climb it will—about 1,600 feet. At points the trail will be steep (as much as a 45 percent grade, though that stretch is mercifully short) and slick. At times, the trail is also co-located with the creek, especially if the mountains are at all wet. In fact, if there's been much rain or if there's any chance of ice, be cautious on this hike. Conditions in the gorge could become hazardous. Don't forget your camera; many places along Little Devils Stairs will make for excellent photographs.

From the parking lot, blue-blazed Little Devils Stairs Trail heads straight into the woods. Before you embark, however, spot and note Keyser Run Fire Road, as you'll be returning this way at the hike's end.

As the blue blazes lead into the forest, cross two streams that are easy to rock-hop. At first, the grade is moderate, but the trail soon draws near Keyser

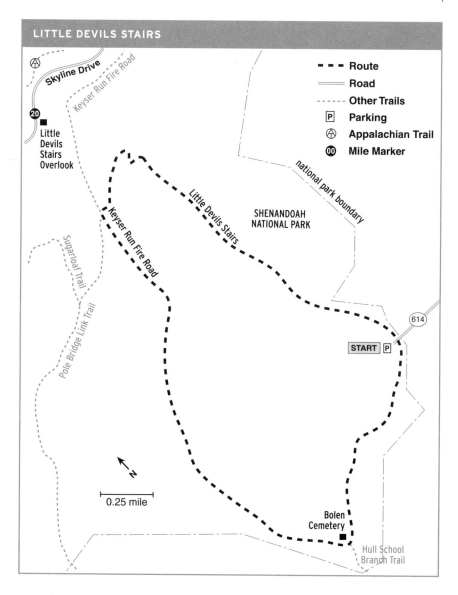

Run, the stream that has eroded the gorge over time. Here, the climbing begins in earnest. Take your time, however, as the steepest areas are also the most scenic. The route crosses Keyser Run numerous times and ascends staircases of stone, passing between forbidding walls of rock. In this area, admire waterfalls but keep an eye on the blue blazes. On a spring afternoon, the sunlight will struggle to find its way into this secluded hollow.

At last, the trail crosses the creek one final time and begins to veer leftward away from the gorge at 1.8 miles, climbing still, but at a less relentless grade,

Hikers negotiate the steep sections of Little Devils Stairs.

as it switchbacks to the intersection known as Fourway at 2.0 miles. Directly across, Pole Bridge Link Trail leads south toward Elkwallow, while Keyser Run Fire Road cuts across the path to the left and the right. Turning right here will bring you to a small parking area off Skyline Drive. Your continuing route turns left to follow the fire road back to the trailhead.

The 3.5-mile descent down yellow-blazed Keyser Run Fire Road will be uneventful as it loses the elevation you worked so hard to gain. The fire road, however, takes a fairly moderate grade, so it will also be pleasant walking. Following the yellow blazes, pass Hull School Trail on your right at 4.3 miles and the Bolen Family Cemetery just a little farther on your left. Eventually, the trail passes a gate and arrives back at the parking lot.

If you're looking to walk a longer route (about 7.9 miles), consider taking Pole Bridge Link Trail from Fourway to Piney Branch Trail, and return to Keyser Run Fire Road via Hull School Trail. Add Piney Ridge Trail to this for an even longer loop.

DID YOU KNOW?

The Bolen Family Cemetery, which the route passes on the left as you descend Keyser Run Fire Road, is a reminder of the settlers who inhabited these hollows before the establishment of the national park in the 1930s. If you have a keen eye, you may be able to spot some remnants of old stone walls and foundations along Little Devils Stairs.

MORE INFORMATION

Shenandoah National Park (nps.gov/shen, 540-999-3500, 800-732-0911 [for emergencies]). Park facilities are generally open from March through late November; a facilities schedule is online. In cases of inclement weather and at night in deer-hunting season (mid-November through early January), call the park to confirm whether Skyline Drive is open to vehicles. Overnight lodging in the park includes lodges, cabins, and campgrounds; visit nps.gov/shen/planyourvisit/lodging.htm or nps.gov/shen/planyourvisit/campgrounds.htm for more information.

NEARBY

A little farther west from the intersection of VA 622 and US 211, Sperryville offers several eateries and shops. A wider range of businesses can be found in Warrenton. If it's more hiking you're after, the north district of Shenandoah will not disappoint. See Jeremy's Run (Trip 13), Overall Run (Trip 11), and Elkwallow (Trip 10).

TRIP 13
JEREMY'S RUN AND KNOB MOUNTAIN

Location: North District, Shenandoah National Park, VA
Rating: Strenuous
Distance: 13.1 miles round-trip
Elevation Gain: 3,164 feet
Estimated Time: 5–8 hours
Maps: PATC, *Map 9, Appalachian Trail and other trails in Shenandoah National Park, North District,* 2009.

The highlight of this wet and wild leg-stretcher is the walk along Jeremy's Run, with its abundance of cascades, pools, and waterfalls, not to mention its many creek crossings.

DIRECTIONS
From I-66, Exit 43A, take US 29 South 13.2 miles to Warrenton. Turn right onto US 211 and drive for 34 miles. West of Sperryville, US 211 twists and turns to meet the park entrance at Thornton Gap (fee). Drive north (right) on Skyline Drive for 7.2 miles to Elkwallow Wayside on your left. Turn into the ample lot and park. *GPS coordinates:* 38° 44.336′ N, 78° 18.564′ W.

TRAIL DESCRIPTION
A bit isolated from Skyline Drive at the Appalachian Trail, you'll need to make a good-sized loop using Knob Mountain Trail to see Jeremy's Run in its entirety. Before beginning this circuit, consider conditions carefully: You'll be crossing the run many times, and if the creek is particularly high, it can be impossible for you stay dry. In warm weather, this route can be very enjoyable, as the cold-water crossings will feel refreshing. No matter how steamy the summer heat, it is probably not prudent to attempt this hike if there's been a great deal of rainfall recently.

From the parking lot, look past the concession shop, to the north, and spot the blue-blazed trail leading into the forest. A few feet into the woods, the trail joins the Appalachian Trail (AT). Turn left and follow the white blazes southbound for about 0.6 mile.

Soon enough, you'll reach an intersection where the AT heads south, or left, and blue-blazed Jeremy's Run Trail continues straight (west). Follow this

JEREMY'S RUN AND KNOB MOUNTAIN

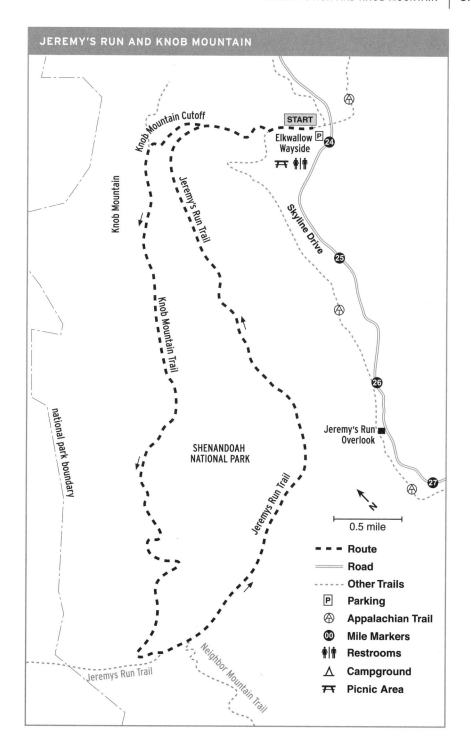

Knob Mountain Cutoff

START

Elkwallow
Wayside

24

Skyline Drive

25

Knob Mountain

Jeremy's Run Trail

Knob Mountain Trail

national park boundary

SHENANDOAH
NATIONAL PARK

26

Jeremy's Run
Overlook

27

Jeremys Run Trail

N

0.5 mile

Jeremys Run Trail

Neighbor Mountain Trail

- - - Route

——— Road

- - - Other Trails

P Parking

Ⓐ Appalachian Trail

⓪⓪ Mile Markers

👫 Restrooms

△ Campground

🏕 Picnic Area

Tackling Jeremy's Run means a multitude of potentially wet creek crossings, like this one.

trail as it descends into the run's drainage. At an intersection at 1.3 miles, Jeremy's Run Trail reaches the creek and continues its descent straight ahead, but Knob Mountain Cut Off Trail branches right. Both are blazed blue. (Take note of this intersection; you'll be returning to it near the end of the hike.) Take Knob Mountain Cut Off Trail to the right, cross the creek, and begin a short but sometimes steep climb to Knob Mountain Trail.

At 1.9 miles, turn left onto now yellow-blazed Knob Mountain Trail. Over the next 2.1 miles, the trail climbs about 680 feet, primarily along an old forest road, before it reaches the summit of Knob Mountain, which is marked by a post, at 3.9 miles. This significant mountain fences in Jeremy's Run on its westward flanks. Though the peak is fairly prominent compared with its neighbors, its summit is wooded and has few views. You may, however, be able to catch occasional glimpses of the valley below, and of Massanutten Mountain to the west.

From Knob Mountain's summit, begin the 1,600-foot descent to the water of the run. Though this is a considerable dropoff, the path is well graded and the footing is not especially rocky. Eventually, the stream becomes audible, and at 6.9 miles the route forces you to ford the run for the first of many crossings. On the far side, turn left onto the blue blazes and immediately pass the intersection for Neighbor Mountain Trail on the right, which offers another opportunity for a different circuit hike (be warned, though, as this circuit is a little longer, at almost 15 miles).

For the next 5.0 miles, the path follows the fairly gentle walk up Jeremy's Run, the highlight of this trip and one of the finest hikes in the park. In the beginning of this section, the trail passes a large waterfall, which makes an excellent spot for a break. (Note the large campsite across the stream.) Each of the crossings provides an excellent opportunity to admire the pools and water-works of the creek. You may spot wildlife: Deer and black bears are common enough in this expansive valley.

Fourteen crossings later (but who's counting?), at 11.9 miles, the route regains the intersection with Knob Mountain Cut Off Trail. Bear right, and continue climbing on the blue blazes until you reach the AT at 12.5 miles. Follow the white blazes until you are virtually at the Elkwallow Wayside. Turn right to enter the parking lot.

If 13 miles seems a bit much, consider visiting Jeremy's Run from its lower trailhead near US 340. Just off VA 611, which leaves VA 340 to head east to-ward the park, there is a parking lot that will enable you to reach the bottom of Jeremy's Run, as described here, after just 1.3 miles of walking. By walking out and back from this trailhead, you can get a taste for what the trail is all about without having to commit to such a demanding loop.

DID YOU KNOW?

Jeremy's Run features some of the best fishing in the park. Fishing is allowed, but it is regulated. To learn more about the rules for fishing in Shenandoah Na-tional Park, see the park service's flyer on the topic: nps.gov/shen/planyourvisit/upload/recreational_fishing_combined_2013.pdf.

MORE INFORMATION

Shenandoah National Park (nps.gov/shen, 540-999-3500, 800-732-0911 [for emergencies]). Elkwallow Wayside—which offers carryout, groceries, camp-ing supplies, and more—is open daily from 9 A.M. to 6 P.M. between April and early November; visit goshenandoah.com for additional concessioner infor-mation. Park facilities are generally open from March through late November; a facilities schedule is online. In cases of inclement weather and at night in deer-hunting season (mid-November through early January), call the park to confirm whether Skyline Drive is open to vehicles. Overnight lodging in the park includes lodges, cabins, and campgrounds, including Mathews Arm

Campground; visit nps.gov/shen/planyourvisit/lodging.htm or nps.gov/shen/planyourvisit/campgrounds.htm for more information.

NEARBY

This section of this book details a number of additional hikes in the north district, including Little Devils Stairs (Trip 12), Elkwallow (Trip 10), and Overall Run (Trip 11). Of course, the central district is not far, either.

The little store at the Elkwallow Wayside sells a number of treats, and concessions may also be had at Mathews Arm, a few miles north along Skyline Drive. If you're in pursuit of more substantial fare, then your best bet is to drive north to Front Royal or south to Sperryville or Luray.

3

CENTRAL SHENANDOAH NATIONAL PARK

THOUGH EUROPEAN SETTLERS ONLY REACHED THE HEIGHTS of what is now Shenandoah National Park as recently as 300 years ago, evidence of human settlement here goes back 8,000 to 9,000 years. Native people were more often visitors than residents, combing the mountains for resources including wild game, nuts and berries, and stone for tools. Around 1750, however, the first settlers began homesteading in the hollows, quickly opening doors for a community of farmers, loggers, and hunters. By the early twentieth century, though, these residents were a barrier to the protection of this land as a national park. For better or worse, in the 1930s at least 500 families were relocated and the Civilian Conservation Corps (CCC) began constructing Skyline Drive, overlooks, and other facilities that make the park what it is today. The CCC's construction work took years, beginning in 1933, two years before the park was officially established; the last CCC camp was disbanded in 1942, shortly after America entered World War II. Much of this human history is still preserved along the trails, particularly in Nicholson, Corbin, and Weakley hollows, where cellar holes and stone walls are ghostly reminders of what these hills were before the park came to be. (For a brief overview of the park and its Wilderness Areas, read the introduction to Section 2; for more on the park's ecology, read the introduction to Section 4.)

Shenandoah National Park's central district encompasses more than 21,000 acres of designated Wilderness between Thornton Gap and Swift Run Gap (after milepost 31 on Skyline Drive to milepost 65.5). Many of the park's overnight options are in this area, including Skyland Resort (milepost 41.7), Big Meadows Lodge and Campground (217 sites, milepost 51), Lewis Mountain Campground and Cabins (milepost 57.5), and four Potomac Appalachian Club Cabins: Corbin, Jones Mountain, Rock Spring, and Pocosin (visit patc.net to make reservations). The Byrd Visitor Center is located at milepost 51. Picnic areas include Pinnacles (milepost 36.5) and South River (milepost 62.5). The segment of Skyline Drive in this district boasts 32 overlooks, as well as access to the park's highest peak, Hawksbill (Trip 19, 4,051 feet).

TRIP 14
MARY'S ROCK

Location: Central District, Shenandoah National Park, VA
Rating: Moderate
Distance: 2.7 miles, round-trip
Elevation Gain: 1,043 feet
Estimated Time: 1–2 hours
Maps: PATC, *Map 10, Appalachian Trail and other trails in Shenandoah National Park, Central District,* 2008.

Get your pulse racing on this climb to the top of the eighth-highest peak in Shenandoah. Stunning 360-degree views and rock-scrambling opportunities await you at the top.

DIRECTIONS
From I-66, Exit 43A, take US 29 South 13.2 miles to Warrenton. Turn right onto US 211 and drive for 34 miles. West of Sperryville, US 211 twists and turns to meet the park entrance at Thornton Gap (fee). Drive south on Skyline Drive to the Meadow Spring Parking Area between mile markers 33 and 34. *GPS coordinates:* 38° 38.300′ N, 78° 18.823′ W.

TRAIL DESCRIPTION
The views from Mary's Rock of the park and the surrounding valleys earn this hike its popularity. At 3,487 feet, this is the eighth-highest point in the park.

From the Meadow Spring Parking Area, cross Skyline Drive and head left up the path. One of the park's ubiquitous concrete trail markers indicates the trailhead. Turn right here onto blue-blazed Meadow Spring Trail, and start with a steady climb. The first 0.25 mile is the toughest, as the path gains about 650 feet in elevation, but the route takes you through a tunnel of mountain laurels—a stunning sight when they're in bloom in spring.

At 0.4 mile, pass the remains of an old homestead as the trail winds its way up the mountain. Soon, at 0.6 mile, arrive at a three-way intersection with the Appalachian Trail (AT). Turn right and begin to follow its white blazes. The AT continues uphill just a bit longer but starts to dip and eventually levels out just beyond 0.75 mile. Great views of the Shenandoah Valley stretch left as you walk along the ridge. Short side trails take you to overlooks, but the real prize is ahead at 1.1 miles as you get your first look at the base of Mary's Rock.

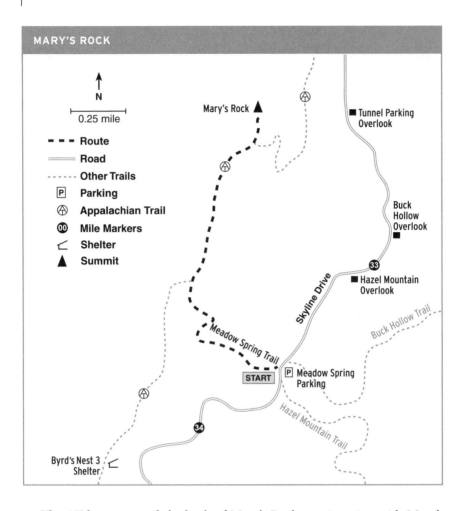

MARY'S ROCK

N
0.25 mile

- - - Route
═══ Road
----- Other Trails
P Parking
Ⓐ Appalachian Trail
⓪⓪ Mile Markers
⊏ Shelter
▲ Summit

Mary's Rock ▲

■ Tunnel Parking Overlook

Buck Hollow Overlook

Skyline Drive

�33

■ Hazel Mountain Overlook

Buck Hollow Trail

Meadow Spring Trail

START | P Meadow Spring Parking

Hazel Mountain Trail

�34

Byrd's Nest 3 Shelter ⊏

The AT loops around the back of Mary's Rock to a junction with Mary's Rock Lookout Trail at 1.2 miles. Take a left onto this spur trail. In just 0.1 mile, the views open up at Mary's Rock itself. To the west, you can see more of the Shenandoah Valley and Massanutten Mountain. To the north, the Thornton Gap park entrance is visible below a few of the park's northern peaks. A short scramble to the top of Mary's Rock earns you even more stunning views of the surrounding area.

To return, simply retrace your steps back to the parking lot.

DID YOU KNOW?

Legends abound about how Mary's Rock got its name, each with its own twist. The first is for the romantics: Francis Thornton brought his wife, Mary, to the top of the mountain to show her the lands they would own together. A more

The views from Mary's Rock are some of the best in the park.

adventurous legend says Thornton's daughter Mary climbed the mountain when she was young and returned with a bear cub under her arm. The last keeps it simple: It was named after Mary Barbee, the wife of sculptor William Randolph Barbee, who was from the area.

MORE INFORMATION

Shenandoah National Park (nps.gov/shen, 540-999-3500, 800-732-0911 [for emergencies]). Park facilities are generally open from March through late November; a facilities schedule is online. In cases of inclement weather and at night in deer-hunting season (mid-November through early January), call the park to confirm whether Skyline Drive is open to vehicles. Overnight lodging in the park includes lodges, cabins, and campgrounds; visit nps.gov/shen/planyourvisit/lodging.htm or nps.gov/shen/planyourvisit/campgrounds.htm for more information.

NEARBY

You'll find no shortage of hikes along Skyline Drive, including Stony Man (Trip 15), and numerous overlooks to give you even better views of the surrounding valleys. Nearby Sperryville has restaurants and small shops, and VA 211 is dotted with wineries, perfect for a post-hike snack and sip.

PUTTING THE NATION TO WORK

The Civilian Conservation Corps (CCC) was the nation's largest public work relief program and formed much of the national park system we enjoy today. One of the most popular components of President Franklin D. Roosevelt's New Deal, the CCC was created to address the devastating and lingering impacts of the Great Depression. When Roosevelt took office, one quarter of the nation's workers were unemployed, most of them young men with no real opportunities.

Established in 1933 and in operation until 1942, the CCC provided jobs for unemployed and unmarried men, ages 18 to 25, from families who had difficulty finding employment. Each participant received $30 a month, $25 of which had to go back to his family. In addition, the men received food, shelter, medical care, and clothing. They had to work for one 6-month period, and could serve up to four periods over two years if they had difficulty finding employment. During its nine years, more than 3 million men participated in the CCC. Nationally, they planted nearly 3 billion trees, constructed more than 800 parks, and supported the construction of buildings and roadways.

The earliest CCC camps were located in Virginia: Camp Roosevelt (a side trip from Trip 31) was the first to be created. Shenandoah National Park was home to the first CCC two camps to be located in national parks: Skyland and Big Meadows. In total, Virginia had had more than 80 CCC camps, with ten either in or near Shenandoah National Park, ranking fourth among states for the number of camps. More than 107,000 men worked for the CCC in Virginia.

The primary objective of CCC work in Virginia was to control erosion and support reforestation, but the most visible legacy may be the work to support the development of a state park system—Virginia had none before 1932—and the work in Shenandoah National Park. The men built overlooks, picnic areas, campgrounds, comfort stations, visitor and maintenance buildings, and signs. They removed most evidence of human habitation in the park, a charge that stirs some debate today (see "A Wonder Way:" Where the Hills Were Once Home). Volunteers also built many of the stone walls along the drive and overlooks. While some of these walls have since been rebuilt, the work was done using the original stone.

World War II and higher employment rates led to the termination of the CCC in 1942, but the work accomplished by the volunteers has lasted for decades. In its final report on the CCC, the state of Virginia noted: "In no state did the CCC make a greater or more lasting contribution to the well-being of its citizens than it did in Virginia."

TRIP 15
STONY MAN

Location: Central District, Shenandoah National Park, VA
Rating: Easy
Distance: 1.5 miles
Elevation Gain: 407 feet
Estimated Time: 1–2 hours
Maps: PATC, *Map 10, Appalachian Trail and other trails in Shenandoah National Park, Central District,* 2008.

Ascending Shenandoah's second-tallest mountain is a short and rewarding hike, probably one of the nicest circuits in the park. Arrive early to avoid the crowds; this is one of the park's most popular hikes.

DIRECTIONS

From I-66, Exit 43A, take US 29 South 13.2 miles to Warrenton. Turn right onto US 211 and drive for 34 miles. West of Sperryville, US 211 twists and turns to meet the park entrance at Thornton Gap (fee). Drive south on Skyline Drive to Skyland parking lot between mileposts 41 and 42. *GPS coordinates:* 38° 35.555′ N, 78° 22.535′ W.

TRAIL DESCRIPTION

This short hike gives a quick reward as you climb to the top of Stony Man Mountain, Shenandoah's second-tallest mountain at 4,014 feet. It's one of the easier and more pleasant hikes in the park, which explains its popularity. Despite its being a short hike, a few trails may make navigation more complicated than other hikes of this difficulty; just keep an eye on the blazes to stay headed in the right direction.

From the parking lot, look for the well-signed trailhead that leads to the white-blazed Appalachian Trail (AT). (At the start, blue-blazed Stony Man Loop Trail and the AT share the same path.) The route starts off with an easy and mild climb. Pass several numbered posts, which are part of a self-guided interpretative nature walk; a guide is available from nearby Skyland Resort.

Arrive at an intersection at 0.4 mile. The AT turns to the right, but follow blue-blazed Stony Man Loop Trail straight through the intersection. The trail quickly splits; going in either direction will get you to the top. (Yellow-blazed Stony Man Horse Trail can create a bit of confusion along this loop; continue

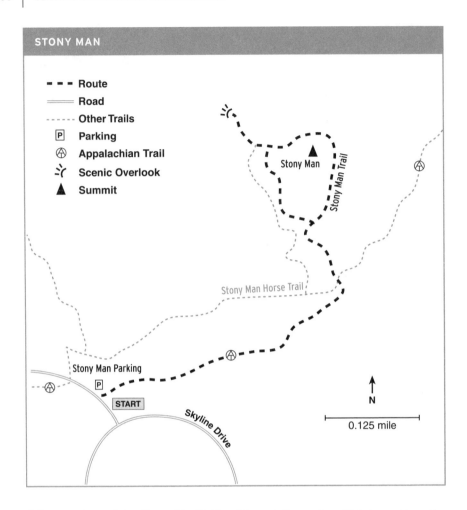

following Stony Man Loop Trail's blue blazes.) From the AT intersection, the trail begins to climb more steadily up the mountain. A well-placed sign at the top directs you to the main vista over the town of Luray and the Shenandoah Valley below, and Massanutten Mountain in the distance. Some side trails lead to equally stunning and less-crowded views.

To complete the loop, continue along blue-blazed Stony Man Loop Trail. Arrive back at the intersection with the AT at 1.0 mile. Turn right onto the AT, and retrace your path back to the parking lot.

DID YOU KNOW?

Skyland Resort, once known as Stony Man Camp, was built before the park came into existence. Constructed in 1895, it was built by George Freeman

Shenandoah's green tunnels are just as famous as the park's many views.

Pollock and designed for wealthy vacationers. The resort was taken over by Shenandoah National Park in 1931, with Skyline Drive being built past it.

MORE INFORMATION

Shenandoah National Park (nps.gov/shen, 540-999-3500, 800-732-0911 [for emergencies]). Pets are not allowed on Stony Man Trail. Park facilities are generally open from March through late November; a facilities schedule is online. In cases of inclement weather and at night in deer-hunting season (mid-November through early January), call the park to confirm whether Skyline Drive is open to vehicles. Overnight lodging in the park includes lodges, cabins, and campgrounds; visit nps.gov/shen/planyourvisit/lodging.htm or nps.gov/shen/planyourvisit/campgrounds.htm for more information.

NEARBY

Skyline Drive is dotted with hikes and overlooks, and Big Meadows Campground gives a good base to explore the area. Nearby hikes include Lewis Falls (Trip 16) and Rose River and Dark Hollow Falls (Trip 18).

TRIP 16
LEWIS FALLS

Location: Central District, Shenandoah National Park, VA
Rating: Moderate
Distance: 3.0 miles
Elevation Gain: 997 feet
Estimated Time: 1–2 hours
Maps: PATC, *Map 10, Appalachian Trail and other trails in Shenandoah National Park, Central District,* 2008.

Lewis Falls is just one of the attractions along this pleasant walk near Big Meadows Campground. Tack on a quick scramble to Blackrock Cliffs for great views of the valley.

DIRECTIONS
From I-66, Exit 43A, take US 29 South 13.2 miles to Warrenton. Turn right onto US 211 and drive for 34 miles. West of Sperryville, US 211 twists and turns to meet the park entrance at Thornton Gap (fee). Drive south on Skyline Drive to the gated service road just south of Big Meadows (milepost 51). The main lot can hold just a few cars; if it is full, head back toward Big Meadows for additional parking options. *GPS coordinates:* 38° 31.019′ N, 78° 26.518′ W.

TRAIL DESCRIPTION
This pleasant ramble near Big Meadows has a bit of everything for the day-hiker: a waterfall, good views, and a climb up to Blackrock for even better views. From the parking lot, pass the yellow gate and start to descend along a yellow-blazed fire road. Continue straight on the fire road through the inter-section with the Appalachian Trail (AT). To the right, a padlocked door appears on the side of the trail: While an odd sight for a day hike, this door covers a spring, which supplies much of the water for facilities in the Big Meadows area.

At 0.25 mile, arrive at blue-blazed Lewis Springs Trail, and turn left to continue the hike. The route narrows from the wide fire road and starts to descend along several switchbacks before reaching Overlook Trail at 0.9 mile. Turn left here.

A rock outcropping just a few steps into Overlook Trail offers the first view of Lewis Falls and of the valley below. To reach it, continue along the trail,

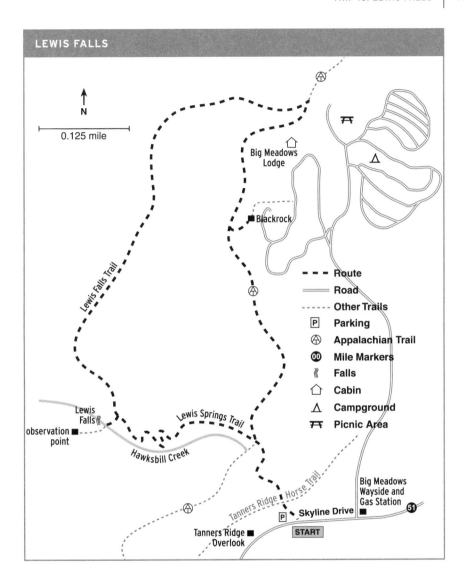

LEWIS FALLS

N

0.125 mile

Big Meadows
Lodge

Blackrock

Lewis Falls Trail

- - - Route
===== Road
----- Other Trails
P   Parking
⚇   Appalachian Trail
⓪⓪   Mile Markers
⟨⟨   Falls
⌂   Cabin
△   Campground
⊓   Picnic Area

Lewis
Falls

observation
point

Lewis Springs Trail

Hawksbill Creek

Tanners Ridge Horse Trail

Big Meadows
Wayside and
Gas Station

Skyline Drive

Tanners Ridge
Overlook

START

across a stream, and down a very rocky path. These rocks can be slippery when wet, but a handrail provides extra support as you make your way to the overlook. From here, you can see the 81-foot-tall Lewis Falls plunge to the valley below.

To continue the hike, return to the intersection with Overlook Trail and turn left onto Lewis Springs Falls Trail. The trail steadily ascends back up to the ridge—a moderate climb that can get steep at times but that can yield nice views. At 2.0 miles, turn right onto the AT and follow the white blazes along a

Overlooks give a good glimpse of the dramatic Lewis Falls.

relatively flat path. To your left, evidence of nearby Big Meadows Campground is visible as the AT skirts close to the lodge.

A rocky overlook provides a good break point and even nicer views of the valley. To get up even higher, turn left at the intersection with blue-blazed Blackrock Trail at 2.4 miles and follow it uphill to the Blackrock Cliffs for more views. (Continuing past the cliffs would bring you to the Big Meadows Lodge, which lies a short distance away.) To continue your hike, retrace your steps back to the AT. Turn left onto the AT, which starts to descend and eventually leads back to the intersection with the fire road you entered on. Turn left and retrace your steps to the parking lot.

DID YOU KNOW?

The Big Meadows Lodge, within sight of the Lewis Falls loop, has a long history. Built in 1939, the lodge is listed on the National Register of Historic Places. It was built with stones cut from nearby Massanutten Mountain, and the interior—the paneling, in particular—was made from what are now nearly extinct chestnut trees.

MORE INFORMATION

Shenandoah National Park (nps.gov/shen, 540-999-3500, 800-732-0911 [for emergencies]). Big Meadows Wayside—which offers full-service dining, groceries, camping supplies, gasoline, and more—is open Sunday through Thursday from 8 A.M. to 5:30 P.M. and Friday and Saturday 8 A.M. to 7 P.M. between April and early November; visit goshenandoah.com for additional concessioner information. Park facilities are generally open March through late November; a facilities schedule is online. In cases of inclement weather and at night in deer-hunting season (mid-November through early January), call the park to confirm whether Skyline Drive is open to vehicles. Overnight lodging in the park includes lodges, cabins, and campgrounds, including the Big Meadows Lodge and Campground; for more information, visit nps.gov/shen/planyourvisit/lodging.htm or nps.gov/shen/planyourvisit/campgrounds.htm.

NEARBY

Skyline Drive is dotted with hikes and overlooks, and Big Meadows Campground gives a good base to explore the area. For a longer outing, this hike can be coupled with nearby Rose River and Dark Hollow Falls (Trip 18).

TRIP 17
SOUTH RIVER FALLS

Location: Central District, Shenandoah National Park, VA
Rating: Moderate
Distance: 4.9 miles
Elevation Gain: 1,914 feet
Estimated Time: 2–3 hours
Maps: PATC, *Map 10, Appalachian Trail and other trails in Shenandoah National Park, Central District,* 2008.

Descend—and then descend some more—to enjoy views of South River Falls, one of the loveliest in the park.

DIRECTIONS
From I-66, Exit 43A, take US 29 South 13.2 miles to Warrenton. Turn right onto US 211 and drive for 34 miles. West of Sperryville, US 211 twists and turns to meet the park entrance at Thornton Gap (fee). Drive south on Skyline Drive to the South River Falls Picnic Area (milepost 63). *GPS coordinates:* 38° 22.875′ N, 78° 31.078′ W.

TRAIL DESCRIPTION
Like many hikes in Shenandoah, South River Falls Trail starts with a descent and ends with a climb. The views of the waterfall, however, lend themselves to a long break before you head back uphill. In warmer weather, the base of the falls provides a nice spot for wading and relaxing.

The blue-blazed trail starts next to the bathrooms at the South River Falls Picnic Area. Follow it into the woods, and quickly arrive at the intersection with the Appalachian Trail (AT). Go straight through the intersection, and keep following the blue blazes of South River Falls Trail. It descends along a fairly rugged path, with some decent stretches of rock hopping.

In 1.0 mile, the trail arrives at the first view of the 83-foot waterfall. An outcropping gives a good vantage point, but the overlook is just a few steps farther down the trail. From here, catch a nice view of the falls as it plunges below.

A more impressive sight is farther down the path but requires some extra work. From the overlook, continue down South River Falls Trail and arrive at a cement post. Turn right to follow the fire road down to the base of the

SOUTH RIVER FALLS

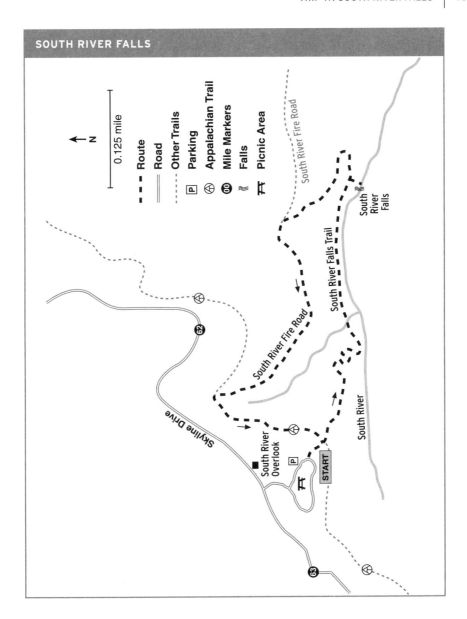

falls. The fire road leads to the river and appears to end. Follow a rocky path upstream to the base of the falls and some pools perfect for wading at 2.3 miles.

After enjoying the falls, follow the fire road back up the hill and arrive again at the cement post. Continue straight on the fire road. (Turning left would bring you back to the overlook.) At the intersection with South River

Factor in some time for wading at the base of South River Falls.

Fire Road, continue straight, following the yellow blazes. The trail makes a long, steady ascent before arriving at an intersection with the AT. Turn left onto the white-blazed AT, and follow its relatively flat path back to the intersection with South River Falls Trail. Turn right, and arrive back at your vehicle.

DID YOU KNOW?

Hikers can get impressive views of the waterfalls, but birders are in luck as well. According to the Virginia Department of Game and Inland Fisheries, this area is one of the prime spots for breeding birds along Skyline Drive. Birders can encounter many species on this path, including: cerulean, Blackburnian, and black-throated blue warblers; northern parula; Louisiana waterthrush; American redstart; white-breasted nuthatch; red-eyed and blue-headed vireos; scarlet tanager; rose-breasted grosbeak; and eastern towhee.

MORE INFORMATION

Shenandoah National Park (nps.gov/shen, 540-999-3500, 800-732-0911 [for emergencies]). Big Meadows Wayside—which offers full-service dining, groceries, camping supplies, gasoline, and more—is open Sunday through Thursday from 8 A.M. to 5:30 P.M. and Friday and Saturday from 8 A.M. to 7 P.M. between April and early November; visit goshenandoah.com for additional concessioner information. Other park facilities are generally open March through late November; a facilities schedule is online. In cases of inclement weather and at night in deer-hunting season (mid-November through early January), call the park to confirm whether Skyline Drive is open to vehicles. Overnight lodging in the park includes lodges, cabins, and campgrounds, including Big Meadows Lodge and Campground; for more information, visit nps.gov/shen/planyourvisit/lodging.htm or nps.gov/shen/planyourvisit/campgrounds.htm.

NEARBY

Skyline Drive is dotted with hikes and overlooks, and Big Meadows Campground gives a good base to explore the area. If you want more waterfalls, nearby hikes include Lewis Falls (Trip 16) and Rose River and Dark Hollow Falls (Trip 18).

TRIP 18
ROSE RIVER AND DARK HOLLOW FALLS

Location: Central District, Shenandoah National Park, VA
Rating: Moderate
Distance: 6.5 miles
Elevation Gain: 1,999 feet
Estimated Time: 3–4 hours
Maps: PATC, *Map 10, Appalachian Trail and other trails in Shenandoah National Park, Central District,* 2008.

With two waterfalls and an easy loop around Big Meadows, this hike makes for a good outing. Lest you think it is too easy, the climb out of Dark Hollow will make sure you get a good workout— surrounded by great views, of course.

DIRECTIONS

From I-66, Exit 43A, take US 29 South 13.2 miles to Warrenton. Turn right onto US 211 and drive for 34 miles. West of Sperryville, US 211 twists and turns to meet the park entrance at Thornton Gap (fee). Drive south on Skyline Drive to Big Meadows Campground (mile marker 51), and park by the amphitheater. *GPS coordinates: 38° 31.842′ N, 78° 26.380′ W.*

TRAIL DESCRIPTION

The Rose River and Dark Hollow loop is a mild one, giving plenty of options for pausing to enjoy the views as you walk. The trail starts from the amphitheater area. Look for a path just to the left of it, and follow it to the intersection with the Appalachian Trail (AT). Turn right and follow the white blazes as the trail makes its way around the campground area. Off to the side, tents and campers pop in and out of view. Some side trails lead back to the campground; just keep following the white blazes.

Fishers Gap Overlook comes into view just as you continue along the trail; enjoy the view then turn right off the AT onto a fire road. Cross Skyline Drive and follow the fire road past a gate. Turn left onto yellow-blazed Skyland–Big Meadows Horse Trail at 1.9 miles. The trail heads downhill for a bit, and then arrives at an intersection at 2.4 miles. Bear right here onto blue-blazed Rose River Trail. The trail gets a bit rockier as it leads to Rose River Falls, a pair of waterfalls. Enjoy the cascades, and then continue along the blue blazes. The

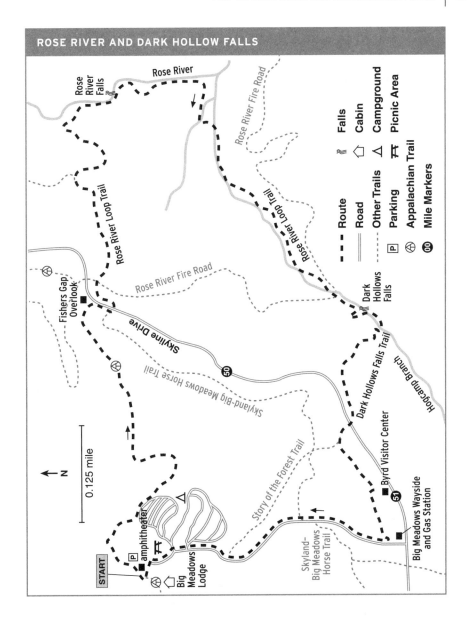

ROSE RIVER AND DARK HOLLOW FALLS

trail swings to the right and follows Hogcamp Branch. It then crosses the stream over a footbridge at 3.5 miles and starts a slight climb uphill. There are views aplenty as the trail continues along the stream.

The trail intersects with Rose River Fire Road. Turn right and follow the fire road as it crosses the stream. Here, the route offers its first view of Dark Hollow Falls, at 4.4 miles, but the better views are still to come. Start following blue-blazed Dark Hollow Trail, and arrive at a good view of the upper falls in

Hikers flock to take in the falls along this pretty hike.

0.2 mile. The trail climbs steeply at times back up the hill before easing out as it arrives at the Dark Hollow Falls Parking Area.

Cross Skyline Drive and follow Story of the Forest Nature Trail. Turn left at the sign for the visitor center, and follow the path past the center, the Big Meadows Wayside, and a small gas station. From here, follow the paved path back into the campground. As you near the camp registration area, cross the road and follow the signs back to the amphitheater and your car.

DID YOU KNOW?

Big Meadows has its place in history: President Franklin D. Roosevelt dedicated the park and Skyline Drive here in 1935. But it has an even longer history than that, one that is still being discovered. Archeologists have found evidence of human habitation as early as 2,000 B.C.

MORE INFORMATION

Shenandoah National Park (nps.gov/shen, 540-999-3500, 800-732-0911 [for emergencies]). Big Meadows Wayside—which offers full-service dining, groceries, camping supplies, gasoline, and more—is open Sunday through Thursday from 8 A.M. to 5:30 P.M. and Friday and Saturday from 8 A.M. to 7 P.M. between April and early November; visit goshenandoah.com for additional concessioner information. Other park facilities are generally open from March through late November; a facilities schedule is online. In cases of inclement weather and at night in deer-hunting season (mid-November through early January), call the park to confirm whether Skyline Drive is open to vehicles. Overnight lodging in the park includes lodges, cabins, and campgrounds, including Big Meadows Lodge and Campground; for more information, visit nps.gov/shen/planyourvisit/lodging.htm or nps.gov/shen/planyourvisit/campgrounds.htm.

NEARBY

Skyline Drive is dotted with hikes and overlooks, and Big Meadows Campground gives a good base to explore the area. For an added challenge, consider tacking on Lewis Falls (Trip 16) to form the bigger hiking loop known as Three Falls.

TRIP 19
HAWKSBILL

Location: Central District, Shenandoah National Park, VA
Rating: Moderate
Distance: 2.8 miles
Elevation Gain: 1,089 feet
Estimated Time: 1–2 hours
Maps: PATC, *Map 10, Appalachian Trail and other trails in Shenandoah National Park, Central District,* 2008.

Challenge yourself with a short, steep climb to Shenandoah's highest peak. The reward: great views and a return route that's all downhill.

DIRECTIONS

From I-66, Exit 43A, take US 29 South 13.2 miles to Warrenton. Turn right onto US 211 and drive for 34 miles. West of Sperryville, US 211 twists and turns to meet the park entrance at Thornton Gap (fee). Drive south on Skyline Drive to the Hawksbill Gap Parking Area, located between mileposts 45 and 46. *GPS coordinates:* 38° 33.372′ N, 78° 23.207′ W.

TRAIL DESCRIPTION

The distance may be short, but the first mile of this hike is certainly a challenge as you gain more than 600 feet to reach the summit of Shenandoah's highest peak.

Small parking lots are on either side of Skyline Drive, but the trailhead is on the western side, marked by an informational sign. Follow the blue blazes for Lower Hawksbill Trail, and get ready to start climbing. The wide and graveled trail itself is easy to follow, but a few rain bars can cause hikers to question the path. Just keep following the blue blazes as the trail threads its way steadily up the mountain.

The top is tantalizingly in view as the climb continues. Stone steps mark the halfway point of the climb, and the trail levels out for a bit, a chance to catch your breath. Keep pressing forward. At 0.7 mile, a concrete post marks the end of the climb. Ahead to the right is the Byrd's Nest Shelter (day use only), and the top of Hawksbill (4,055 feet). Pass in front of the shelter and enjoy the views. A viewing platform, just a bit farther past the shelter at 0.8 mile, gives even better views to the west, north, and east. Skyline Drive is within sight

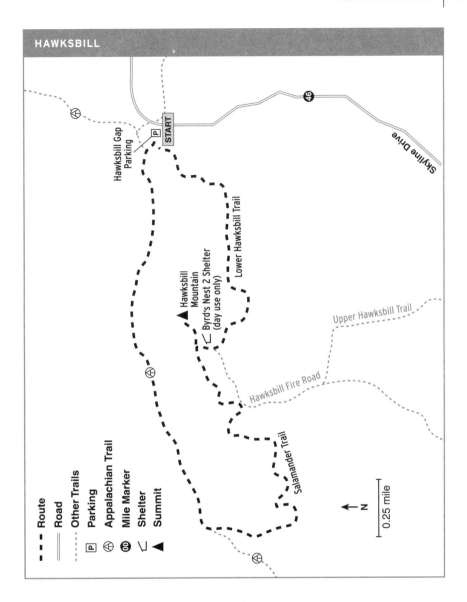

HAWKSBILL

Hawksbill Gap Parking

START

Lower Hawksbill Trail

Hawksbill Mountain

Byrd's Nest 2 Shelter (day use only)

Upper Hawksbill Trail

Hawksbill Fire Road

Salamander Trail

Skyline Drive

Route
Road
Other Trails
Parking
Appalachian Trail
Mile Marker
Shelter
Summit

N
0.25 mile

below, the rocky crags of Old Rag (Trip 21) can be seen to the east, and the Shenandoah Valley and Massanutten Mountain are to the west.

To continue the hike, head back past the shelter and to the concrete post. (You can shorten the described route by heading to the left at the post and retracing your steps back down the trail.) Make a slight turn to the right and follow the blue blazes, and quickly arrive at another concrete post at 0.9 mile. Turn right here to gain Salamander Trail, also blue blazed, which enters the woods. Pass several nice viewing points, and follow the trail as it winds its way

The viewing platform atop Hawksbill looks out over Old Rag to the east and Massanutten Mountain and the valley to the west.

around the mountain. Once again, the trail is obvious but rain bars can give cause for pause. Keep following the blue blazes.

The trail makes its way gently downhill until it intersects with the Appalachian Trail (AT), which you'll spy coming in from the side at 1.7 miles. Another concrete post marks the intersection. Turn right onto the AT, and follow the white-blazed path as it continues around the mountain. Good views of the gap and mountain greet you as you start on the AT, and interesting rock formations provide interest on the right. Three talus fields in short succession at 2.2 miles mark a bit of rock hopping. The trail remains rocky for a bit, but eventually levels out.

Skyline Drive and the parking lot will pop into sight as you round the last bend in the trail. Resist the temptation to cut through the trees to get to your car faster; in just a few minutes, a concrete post at 2.7 miles marks a spur trail to the parking lot.

DID YOU KNOW?

Peregrine falcons and balsam fir are two unique findings on Hawksbill's summit. In an attempt to restore the peregrine population, the park launched a Peregrine Falcon Restoration Project and had a successful nesting attempt at Hawksbill. The bird was removed from the Endangered Species List in 1999 but is still considered to be a threatened species. Hawksbill is also one of the few places where balsam fir, a tree typical of northern New England, can be found in the park.

MORE INFORMATION

Shenandoah National Park (nps.gov/shen, 540-999-3500, 800-732-0911 [for emergencies]). Park facilities are generally open from March through late November; a facilities schedule is online. In cases of inclement weather and at night in deer hunting season (mid-November through early January), call the park to confirm whether Skyline Drive is open to vehicles. Overnight lodging in the park includes lodges, cabins, and campgrounds; for more information, visit nps.gov/shen/planyourvisit/lodging.htm or nps.gov/shen/planyourvisit/campgrounds.htm.

NEARBY

Nearby Sperryville has restaurants and small shops, and VA 211 is dotted with wineries, perfect for a post-hike snack and sip. If you're looking for a strenuous outing, couple this hike with Whiteoak and Cedar Run (Trip 22). Consider starting the climb up Cedar Run, crossing Skyline Drive, and continuing to climb up to Hawksbill before descending back to the drive and then down Whiteoak.

TRIP 20
RAPIDAN CAMP

Location: Central District, Shenandoah National Park, VA
Rating: Moderate
Distance: 7.5 miles, round-trip
Elevation Gain: 1,623 feet
Estimated Time: 3–5 hours
Maps: PATC, *Map 10, Appalachian Trail and other trails in Shenandoah National Park, Central District,* 2008.

Visit President Hoover's retreat and enjoy a picturesque stretch of the Appalachian Trail along Hazeltop Mountain.

DIRECTIONS

From I-66, Exit 43A, take US 29 South 13.2 miles to Warrenton. Turn right onto US 211 and drive for 34 miles. West of Sperryville, US 211 twists and turns to meet the park entrance at Thornton Gap (fee). Drive south on Skyline Drive to the parking lot for Milam Gap between mileposts 52 and 53. *GPS coordinates:* 38° 30.025′ N, 78° 26.732′ W.

TRAIL DESCRIPTION

Toward the back of the parking lot, on the south side, you should be able to spot a spur trail that takes you, in very short order, to the Appalachian Trail (AT). Turn left (south) onto the white-blazed AT and cross Skyline Drive. On the opposite side of the road, the AT heads to the right, while blue-blazed Mill Prong Trail (your route) begins its descent toward Rapidan Camp on the left.

Head left, follow the blue blazes, and start this pleasant descent. About 1.0 mile later, the trail arrives at an intersection with Mill Prong Horse Trail. Bear right to follow the yellow blazes as the horse trail continues the descent. At 1.5 miles, pass Big Rock Falls on your right—a bonus on this hike, as the waterfalls are lovely and the pool deep enough for a dip—then cross the creek. Arrive at a forest road that cuts across your path at 1.8 miles. Note this place: When you return from visiting Rapidan Camp, your route to Laurel Prong Trail will head to the right (south).

To reach Rapidan Camp, continue straight ahead on the paved path. Though only a few houses remain, the camp is still a striking historical site,

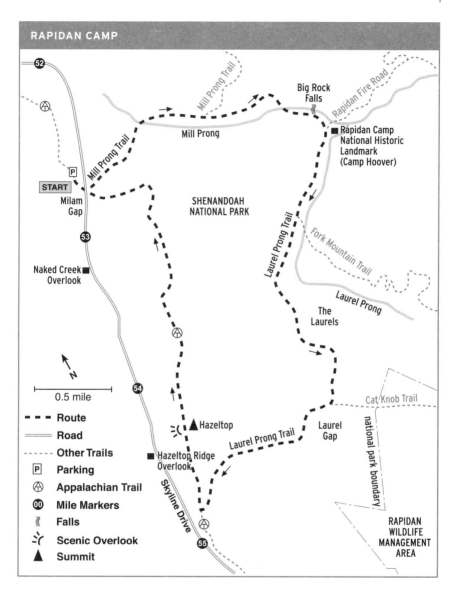

RAPIDAN CAMP

52

Mill Prong Trail

Big Rock
Falls

Rapidan Fire Road

Mill Prong

Rapidan Camp
National Historic
Landmark
(Camp Hoover)

P

START

Milam
Gap

SHENANDOAH
NATIONAL PARK

Laurel Prong Trail

Fork Mountain Trail

53

Naked Creek
Overlook

Laurel Prong

The
Laurels

N

0.5 mile

54

Cat Knob Trail

Laurel
Gap

national park boundary

- - - Route

Road

Hazeltop

Laurel Prong Trail

Other Trails

Hazeltop Ridge
Overlook

P Parking

Skyline Drive

Appalachian Trail

00 Mile Markers

Falls

Scenic Overlook

Summit

55

RAPIDAN
WILDLIFE
MANAGEMENT
AREA

with its rustic buildings appearing out of the foliage. A number of signs detail the history of this place, where President Herbert Hoover relaxed from the stress of governing the country during the Great Depression. The White House physician of the day called the camp "one of the most relaxing places that I have ever known." Conversely, the leader of the Marine Corps construction team that worked on the site between 1929 and 1932 described the job as one of the most challenging in his career because of the surrounding terrain.

Rapidan Camp's outdoor fireplace served as the setting for many photos during President Hoover's visits. (Photo courtesy Hua Davis)

(Rapidan Camp exhibits are open intermittently; check at Byrd Visitor Center for current hours.)

Once you've completed your walking tour, return to the post where the pavement ends at the forest road, and turn left (south) to begin Laurel Prong Trail. Pass a placard, on the right, for Five Tents, then reach a somewhat confusingly marked fork in the trail on the edge of Rapidan Camp at 2.2 miles. Do not take the footpath to the left (it leads to a dam in the forest and a dead end); instead, follow the forest road (Laurel Prong Trail) to the right. Blue blazes appear eventually. The trail climbs gently at first to an intersection with Fork Mountain Trail at 2.7 miles.

Beyond this intersection, the trail makes its way through a beautiful woodland section known as the Laurels. At a sharp righthand bend, pass a campsite at 3.4 miles, and begin climbing more steeply. Just beyond 4.0 miles, the trail reaches a ridgeline where Cat Knob Trail heads east, also on blue blazes. Turn right, and continue climbing more gently as the path works its way along the contour lines of Hazeltop Mountain. Some views may be possible here, depending on the time of year.

At last, Laurel Prong Trail ends at the AT, just south of Hazeltop at 5.0 miles. Turn right and complete the hike up this mountain. Beyond its summit is a spur trail at 5.5 miles that leads to a view westward. This view makes the short side trip entirely worthwhile. The AT continues northward and makes fine, pleasant walking as it descends toward Milam Gap. Keep an eye out here, especially in summer; if the berries are out, the bears will likely be out as well. Michael spotted the largest black bear he's ever seen on this stretch.

At 7.4 miles, the trail returns to Milam Gap and the intersection with Mill Prong Trail. Cross Skyline Drive and return to your vehicle.

DID YOU KNOW?

Rapidan Camp, or Camp Hoover, was the Camp David of its day, as President Hoover used the camp to host visiting luminaries throughout the 1930s. President Roosevelt found the surroundings too rugged for his liking and had Camp David constructed as a presidential retreat. Jimmy Carter was the last president to visit Rapidan Camp.

MORE INFORMATION

Shenandoah National Park (nps.gov/shen, 540-999-3500, 800-732-0911 [for emergencies]). Park facilities are generally open from March through late November; a facilities schedule is online. In cases of inclement weather and at night in deer-hunting season (mid-November through early January), call the park to confirm whether Skyline Drive is open to vehicles. Overnight lodging in the park includes lodges, cabins, and campgrounds; visit nps.gov/shen/planyourvisit/lodging.htm or nps.gov/shen/planyourvisit/campgrounds.htm for more information.

To learn more about Rapidan Camp, visit nps.gov/shen/historyculture/rapidancamp.htm; for ranger-led tour information, visit nps.gov/shen/planyourvisit/rangerprograms.htm.

NEARBY

There is no shortage of excellent hikes in the central district of the Shenandoah. The waysides at Big Meadows (milepost 51) or Skyland (between mileposts 41 and 42) make great stopping points. If you're heading back into the DC metropolitan area, consider stopping in Sperryville or Warrenton.

PRESIDENTS IN SHENANDOAH

"The passage of the Patowmac [*sic*] through the Blue Ridge is perhaps one of the most stupendous scenes in Nature. You stand on a very high point of land. On your right comes up the Shenandoah, having ranged along the foot of the mountain a hundred miles to seek a vent. On your left approaches the Patowmac [*sic*] in quest of a passage also. In the moment of their junction they rush together against the mountain, rend it asunder and pass off to the sea....This scene is worth a voyage across the Atlantic."

–Thomas Jefferson, *Notes on the State of Virginia* (1785)

Given the proximity of the Shenandoah Valley to Washington, DC, it is no surprise that the land has left its mark on the writings and biographies of more than a few American presidents. In the eighteenth century, Thomas Jefferson admired the view of the confluence of the Potomac and Shenandoah rivers, where the settlement of Harpers Ferry now stands. Modern-day hikers can visit Jefferson Rock in Trip 1, or enjoy other awe-inspiring views from Maryland Heights or Loudoun Heights (Trips 1 and 2).

Not only were several of the nation's first presidents–George Washington, Thomas Jefferson, and James Madison–Virginians who knew the Shenandoah Valley intimately, but others also made homes in the Blue Ridge and the Shenandoah Valley. In the late 1920s and early 1930s, before the Shenandoah National Park was founded, Herbert Hoover established Rapidan Camp as a summer retreat where he could escape the heat and turmoil of the city, enjoy the mountain air, and indulge his favorite pastime of fishing. Long before George W. Bush called Crawford, Texas, home and before Barack Obama relaxed at Martha's Vineyard, Hoover's modest "Brown House" was a fact of the political landscape. Visit Rapidan Camp, or Camp Hoover, on Trip 20.

On July 3, 1936, Franklin Delano Roosevelt dedicated Shenandoah National Park, describing it as part of a larger social project of ending "involuntary idleness of thousands of young men" through the work of the Civilian Conservation Corps (CCC). Roosevelt reportedly found Rapidan Camp too primitive for his tastes, but he established CCC camps throughout the Blue Ridge. Camps throughout the Shenandoah Valley were models for the rest of the nation during Roosevelt's New Deal, which brought Americans back to work. (See Putting the Nation to Work)

TRIP 21
OLD RAG

Location: Central District, Shenandoah National Park, VA

Rating: Strenuous

Distance: 9.0 miles round-trip

Elevation Gain: 2,812 feet

Estimated Time: 4–7 hours

Maps: PATC, *Map 10, Appalachian Trail and other trails in Shenandoah National Park, Central District,* 2008; *Old Rag Area* (National Park Service)

No other hike in the Shenandoah Valley rivals the fame of the scramble along Old Rag's Ridge Trail. If you're going to do only one hike in the area, this might very well be the one. But come prepared— the Class 3 terrain atop is as challenging as it is rewarding.

DIRECTIONS

From I-66, Exit 43A, take US 29 South 13.2 miles to Warrenton. Turn right onto US 211 west toward Sperryville. In 27.0 miles, take a left onto US 522 South, cross the creek, then take another left to remain on US 522 South. About 0.7 miles later, turn right onto VA 231 South. In 7.8 miles, turn right onto VA 600. Follow this road for 3.2 miles to the end of public access. A parking lot is on your left, and there is a small ranger station in the parking lot's corner. *GPS coordinates:* 38° 34.233′ N, 78° 17.187′ W.

TRAIL DESCRIPTION

Old Rag is one of the best hikes in the region, and everybody knows it. Mid-morning on a beautiful spring day, count on finding this parking lot full to bursting and plan on encountering a few thousand of your best friends on the mountain. For more solitude, come on a weekday or on a day when the weather is less than ideal. Even then, this is a very popular hike; expect to wait in lines at some of the obstacles. The terrain at ridgeline is challenging and will likely require you to use your hands to pull yourself up and over the rocks; if you're uncomfortable with very rocky terrain, this may not be an ideal hike for you.

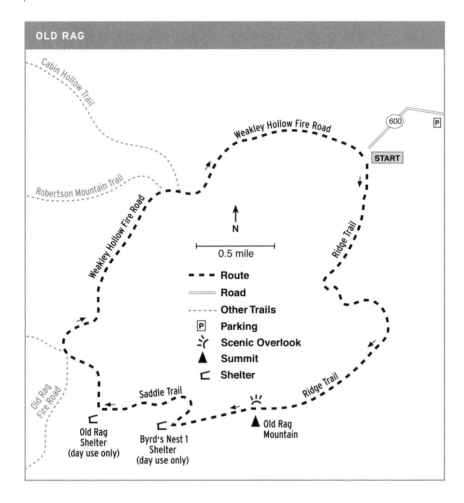

OLD RAG

While Old Rag is justly famed for its approximately mile-long scramble atop its ridgeline, for the first 0.9 miles, the trail is simply a road that passes a few cottages. Pass Nicholson Hollow Trail on the right at 0.5 mile and then, at 0.9 mile, arrive at the trailhead for blue-blazed Ridge Trail, which you will follow to Old Rag's summit. Note this location carefully; you're about to head south on Ridge Trail now, but you'll be returning to this point from the west on Weakley Hollow Fire Road.

A goodly amount of climbing awaits you, with 3.0 miles and 2,400 feet of gain to the summit. Ridge Trail begins by climbing gently through the forest, but it soon starts to switchback along some rather typical Virginia hollows. In its upper reaches, there are fewer switchbacks, but the trail continues to climb. Just before it reaches the ridgeline, it becomes quite steep and rocky. The path

A hiker ducks below a boulder just shy of Old Rag's summit.

reaches a viewpoint, and then shortly thereafter, at nearly 3.0 miles, meets the first obstacle: a slabby affair you must either crawl through or clamber up.

From this point forward, over the next 0.8 mile, you'll be scrambling to reach the summit. Although the trail does continue climbing over this stretch, it won't feel especially vertical, as you'll be concentrating on the moves necessary to overcome the obstacles. You'll lower yourself into cracks, edge out around shelves, pass through a cave or two, climb up through chimneys, jump over fissures, and embrace many, many rocks. Throughout this section, keep your eye open for the blue blazes, which can be tricky to find in some of the slabbier areas. But no fear—there are often several ways to pass an obstacle (some more scrambly than others), and it would be quite hard to lose the ridgeline.

The terrain on the ridge is considered Class 3 in the Yosemite Decimal System, which means that you'll periodically need your hands to advance but ropes are not required. There is little exposure to speak of, and none of the moves aspire to Class 4 terrain (the first class that the Yosemite Decimal System truly considers "climbing," which is often aided by ropes). If you use trekking poles, affix them to your pack, as they are more encumbrances than aids when scrambling. Make sure that you always have three points in firm contact with rock before moving a fourth.

Old Rag's summit is just beyond the stretch of scrambles at 3.9 miles. Clamber up any one of a number of boulders for expansive views of the Shenandoah region. Relax, enjoy a bite, and perhaps a nap, before it's time to complete this classic trip.

Your descent begins with a series of switchbacks, which takes you just over 0.6 mile and 550 vertical feet down to the Byrd's Nest No. 1 Shelter (day use only). Turn hard right here, and traverse left then right across the mountain, losing 670 feet before reaching the Old Rag Shelter at 5.3 miles. From here, walk just 0.4 miles farther on a forest road to reach Weakley Hollow Fire Road. Turn right and follow the fire road past Robertson Mountain Trail at 6.7 miles and Corbin Hollow Trail at 6.8 miles, both on the left. The route eventually crosses a few bridged creeks before returning to the trailhead for Ridge Trail just beyond 8.0 miles.

Follow the road for 1.0 mile back to the parking lot and your waiting vehicle.

DID YOU KNOW?

Old Rag, the mountain's official name, is actually a shorter version of "Old Raggedy Top," as it is often known. As you're driving in on US 211 toward Shenandoah, you should be able to spot the distinctively ragged line of Old Rag's rocky summit, which stands out against the more typically wooded Mid-Atlantic peaks.

MORE INFORMATION

Shenandoah National Park (nps.gov/shen, 540-999-3500, 800-732-0911 [for emergencies]). Park facilities are generally open from March through late November; a facilities schedule is online. In cases of inclement weather and at night in deer hunting season (mid-November through early January), call the park to confirm whether Skyline Drive is open to vehicles. Overnight lodging in the park includes lodges, cabins, and campgrounds; visit nps.gov/shen/planyourvisit/lodging.htm or nps.gov/shen/planyourvisit/campgrounds.htm for more information.

If you're looking to have Old Rag's summit all to yourself (albeit by means of an overnight trip), consult *AMC's Best Backpacking in the Mid-Atlantic*.

NEARBY

Sperryville is the closest town, and there are a few eateries there, but the nearest town with a full array of services is Warrenton. Of course, there are many hikes in the near vicinity of Old Rag, including Hawksbill (Trip 19), Whiteoak and Cedar Run (Trip 22), and many others.

TRIP 22
WHITEOAK AND CEDAR RUN

Location: Central District, Shenandoah National Park, VA
Rating: Moderate
Distance: 8.0 miles
Elevation Gain: 2,720 feet of gain
Estimated Time: 3–6 hours
Maps: PATC, *Map 10, Appalachian Trail and other trails in Shenandoah National Park, Central District,* 2008.

Not only is this hike one of the great classics of Shenandoah National Park and of Virginia more generally, but it is also a strong contender for the best waterfall hike in the state.

DIRECTIONS

From I-66, Exit 43A, take US 29 South 13.2 miles to Warrenton. Turn right onto US 211 west toward Sperryville. In 27.0 miles, take a left onto US 522 South, cross the creek, then take another left to remain on US 522 South. About 0.7 miles later, turn right onto VA 231 South and drive 10 miles to the junction with VA 643. Turn right here at a sign for Whiteoak. After about 4 miles, take another right onto Weakley Hollow Road. The parking lot for Whiteoak and Cedar Run is about 3.6 miles away, on the left. This lot can become quite crowded when the weather is good. *GPS coordinates:* 38° 32.316′ N, 78° 20.878′ W.

TRAIL DESCRIPTION

To begin this classic and much-loved Shenandoah hike, start by walking to the back of the parking lot past the ranger station. A bridge takes you over the creek. At this point, you're walking on blue-blazed Whiteoak Trail, which quickly arrives at an intersection. The left fork leads up Cedar Run, the described route; the right, up Whiteoak Canyon. Though you can certainly walk Whiteoak Canyon first, Cedar Run is the steeper trail; you'll likely be more comfortable climbing it and then descending the less steep, though certainly challenging, Whiteoak Canyon Trail.

Bear left and begin climbing Cedar Run Trail, which is also blue-blazed. At first, it climbs fairly gently through the run's lower reaches, with the creek on your left. At 0.6 mile, the route reaches an intersection with Cedar Run–Whiteoak Link Trail. Continue straight ahead.

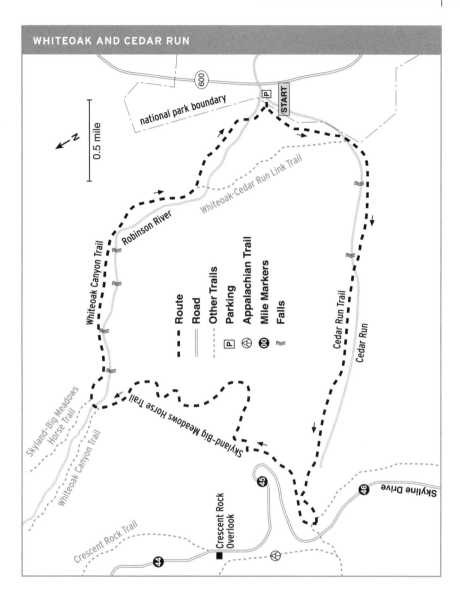

Cedar Run Trail reaches the stream, crosses to the left, bears sharply left, and begins switchbacking its way up the mountain, at times very steeply. Over the next 2.4 miles, you'll climb 2,020 feet and enjoy quite a good workout. The trail alternates between climbing steeply, easing off for stretches before arriving at the falls, cascades, and slides of Cedar Run. Take the time to enjoy these slides, as they are the highlight of this portion of the trail. The slide at 1.5 miles, in particular, is often crowded with hikers cooling themselves in its pool.

A visitor enjoys one of the many beautiful waterfalls in Shenandoah's Whiteoak Canyon.

Beyond this fall, the trail crosses the creek again to the right. It continues to climb steadily, but the steepest parts mercifully are over. The forest opens out as the trail emerges from the narrow hollow and eventually veers away from the creek. Just shy of Skyline Drive at 3.1 miles, Skyland–Big Meadows Horse Trail approaches from the right; from this point, the horse trail leads 2.2 miles to its junction with Whiteoak Canyon Trail.

The good news is that it's all downhill from here. Turn right onto the yellow-blazed horse trail and begin the traverse to Whiteoak Canyon. Pass a spur trail to a parking lot on your left at 3.7 miles. Eventually, the big, broad, and easy path reaches, at 5.2 miles, the creek that flows down toward the falls of Whiteoak Canyon. Rock-hop across to join blue-blazed Whiteoak Canyon Trail. There is actually a bridge a little farther upstream, if you prefer.

The next 1.5 miles of descent are the highlight of this hike. Whiteoak Canyon Trail plummets down the canyon, sometimes rather steeply, bringing you a number of viewpoints of the cascades. At times it veers away from the falls to make its way past the steepest cascades, only to bring you back to the water. Take the time to explore. Not only are there excellent points for photography and relaxing, but there are a number of fine swimming holes as well. You'll pass the upper falls at 5.75 miles and then the lower at 6.5 miles. The trail crosses a tributary creek and follows the stream through the lower reaches of the canyon. Though the falls here are less dramatic, the excellent swimming pools more than make up for it.

When the trail has become nearly flat you'll know you're almost at the hike's end. Pass Cedar Run–Whiteoak Link Trail at 7.1 miles and then rejoin with Cedar Run itself at 7.8 miles. Bear left. The parking is just ahead at 8.0 miles.

DID YOU KNOW?

While the highest waterfall in Shenandoah National Park is 93-foot Overall Run (Trip 11), you won't feel shorted by the falls of Cedar Run or Whiteoak. Lower and Upper White Falls, in particular, will not disappoint, as you're able to get much better vantage points than with Overall Run. Of course, the highest waterfall in Virginia is Jefferson National Forest's Crabtree Falls (Trip 40) with five major cascades that fall a total of more than 1,000 feet. The highest single drop is 400 feet.

MORE INFORMATION

Shenandoah National Park (nps.gov/shen, 540-999-3500, 800-732-0911 [for emergencies]). Park facilities are generally open from March through late November; a facilities schedule is online. In cases of inclement weather and at night in deer-hunting season (mid-November through early January), call the park to confirm whether Skyline Drive is open to vehicles. Overnight lodging in the park includes lodges, cabins, and campgrounds; visit nps.gov/shen/planyourvisit/lodging.htm or nps.gov/shen/planyourvisit/campgrounds.htm for more information.

NEARBY

The variety and quality of hikes near the central district of Shenandoah may be among the best on the East Coast. If you're looking to increase the difficulty of this hike, consider adding on the stretch to Hawksbill's summit (see Trip 19), which will mean that you'll have climbed from the base of the valley to its highest point. Consider starting by climbing up Cedar Run, crossing Skyline Drive, and continuing to climb up to Hawksbill, before descending back to the Drive and then down Whiteoak. For an additional and much more challenging variant, from Hawksbill, descend to the AT, hike north to Skyland, and then descend the Whiteoak Canyon Trail (about 13 miles).

Sperryville, Virginia, is the closest town, though a wider ranges of good and services are available in Warrenton, if you're headed back into Washington, DC.

4

SOUTH SHENANDOAH NATIONAL PARK

THE PARK'S 200,000 ACRES LIE BETWEEN the Virginia Piedmont and the Shenandoah Valley, providing a diverse array of habitats that shelter migratory birds, originate headwaters of three river drainages, and nurture a host of rare and notable plant and animal species.

When Shenandoah National Park was founded in 1940, just 85 percent of the land was forested; the rest was either natural grassland or had been cultivated. Surveys in 1987 and 2009 showed that 95 percent of the park was forested, though over time the types of forests had changed because of disease, extreme weather, and pests such as the gypsy moth and the hemlock woolly adelgid. Most of the park supports oak-hickory forests, but chestnut–red oak forests also occur, as do tulip poplar, cove hardwood, and small sections of spruce-fir forests. In the understory, look for hepatica, bloodroot, trillium, purple and yellow violets, pink lady's slippers, bluets, columbine, oxeye daisy, milkweed, and 852 other species of wildflowers. Visit in June to see the mountain laurel in bloom. Fern, grasses, lichens, mosses, and liverworts fill the spaces between, flourishing on the forest floor, on dry cliff faces, in muddy streambeds, and in the acidic soils at higher elevations. If you're visiting in the wet seasons of spring or fall, you'll likely see the park's 400 mushroom species in at their peak of development.

More than 200 species of animals either reside in or pass through Shenandoah National Park. Most visitors see the abundant white-tailed deer, but black bears, bobcats, big brown bats, and other smaller, elusive species are present. Approximately 100 species of birds breed in the park; common species include the broad-winged hawk, Carolina wren, ovenbird, and eastern towhee, among many others. Ten species of amphibians reside here, including the endangered Shenandoah salamander, found only in the park.

(For a brief overview of the park and its Wilderness Areas, see the introduction to Section 2; for more on the park's history, see the introduction to Section 3.)

Shenandoah National Park's southern district, which stretches from Swift Run Gap to the Rockfish Gap, encompasses more than 33,000 acres of designated Wilderness, most of which are to the west. The final 39 miles of Skyline Drive traverses this district, from milepost 65.5 to milepost 104.6. Park facilities are sparser here: A ranger station is located at Simmons Gap (milepost 73) and the Dundo Group Camp (still a picnic spot in early 2015, but group camp sites are set to open shortly) is located farther south at milepost 83.5. The most developed area in the district is Loft Mountain, which includes 219 campsites and an information center. The Potomac Appalachian Trail Club operates a number of cabins in the area, including the Doyles River Cabin (visit patc.net to make reservations). Thirty-one overlooks dot Skyline Drive in this stretch of the park. Hightop Mountain, the district's highest peak at 3,587 feet, is just south of the Swift Run Gap entrance station (Trip 24).

TRIP 23
FRAZIER DISCOVERY TRAIL–
LOFT MOUNTAIN LOOP

Location: South District, Shenandoah National Park, VA
Rating: Easy
Distance: 1.3 miles
Elevation Gain: 494 feet
Estimated Time: 1 hour
Maps: *Map 11: Appalachian Trail and Other Trails in Shenandoah National Park South District* (PATC)

While this short hike is a steep climb for some, the views at the top are well worth the effort.

DIRECTIONS
From the north: From I-66, Exit 43A, take US 29 South 54.5 miles to its junction with VA 33 in Ruckersville. Turn right (west) onto VA 33 and continue 14.4 miles to the park's Swift Run Gap entrance (fee). Head left (south) onto Skyline Drive to the Loft Mountain Wayside (between mileposts 79 and 80).

From the south: From I-64, Exit 99 (US 250), follow signs for Skyline Drive and enter the park through the Rockfish Gap entrance (fee). Drive north on Skyline Drive for 25.9 miles, then turn right into the Loft Mountain Wayside (between mileposts 79 and 80). *GPS coordinates:* 38° 15.741′ N, 78° 39.677′ W.

TRAIL DESCRIPTION
On Frazier Discovery Trail, you'll sample all that Shenandoah has to offer in just over a mile: a quick and steep climb, excellent views, and reminders of the people who once lived in these mountains. This quick loop gets down to business with an uphill climb on Loft Mountain but then eases out once along the ridge before dipping back down the mountain.

To start the hike, cross Skyline Drive and head up the paved path that runs alongside the entrance to the campground. Arrive quickly at an intersection with Frazier Discovery Trail, and turn left onto the dirt path. (The path continuing straight ahead leads into the campground.) Again, rather quickly, the trail splits. Going in either direction will take you around the loop; this description follows the loop clockwise, turning left first. If you are interested

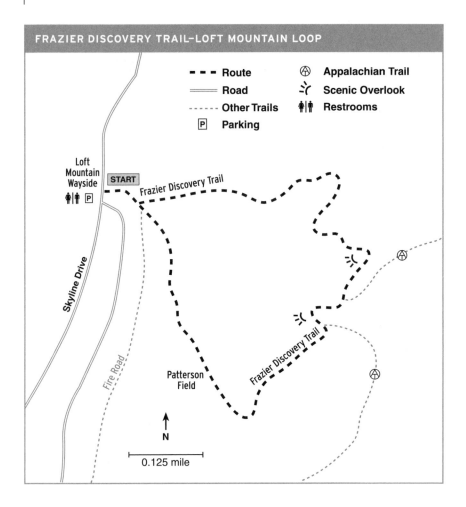

in learning more about the trail, the metal box at this intersection contains trail guides.

From this initial left turn, the trail starts to climb, sometimes a bit steeply, and at 0.4 mile passes a large rock overhang that offers an impressive bit of shelter to the ground below. Pass the overhang, and arrive at the first of two vistas. From either spot, you can see a wide array of peaks in the southern Shenandoah district, including Trayfoot Mountain (Trip 27), Austin Mountain, Lewis Peak, and Rockytop. In the distance, if the sky is clear, you can even see the Massanuttens and catch a glimpse of the Shenandoah Valley. Soon after the second vista, Frazier Discovery trail intersects the white-blazed Appalachian Trail (AT) at 0.6 mile. Turn right onto the AT and follow the trail for

A dramatic overhang is one of the many sights along this pleasant hike.

a short bit, passing another overlook. At 0.75 mile, arrive at another junction with Frazier Discovery Trail. The AT continues straight ahead; instead, follow Frazier Discovery Trail's blue blazes to the right as it descends the mountain.

This half of the hike is quite different from the first part, wending through older pasture land that was known as Patterson Field. The Patterson family owned much of the land surrounding Loft Mountain, and the Frazier family watched over their cattle and lived in a house that used to be located near the wayside. The cattle grazed in this field, which has since returned to a wilder state. The Fraziers moved away when officials revealed plans for building a national park.

Keep following the blue blazes back to the start of the loop. Retrace your steps back to the paved path and to the parking lot.

DID YOU KNOW?

Loft Mountain Campground isn't actually on Loft Mountain. The campground, the largest in the park, is perched on Big Flat Mountain, but Big Flat Mountain Campground just doesn't quite have the same ring.

MORE INFORMATION

Shenandoah National Park (nps.gov/shen, 540-999-3500, 800-732-0911 [for emergencies]). Pets are not allowed on the Frazier Discovery Trail. Loft Mountain Wayside sells groceries, camping and hiking supplies, and gifts and is open daily from 9 A.M. to 6 P.M. between mid-April and early November; visit goshenandoah.com for additional concessioner information. Park facilities are generally open from March through late November; a facilities schedule is online. In cases of inclement weather and at night in deer-hunting season (mid-November through early January), call the park to confirm whether Skyline Drive is open to vehicles. Overnight lodging in the park includes lodges, cabins, and campgrounds, including Loft Mountain Campground; visit nps.gov/shen/planyourvisit/lodging.htm or nps.gov/shen/planyourvisit/campgrounds.htm for more information.

NEARBY

The towns of Harrisonburg and Crozet are good stopping points for hikers on their way in or out of the southern stretch of Shenandoah National Park. The next-closest trips are Riprap Hollow (Trip 29) and Blackrock (Trip 28). The hikes in this section (Trips 23–29) are all within about 30 minutes of one another and within an hour's drive of the central district hikes on Skyline Drive (Trips 14–20). Make your trip more challenging by adding Riprap (Trip 29) to your route.

PRESERVING THE NIGHT SKY

At night from the many overlooks in the Shenandoah Valley, you can see the twinkling of town lights below. For some, they are an added attraction to the views, but to others, they are a sign that our night skies are disappearing. An estimated two-thirds of people in the United States live in areas where they cannot see the Milky Way. Look at any map that tracks light pollution, and the East Coast lights up brilliantly. (Visit darksky.org/resources/images for maps and images.)

Disappearing night skies mean fewer stars to enjoy, but it also affects the nocturnal habits of some animals. For example, birds rely on stars for navigation, and some believe the moth population is being impacted by unnatural light.

As national parks become one of the few places where night skies are visible, the National Park Service has taken up the charge of preserving not only the environment we see around us, but also the one above us. Since 2001, its Night Skies Team has been measuring the impact of light pollution in 100 parks, finding that every park has been impacted by light pollution.

Fortunately, there are solutions at hand. An estimated 30 percent of all light produced in the United States is wasted. Park officials have been teaming with local communities to reduce the impact of light pollution. In the Shenandoah Valley, officials have erected zoning codes to reduce light use.

In Shenandoah National Park itself, the park staff is looking at ways to reduce light pollution. For example, light fixtures at the Big Meadows Wayside had shields installed on them to reduce glare, and staff members are looking at other ways to improve area and walkway lights. Since 2000, Big Meadows has been hosting night sky programs to raise awareness of the night sky and of what park visitors can do to make a difference.

TRIP 24
HIGHTOP MOUNTAIN

Location: South District, Shenandoah National Park, VA
Rating: Easy
Distance: 3.5 miles, round-trip
Elevation Gain: 999 feet
Estimated Time: 2–3 hours
Maps: *Map 11: Appalachian Trail and Other Trails in Shenandoah National Park South District* (PATC)

Stretch your legs on this steady uphill hike to the top of Hightop Mountain and a scenic spot for a good, long break.

DIRECTIONS

From I-66, Exit 43A, take US 29 South 54.5 miles to its junction with VA 33 in Ruckersville. Turn right (west) onto VA 33 and continue 14.4 miles to the park's Swift Run Gap entrance (fee). Head left (south) onto Skyline Drive to the Smith Roach Parking Area (between mileposts 69 and 70). *GPS coordinates:* 38° 19.717′ N, 78° 34.498′ W.

TRAIL DESCRIPTION

Hightop Mountain may not be one of the better-known hikes in Shenandoah National Park, but its lovely stretch on the Appalachian Trail (AT) is a perfect introduction to the trails in the southern part of the Shenandoah, which tend to be less crowded and a little wilder. Starting the hike from the Smith Roach Gap parking lot rather than the Hightop parking area makes for a longer hike, but this approach gives a more gradual climb to the top. With an easy path that isn't too rocky, this is a perfect route for a leisurely stroll.

To start the hike, head past the yellow gate and then make a quick left turn onto the AT (white blazes). The trail maintains a steady climb until you reach to the top, giving you a chance to take your time and enjoy your surroundings as you meander up the mountain.

At just under 1.0 mile, the AT intersects Smith Roach Gap Fire Road; pass through the intersection and stay on the AT. Shortly after this intersection, a blue-blazed spur trail departs on the left. Your route lies straight ahead on the AT, but if you're interested in a quick diversion, follow the blue blazes to and from Hightop Hut, one of the many shelters along the AT in Shenandoah.

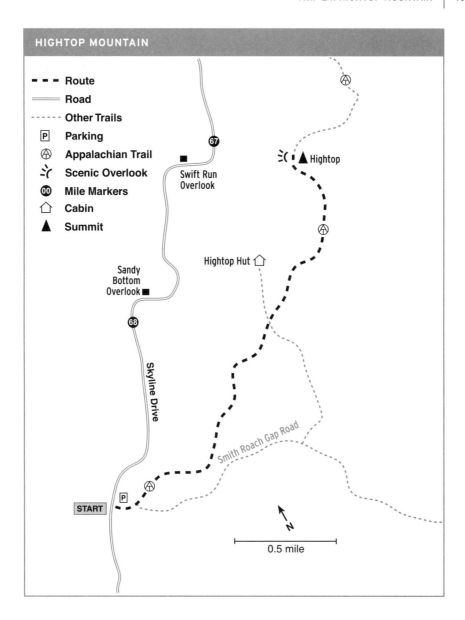

HIGHTOP MOUNTAIN

- - - Route
=== Road
----- Other Trails
P Parking
⊕ Appalachian Trail
⅔ Scenic Overlook
00 Mile Markers
⌂ Cabin
▲ Summit

67

Swift Run
Overlook

⅔ ▲ Hightop

⊕

Hightop Hut ⌂

Sandy
Bottom
Overlook ■

68

Skyline Drive

Smith Roach Gap Road

⊕

START P

N

0.5 mile

The trail continues to make its way up the mountain, passing a covered spring to the right. Shortly after the spring, the trail flattens out slightly. Some social trails lead off to campsites, but stay straight on the AT, and at 1.7 miles arrive at an overlook with views of Skyline Drive and some of the peaks farther south in the park.

After enjoying the views, retrace your steps back down the mountain and to the parking lot.

These ubiquitous stone pillars serve as helpful trail markers throughout Shenandoah—on and off the Appalachian Trail.

DID YOU KNOW?

Hightop Hut is just shy of a milestone for AT thru-hikers: The shelter is just 899 miles from Springer Mountain, Georgia, and 1,286 miles from Katahdin, Maine.

MORE INFORMATION

Shenandoah National Park (nps.gov/shen, 540-999-3500, 800-732-0911 [for emergencies]). Loft Mountain Wayside (milepost 79.5) sells groceries, camping and hiking supplies, and gifts and is open daily from 9 A.M. to 6 P.M. between mid-April and early November; visit goshenandoah.com for additional concessioner information. Park facilities are generally open from March through late November; a facilities schedule is online. In cases of inclement weather and at night in deer-hunting season (mid-November through early January), call the park to confirm whether Skyline Drive is open to vehicles. Overnight lodging in the park includes lodges, cabins, and campgrounds, including Loft Mountain Campground; visit nps.gov/shen/planyourvisit/lodging.htm or nps.gov/shen/planyourvisit/campgrounds.htm for more information.

NEARBY

The towns of Harrisonburg and Crozet are good stopping points for hikers on their way in or out of Shenandoah. For another short hike in the area, tackle Frazier Discovery Trail on Loft Mountain (Trip 23). The hikes in this section (Trips 23–29) are all within about 30 minutes of one another and within an hour's drive of the central district hikes on Skyline Drive (Trips 14–20).

TRIP 25
DOYLES RIVER, JONES RUN FALLS

Location: South District, Shenandoah National Park, VA
Rating: Moderate
Distance: 8.0 miles round-trip
Elevation Gain: 2,267 feet gain
Estimated Time: 3–5 hours
Maps: *Map 11: Appalachian Trail and Other Trails in Shenandoah National Park South District* (PATC)

In springtime, the falls along Doyles River and Jones Run may make for the most attractive waterfall walk in Virginia.

DIRECTIONS

From the north: From I-66, Exit 43A, take US 29 South 54.5 miles to its junction with VA 33 in Ruckersville. Turn right (west) onto VA 33 and continue 14.4 miles to the park's Swift Run Gap entrance (fee). Head left (south) onto Skyline Drive to the Jones River trailhead parking lot on the left near milepost 84.

From the south: From I-64, Exit 99 (US 250), follow signs for Skyline Drive and enter the park through the Rockfish Gap entrance (pay fee). Drive north on Skyline Drive for 21.2 miles, then turn right into the Jones River trailhead parking lot, just shy of milepost 84.

GPS coordinates: 38° 13.802′ N, 78° 43.577′ W.

TRAIL DESCRIPTION

The first 2.4 miles of this loop descends 1,272 feet, past Jones Run Falls and to a low point in the valley; the second 2.2 miles will vault you higher as you gain 1,506 feet on what is by far the most strenuous part of this route. The incredible views of Doyles River Falls will make it worth the effort. The final 3.4 miles on the Appalachian Trail (AT) rolls along far more placidly.

From the parking lot, follow the blue-blazed trail from the back of the lot to an intersection with the white-blazed AT, which crosses your path from left to right. Note this intersection; you'll be returning to it at the end of the hike.

At first the trail drops down through a fairly mild series of switchbacks as it approaches Jones Falls. As this is one of the most popular trails in this part

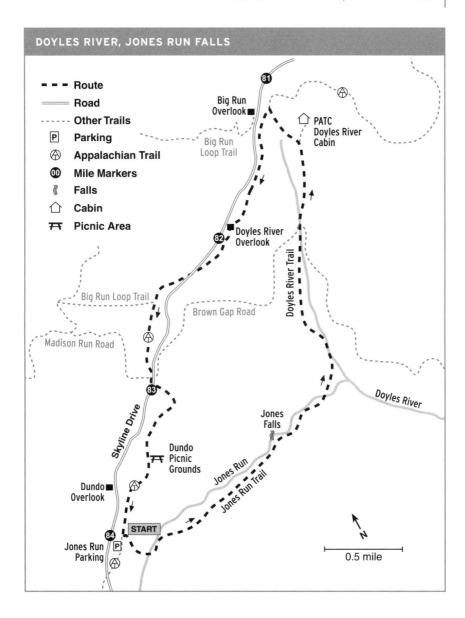

DOYLES RIVER, JONES RUN FALLS

- - - Route
—— Road
····· Other Trails
P Parking
Ⓐ Appalachian Trail
⓪⓪ Mile Markers
Falls
⌂ Cabin
Picnic Area

Big Run
Overlook ■

PATC
Doyles River
Cabin

Big Run
Loop Trail

Doyles River
Overlook

Doyles River Trail

Big Run Loop Trail

Brown Gap Road

Madison Run Road

Skyline Drive

Doyles River

Jones
Falls

Dundo
Picnic
Grounds

Jones Run

Jones Run Trail

Dundo ■
Overlook

START

Jones Run
Parking

N

0.5 mile

of the park, the path is well maintained and well graded. Eventually, the trail approaches the creek more closely and reaches an area where the water forms a steep slide over the stone. The trail switchbacks over a broad rim and brings you down into the bowl of Jones Run Falls itself at 1.6 miles.

Follow the trail as it parallels the creek on the right and, at 2.4 miles, finally arrives at the intersection with Doyles River Trail, which has descended the

The terraced waterfall of Upper Doyles River is an attractive rest spot for footsore explorers, especially on a warm summer's day.

mountain from the left, also following blue blazes. This V-shaped valley is the lowest point on the trail; the route's big climb is ahead.

Follow Doyles River Trail's blue blazes back up the mountain. The path first arrives at the Lower Doyles River Falls at 3.1 miles. A steep spur trail takes you down to explore. Although you may find it difficult to believe, Upper Doyles River Falls is even more attractive. Continue up Doyles River Trail another 0.4 mile; a short trail leads to the base of the two terraces over which the water cascades. If you like, get close enough to feel the spray. Do be careful, as approaching the waterfall involves some scrambly moves on rocks that may be slick.

From here, the climb becomes a bit more of a chore as the trail leaves the falls and ascends—step by laborious step—toward Skyline Drive and the AT. Pass Brown Gap Road at 3.8 miles. In another 0.5 mile, your route intersects a trail on the right that leads to the Potomac Appalachian Trail Club's Doyles River Cabin; continue on Doyles River Trail, which can be steep at times, but is very frequently walked and quite well maintained. At 4.6 miles, just shy of the parking lot on Skyline Drive, the path intersects the AT. Turn left (or south) on the white blazes.

Though this final section is fairly gentle, it does involve some rolling terrain. At first, the trail runs along the east (or left) side of Skyline Drive. Pass through the parking lot at Doyles River Overlook, cross the drive, and hike to Brown Gap at 6.7 miles. From this point, the AT crosses Skyline Drive, climbs slightly, and then passes alongside the Dundo Picnic Grounds at 7.4 miles. In another 0.6 mile, the trail reaches the intersection with the AT from which you started. Turn right to return to the parking lot.

DID YOU KNOW?

Although Jones River and Doyles River lay claim to the most attractive water-falls in Shenandoah National Park, they are not the tallest. That honor falls to Overall Run (Trip 11), which at 93 feet measures more than any other falls in the park. Unfortunately, Overall Run suffers in dry spells and is not as easily viewed. Nearby in Jefferson National Forest, Apple Orchard Falls (Trip 43) feels more vertical. Crabtree Falls (Trip 40), also in Jefferson National Forest, claims the honor of being not only the highest falls in Virginia but also the highest east of the Mississippi.

MORE INFORMATION

Shenandoah National Park (nps.gov/shen, 540-999-3500, 800-732-0911 [for emergencies]). Loft Mountain Wayside (milepost 79.5) sells groceries, camping and hiking supplies, and gifts and is open daily from 9 A.M. to 6 P.M. between mid-April and early November; visit goshenandoah.com for additional conces-sioner information. Park facilities are generally open from March through late November; a facilities schedule is online. In cases of inclement weather and at night in deer-hunting season (mid-November through early January), call the park to confirm whether Skyline Drive is open to vehicles. Overnight lodging in the park includes lodges, cabins, and campgrounds, including Loft Mountain Campground; for more information, visit nps.gov/shen/planyourvisit/lodging .htm or nps.gov/shen/planyourvisit/campgrounds.htm.

NEARBY

You won't lack for hiking in the wild southern district of Shenandoah. The hikes in this section (Trips 23–29) are all within about 30 minutes of one an-other and within an hour's drive of the central district hikes on Skyline Drive (Trips 14–20). The trailhead for Blackrock (Trip 28) is just another mile south on Skyline Drive.

Harrisonburg, Virginia, to the north, and Staunton, Virginia, to the south, offer a broad array of goods and services.

TRIP 26
BIG RUN, BROWN MOUNTAIN LOOP

Location: South District, Shenandoah National Park, VA
Rating: Moderate
Distance: 9.3 miles loop
Elevation Gain: 2,464 feet gain
Estimated Time: 4–7 hours
Maps: *Map 11: Appalachian Trail and Other Trails in Shenandoah National Park South District* (PATC)

Reachable only by circuitous routes, Big Run's most picturesque pools, cascades, and falls are hidden gems of Shenandoah National Park.

DIRECTIONS

From the north: From I-66, Exit 43A, take US 29 South 54.5 miles to its junction with VA 33 in Ruckersville. Turn right (west) onto VA 33 and continue 14.4 miles to the park's Swift Run Gap entrance (fee). Head left (south) onto Skyline Drive to Brown Mountain Overlook on the right (between mileposts 76 and 77).

From the south: From I-64, Exit 99 (US 250), follow signs for Skyline Drive and enter the park through the Rockfish Gap entrance (fee). Drive north on Skyline Drive for 28.5 miles to Brown Mountain Overlook, on the left.

GPS coordinates: 38° 17.537′ N, 78° 39.477′ W.

TRAIL DESCRIPTION

Take time before beginning the hike to survey your route from the overlook. Directly ahead of you, spot the rocky ridgeline of Brown Mountain. You will descend to the saddle beneath you, then reascend to this ridgeline, which you'll follow westward until you drop down to Big Run. From there, the route doubles back on itself, following Big Run east toward Skyline Drive. Directly beneath you is Rocky Mountain Run, which you'll follow as it climbs away from Big Run, to the saddle, and then back to the overlook where you stand. You'll need to ford a few runs on this route. In drier seasons, you might be able to rock-hop over these fords and reach the other side with dry feet, but always be prepared to get your feet wet, no matter the conditions. If there's been considerable rainfall recently, be cautious at these crossings.

Once you start hiking, you'll descend about 500 feet over 0.6 mile, following the blue blazes of Brown Mountain Trail, to reach the intersection with

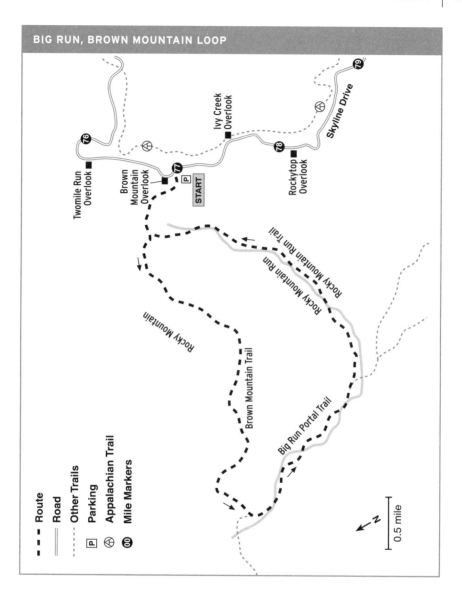

Rocky Mountain Trail on the left, also blue blazed. Take careful note of this point, as you'll return here near the end of the hike. For now, climb away from the saddle on Brown Mountain Trail, which switchbacks its way to the ridgeline, gaining about 450 feet. The footway opens out to a series of rocky views. Scramble up for a look back toward Skyline Drive.

Over the next 1.3 miles, Brown Mountain Trail generally follows this ridgeline as it weaves its way westward toward the park's periphery. Generally, the terrain is rolling. Keep your eye out for side paths that will take you to various interesting viewpoints. Eventually, the trail runs out of mountain and begins

Big Run can be seen from the rocky prominences of Brown Mountain.

to switchback vigorously down toward Big Run. Scope out the rockslides on the northern face of Rockytop, and listen for the sound of rushing water. After about 1,700 feet of total descent and 4.6 total miles, the path reaches two park posts and passes by the metal bridge leading over the river, on the right, to Rockytop Trail.

Stay left and follow Big Run Portal Trail, blazed in yellow. At first, this trail stays to the north of the stream, passing by a few campsites. Soon enough, it crosses the run at the first of four fords. The trail crosses first to the south, then the north, then the south, and finally the north once again over the next 1.5 miles. The hiking here is generally easy, as it follows an old road grade that stays fairly flat. Take time to explore, as Big Run is the star of this hike.

After the fourth ford, at 6.0 miles, the trail reaches a truly magnificent swimming hole that stays deep enough to enjoy even in fairly dry weather. Seize this opportunity for a break, a dip, and a picnic. Don't leave until you're refreshed, as you have the climb back to Skyline Drive ahead of you.

Immediately after you leave the swimming hole, the route intersects blue-blazed Rocky Mountain Run Trail on the left. Turn left, leave Big Run, and begin to climb. At first, the path's grade is fairly gentle as it cuts through a deep and dark valley that sees few visitors. In season, you might find berries and bears along the path, as Michael did. The trail passes by a nice campsite at the base of a little waterfall. Then, grin and bear it as the climbing becomes steeper, the path eventually switchbacking—quite indirectly—as it nears the saddle, noted above.

At 8.6 miles, the trail reaches the saddle. Turn right onto Brown Mountain Trail and climb the remaining 500 feet and 0.6 mile to the overlook.

DID YOU KNOW?

Big Run is the park's largest drainage, emptying a vast watershed and draining into the north fork of the Shenandoah River. To get a sense of how large is the valley that Big Run occupies, climb Blackrock (see Trip 29). From its summit, you can see Big Run's capacious valley to the north, guarded to the west by Rockytop and Brown Mountain.

MORE INFORMATION

Shenandoah National Park (nps.gov/shen, 540-999-3500, 800-732-0911 [for emergencies]). Loft Mountain Wayside (milepost 79.5) sells groceries, camping and hiking supplies, and gifts and is open daily from 9 A.M. to 6 P.M. between mid-April and early November; visit goshenandoah.com for additional concessioner information. Park facilities are generally open from March through late November; a facilities schedule is online. In cases of inclement weather and at night in deer-hunting season (mid-November through early January), call the park to confirm whether Skyline Drive is open to vehicles. Overnight lodging in the park includes lodges, cabins, and campgrounds, including Loft Mountain Campground; for more information, visit nps.gov/shen/planyourvisit/lodging .htm or nps.gov/shen/planyourvisit/campgrounds.htm.

NEARBY

The hikes in this section (Trips 23 through 29) are all within about 30 minutes of one another and within an hour's drive of the central district hikes on Skyline Drive (Trips 14 through 20). The nearest trips are Hightop Mountain (Trip 24) and Jones Run and Doyles River (Trip 25).

For supplies, visit the Loft Mountain Wayside or campground store, or leave the park to shop at Harrisonburg, the nearest city.

TRIP 27
TRAYFOOT MOUNTAIN AND PAINE RUN LOOP

Location: South District, Shenandoah National Park, VA
Rating: Strenuous
Distance: 9.2 miles
Elevation Gain: 2,500 feet
Estimated Time: 5–6 hours
Maps: *Map 11: Appalachian Trail and Other Trails in Shenandoah National Park South District* (PATC)

The stretch along the ridgeline is one of the nicest in the park, and one of the highlights comes early—the near-360-degree views from Blackrock.

DIRECTIONS

From the north: From I-66, Exit 43A, take US 29 South 54.5 miles to its junction with VA 33 in Ruckersville. Turn right (west) onto VA 33 and continue 14.4 miles to the park's Swift Run Gap entrance (fee). Head left (south) onto Skyline Drive to the Blackrock Gap Parking Area (between mileposts 87 and 88).

From the south: From I-64, Exit 99 (US 250), follow signs for Skyline Drive and enter the park through the Rockfish Gap entrance (fee). Drive north on Skyline Drive for 25.9 miles, then turn right into the Blackrock Gap Parking Area (between mileposts 87 and 88). *GPS coordinates:* 38° 12.405′ N, 78° 44.983′ W.

TRAIL DESCRIPTION

The Trayfoot Mountain and Paine Run Loop is another excellent example of southern Shenandoah National Park's rugged hiking. This route starts and ends with a climb, making it a good hike if you're looking for a challenge. Save your energy for the end, however; the trail climbs steadily for more than 3.0 miles back to the parking lot.

From the parking lot, cross Skyline Drive and look for the concrete post marking the Appalachian Trail (AT). Turn left onto the white-blazed AT and start to follow it uphill. The trail will cross Skyline Drive again, and continue on its steady climb. Stay straight on the AT, passing an intersection with a spur trail at 0.7 mile. (Following the blue-blazed spur will lead you to Blackrock Hut.)

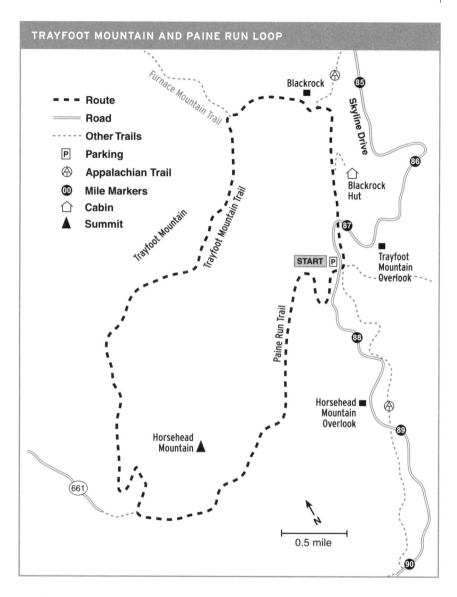

TRAYFOOT MOUNTAIN AND PAINE RUN LOOP

- - - Route
═══ Road
----- Other Trails
P Parking
Ⓐ Appalachian Trail
⓪⓪ Mile Markers
⌂ Cabin
▲ Summit

Furnace Mountain Trail

Blackrock
85
Skyline Drive
86
Blackrock Hut
87
Trayfoot Mountain Overlook

Trayfoot Mountain

Trayfoot Mountain Trail

START P

N

Paine Run Trail

88

Horsehead Mountain Overlook
Ⓐ
89

Horsehead Mountain ▲

661

↑ N

├──────────────┤
0.5 mile

90

The trail continues to climb, and at 1.1 miles intersects Trayfoot Mountain Trail. Stay on the AT and keep following the white blazes. Famed Blackrock lies just past this intersection, and it is well worth taking a break here to scramble to the top for 360-degree views of the park and out to the valley.

Once you are ready to continue, the AT loops around Blackrock and arrives at Blackrock Spur Trail at 1.25 miles. Turn left onto the blue-blazed spur trail, which leads through a maze of slabs and to an intersection with blue-blazed

The path from Blackrock leads hikers through a maze of slabs before entering the woods again.

Trayfoot Mountain Trail at 1.4 miles. Bear right and follow Trayfoot Mountain Trail as it makes its way farther up the mountain, passing an intersection with Furnace Mountain Trail at 2.0 miles and eventually arriving at Trayfoot's 3,371-foot summit at 2.2 miles.

The next stretch of the trail is pleasant, running up and down along the ridge, occasionally opening up for views across the valley. The trail eventually heads straight toward another outcropping that gives a good view of Buzzard Rock at 5.2 miles.

From here, the route turns sharply to the left and starts making its way downhill. Arrive at Paine Run Trail at 5.8 miles, and turn left to start following it. Paine Run Trail (yellow blazes) crosses the run a few times as it starts to make its way back uphill. The climb at first is a mild one, and the wide trail switches between a sandy and rocky path to one more packed down. It also can be rather exposed to the sun, especially in summer, as the area is still recovering from a forest fire that occurred several years ago.

The mild climb eventually gets a little tougher as it makes a sharp turn to the right and begins a series of steep and long switchbacks to the top before arriving at the parking lot.

DID YOU KNOW?

Little evidence remains of the Blackrock Springs Hotel, which was located along Paine Run Road. The first mention of this resort appeared in a newspaper from 1835, and its seven springs were touted as able to heal gout and even baldness. The property switched hands several times over the years, and cottages and a boarding house sprang up nearby. In 1909, the hotel and cottages were destroyed in a fire, but the boarding house was spared. It—and its bowling alley—remained in operation until the park was established.

MORE INFORMATION

Shenandoah National Park (nps.gov/shen, 540-999-3500, 800-732-0911 [for emergencies]). Loft Mountain Wayside (milepost 79.5) sells groceries, camping and hiking supplies, and gifts and is open daily from 9 A.M. to 6 P.M. between mid-April and early November; visit goshenandoah. com for additional concessioner information. Park facilities are generally open from March through late November; a facilities schedule is online. In cases of inclement weather and at night in deer-hunting season (mid-November through early January), call the park to confirm whether Skyline Drive is open to vehicles. Overnight lodging in the park includes lodges, cabins, and campgrounds, including Loft Mountain Campground; for more information, visit nps.gov/shen/planyourvisit/lodging.htm or nps .gov/shen/planyourvisit/campgrounds.htm.

NEARBY

The towns of Harrisonburg and Crozet are good stopping points for hikers on their way in or out of Shenandoah. Loft Mountain—and its wayside—is a few miles north on Skyline Drive. You could also opt to just see Blackrock by a gentler route from the Blackrock Summit Parking Area at milepost 85 (Trip 28). The hikes in this section (Trips 23 through 29) are all within about 30 minutes of one another and within an hour's drive of the central district hikes on Skyline Drive (Trips 14 through 20).

TRIP 28
BLACKROCK

Location: South District, Shenandoah National Park, VA
Rating: Easy
Distance: 1.2 miles, round-trip
Elevation Gain: 300 feet gain
Estimated Time: 1–1.5 hours
Maps: *Map 11: Appalachian Trail and Other Trails in Shenandoah National Park South District* (PATC)

This gentle and short hike leads to one of the most compelling vistas in Virginia, an awe-inspiring 360-degree view of the south district of the Shenandoah

DIRECTIONS
From the north: From I-66, Exit 43A, take US 29 South 54.5 miles to its junction with VA 33 in Ruckersville. Turn right (west) onto VA 33 and continue 14.4 miles to the park's Swift Run Gap entrance (fee). Head left (south) onto Skyline Drive to the Blackrock Summit Parking Area (between mileposts 84 and 85).

From the south: From I-64, Exit 99 (US 250), follow signs for Skyline Drive and enter the park through the Rockfish Gap entrance (pay fee). Drive north on Skyline Drive, past the Blackrock Gap Parking Area (between mileposts 88 and 87), to the Blackrock Summit Parking Area (between mileposts 85 and 84). *GPS coordinates: 38° 13.368′ N, 78° 43.997′ W.*

TRAIL DESCRIPTION
Few trails, especially in this region, offer such reward for so little effort.

From the parking lot, look westward to find the big and broad spur trail leading to the Appalachian Trail (AT). The blue blazes mark Trayfoot Mountain Trail. This path climbs some as it leads about 800 feet to an intersection with the AT's hallmark white blazes. Turn left and head south on the AT. (Trayfoot Mountain Trail also continues to the summit of Blackrock, though by a slightly different path, on the left.)

The AT climbs about 150 feet in elevation, but the grade never approaches anything resembling steep. The mountain rises above you on the left, and with

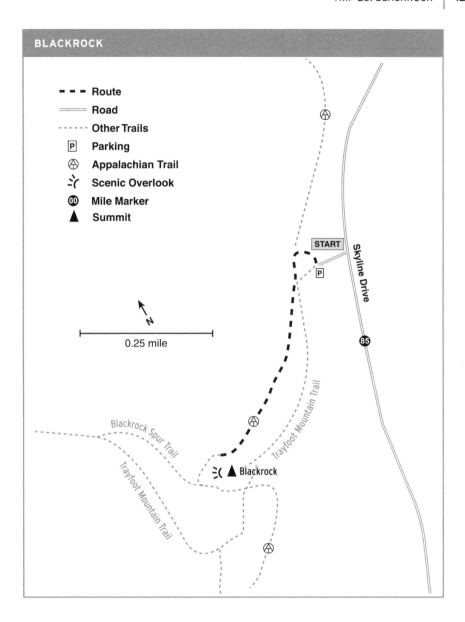

BLACKROCK

--- Route
=== Road
----- Other Trails
P Parking
Ⓐ Appalachian Trail
⛅ Scenic Overlook
⓪⓪ Mile Marker
▲ Summit

START

Skyline Drive

P

N

0.25 mile

85

Blackrock Spur Trail

Trayfoot Mountain Trail

Trayfoot Mountain Trail

⛅ ▲ Blackrock

a keen eye you can also spot the blue-blazed trail shadowing the AT through the forest. After about 0.5 mile, the AT crosses a rockfall and descends to the right. Be careful as you cross this field as the footing is somewhat treacherous. Look left for a view of the top, and start to gain an appreciation for this vantage point.

Just past the rockfall, the trail reaches a post marking an intersection with Trayfoot Mountain Trail. Leave the AT and scramble over the boulders to

From the summit of Blackrock you'll enjoy expansive views of the southern district of the Shenandoah.

reach the summit's garden of rocks. Take your time and be sure of your foot placement, but the scrambling isn't too difficult.

From the top, the view is spectacular, especially westward. To the right, you have a wide-ranging vantage that takes in all of Big Run's drainage—the largest in the park—as well as Brown Mountain, Rockytop, Austin Mountain, and a number of additional peaks familiar to frequent day-hikers. Directly ahead is the formidable ridgeline of Trayfoot Mountain and Furnace Mountain (Trip 27). On your left, spot the valley of Paine Run.

Savor this view, which makes an especially good sunrise or sunset hike, as the trail is not especially problematic to follow in the dark; just make sure to bring your headlamp or a flashlight. Once you're ready, retrace your route to return to your vehicle.

DID YOU KNOW?

Blackrock is one of just five true 360-degree views in the park. The others are Hawksbill (Trip 19), Mary's Rock (Trip 14), Old Rag (Trip 21), and Bear Fence (as this one is for the intrepid, it is not described in this book). Though there are many other fine views in the Shenandoah region, its lush vegetation does tend to cut down on the sweeping panoramas from its summits.

MORE INFORMATION

Shenandoah National Park (nps.gov/shen, 540-999-3500, 800-732-0911 [for emergencies]). Loft Mountain Wayside (milepost 79.5) sells groceries, camping and hiking supplies, and gifts and is open daily from 9 A.M. to 6 P.M. between mid-April and early November; visit goshenandoah.com for additional concessioner information. Park facilities are generally open March through late November; a facilities schedule is online. In cases of inclement weather and at night in deer-hunting season (mid-November through early January), call the park to confirm whether Skyline Drive is open to vehicles. Overnight lodging in the park includes lodges, cabins, and campgrounds, including Loft Mountain Campground; for more information, visit nps.gov/shen/planyourvisit/lodging .htm or nps.gov/shen/planyourvisit/campgrounds.htm.

NEARBY

If you're looking for another short hike nearby, Frazier Discovery Trail (Trip 23) starts from the Blackrock Gap Parking Area just a few miles south. You could opt to just see Blackrock as part of a more challenging route to tackle Trayfoot Mountain (Trip 27). The hikes in this section (Trips 23 through 29) are all within about 30 minutes of one another and within an hour's drive of the central district hikes on Skyline Drive (Trips 14 through 20).

For post-hike refreshment, your best bets are along your route homeward, perhaps Waynesboro to the south or Warrenton to the north. The Loft Mountain Wayside also makes a good spot for a break.

TRIP 29
RIPRAP HOLLOW

Location: South District, Shenandoah National Park, VA
Rating: Strenuous
Distance: 9.1 miles
Elevation Gain: 2,365 feet
Estimated Time: 5–6 hours
Maps: *Map 11: Appalachian Trail and Other Trails in Shenandoah National Park South District* (PATC)

With a swimming hole, sweeping views, and waterfalls, this valley offers some of the best hiking in the southern Shenandoah district.

DIRECTIONS
From the north: From I-66, Exit 43A, take US 29 South 54.5 miles to its junction with VA 33 in Ruckersville. Turn right (west) onto VA 33 and continue 14.4 miles to the park's Swift Run Gap entrance (fee). Head left (south) onto Skyline Drive to the Riprap Parking Area (just past milepost 90).

From the south: From I-64, Exit 99 (US 250), follow signs for Skyline Drive and enter the park through the Rockfish Gap entrance (fee). Drive north on Skyline Drive to the Riprap Parking Area (just past milepost 90). *GPS coordinates:* 38° 10.656′ N, 78° 45.914′ W.

TRAIL DESCRIPTION
Many describe Riprap as one of the better hikes in Shenandoah. After doing this hike, you'd be hard pressed to disagree. Hike this in summer, when you can take advantage of a cooling break in the swimming hole—but it is all uphill from here.

From the parking lot, head along the blue-blazed trail. In just a few yards, arrive at an intersection with the Appalachian Trail (AT) and turn right. The white-blazed AT heads uphill for a bit and then arrives at another intersection in 0.5 mile, this time with blue-blazed Riprap Trail. Turn left onto Riprap Trail and follow it as it dips and climbs to Calvary Rocks at 1.2 miles, giving you the first vista of the hike.

The second view isn't too far away. Continue along the trail past Chimney Rock at 1.5 miles to more views of the surrounding area. From here, the trail starts to head downhill. It's a pleasant hike with an occasional steep descent

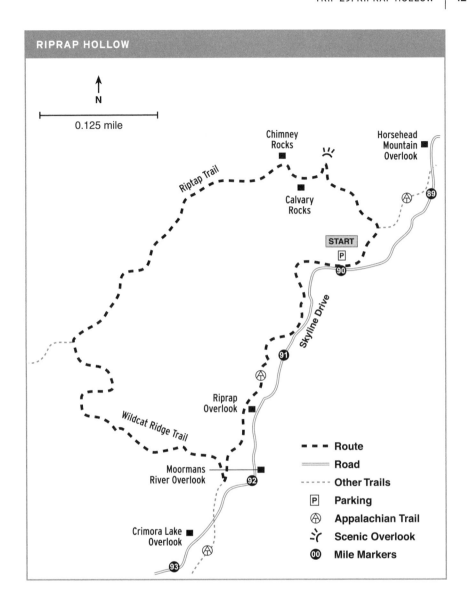

RIPRAP HOLLOW

N

0.125 mile

Chimney
Rocks

Horsehead
Mountain
Overlook

Riptap Trail

Calvary
Rocks

89

START

P

90

Skyline Drive

91

Riprap
Overlook

Wildcat Ridge Trail

Moormans
River Overlook

92

- - - **Route**

───── **Road**

----- **Other Trails**

P   **Parking**

Ⓐ   **Appalachian Trail**

⁖ᒼ   **Scenic Overlook**

⓪⓪   **Mile Markers**

Crimora Lake
Overlook

93

that eventually flattens out for a bit as it starts to follow a streambed. At 3.2 miles, the stream that has been running to your side erupts into a cascade as it passes through a small gorge.

The trail climbs uphill briefly, then dips back down to the stream, crosses over it, and leads to a deep swimming hole at 3.6 miles. Wade along the shallow parts or, if you're feeling brave, plunge into the water and go for a quick swim.

From here, the hike continues alongside the stream. Arrive at an intersection with Wildcat Ridge Trail at 4.1 miles and turn left. The route crosses the

Hikers will find themselves pausing several times to enjoy waterworks along this trip.

stream twice before the real workout begins. For the next 2.5 miles, the trail climbs back up to the ridge—steeply at times—before arriving at the intersection with the AT at 6.5 miles. Turn left onto the AT and follow the white blazes. From here, the trail flattens out with occasional dips and rises and leads back to the original spur trail and the parking lot.

DID YOU KNOW?

The rocks at Calvary Rocks are among the "youngest" in the park, evidence of the shifts that led to the creation of the Shenandoah Mountains. The plates that make up North America, Europe, and North Africa collided, closing the ocean that was formed and pushing up sediment from that ocean to become the Appalachian Mountains. Some of these sedimentary rocks can be seen in the park, more so in the southern part of the park, where they are exposed. Part of the Chilhowee Group, these white quartzite rocks are roughly 500 million years young and are part of the Erwin Formation.

MORE INFORMATION

Shenandoah National Park (nps.gov/shen, 540-999-3500, 800-732-0911 [for emergencies]). Loft Mountain Wayside (milepost 79.5) sells groceries, camping and hiking supplies, and gifts and is open daily from 9 A.M. to 6 P.M. between mid-April and early November; visit goshenandoah.com for additional concessioner information. Park facilities are generally open from March through late

November; a facilities schedule is online. In cases of inclement weather and at night in deer-hunting season (mid-November through early January), call the park to confirm whether Skyline Drive is open to vehicles. Overnight lodging in the park includes lodges, cabins, and campgrounds, including Loft Mountain Campground; for more information, visit nps.gov/shen/planyourvisit/lodging. htm or nps.gov/shen/planyourvisit/campgrounds.htm.

NEARBY

The towns of Harrisonburg and Crozet are good stopping points for hikers on their way in or out of Shenandoah. Loft Mountain—and its wayside—is a few miles north on Skyline Drive. The hikes in this section (Trips 23 through 29) are all within about 30 minutes of one another and within an hour's drive of the central district hikes on Skyline Drive (Trips 14 through 20). The nearest hikes to this trailhead are Trayfoot Mountain (27) and Frazier Discovery Trail (Trip 23).

5

MASSANUTTEN MOUNTAIN

WEST OF SHENANDOAH NATIONAL PARK, the Shenandoah River's South Fork etches a path around the foot of three long, parallel ridges. Though officially named Massanutten Mountain collectively, hikers more often refer to the ridges as the Massanuttens. With a peak elevation of 2,922 feet, these ridges stretch across 45 miles, bisecting the Shenandoah Valley.

Much of the land here is protected by the George Washington National Forest, which encompasses more than 1 million acres of land (95 percent of which is in Virginia; the rest is in West Virginia). Together, the administratively combined George Washington and Jefferson National Forests protect more than 1.8 million acres of land in Virginia, West Virginia, and Kentucky. On Massanutten Mountain, 10,000 acres of forest on the west face have been identified as a sensitive viewshed, limiting the impact that development of roads and trails can have on the beauty of these wild ridges. Other projects to improve recreation resources, protect the forest against human impact, limit the effects of natural threats like the gypsy moth and wooly adelgid, and expand interpretative programs are underway.

This mountain and the valley it surrounds nearly served as the Continental Army's last refuge against the British Army during the American Revolution, but the siege of Yorktown swayed the course of history, and retreat to Fort Valley was unnecessary.

When you're visiting the area, stop by the Massanutten Visitor Center on VA 211 in New Market for more information about the natural and cultural history of this singular area. Or, stop for a walk on the 0.5-mile, handicap-accessible Storybook Trail (VA 211 to FR 274, then 1.5 miles to Storybook Trail) for an outdoor, interpretative experience.

TRIP 30
BUZZARD ROCK

Location: Massanutten Mountain, George Washington National Forest, VA
Rating: Strenuous
Distance: 9 miles
Elevation Gain: 3,433 feet gain
Estimated Time: 4–6 hours
Maps: *Map G: Trails in the Massanutten Mountain—North Half, Signal Knob to New Market Gap* (PATC)

The dramatic knife-edge ridge of Buzzard Rock offers a commanding view of Fort Valley and the South Fork of the Shenandoah River.

DIRECTIONS

From I-66, Exit 6 in Front Royal, turn left (south) onto US 340. After about 1.2 miles, turn right onto VA 55 and head west for about 5 miles. Turn left on Fort Valley Road/VA 678 and enter the national forest. Continue about 4 miles south along Fort Valley Road to the sign for the Elizabeth Furnace Recreation area on the left. There are several turnoffs—you want the one for the family campground. Turn left, cross the bridge over Passage Creek, and park in the parking lot. *GPS coordinates:* 38° 55.668′ N, 78° 19.759′ W.

TRAIL DESCRIPTION

From the parking lot, look east toward the ridge of Massanutten Mountain. You should be able to discern a gap along the ridgeline. This is Shawl Gap, and it will be your intermediary destination as you make your way from Elizabeth Furnace to Buzzard Rock.

When you're ready to get started, walk back along the road you drove in on until you reach the near side of the bridge. Look right and you should see the orange and blue blazes headed along Passage Creek. This is the beginning point of the hike. For the first 2.4 miles, both colors mark Massanutten Trail (orange blazes) as it shares the footway with Tuscarora Trail (blue blazes). Grab the trail and follow along the bank of the creek, passing by, no doubt, a number of anglers, who especially relish this area. Pass some signage for Pig Iron and Charcoal Interpretive Trail, which explains how iron was produced

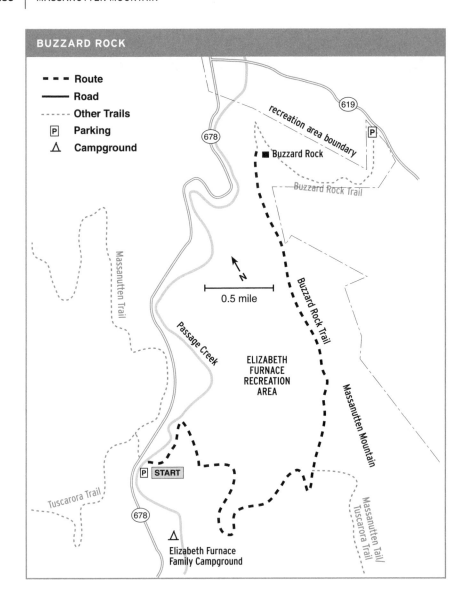

BUZZARD ROCK

- - - Route
—— Road
----- Other Trails
P Parking
△ Campground

619

recreation area boundary

678

P

■ Buzzard Rock

Buzzard Rock Trail

Massanutten Trail

N

0.5 mile

Passage Creek

Buzzard Rock Trail

ELIZABETH
FURNACE
RECREATION
AREA

Massanutten Mountain

P START

Tuscarora Trail

678

Massanutten Tail/
Tuscarora Trail

△

Elizabeth Furnace
Family Campground

in the old stone furnaces. Keep your eyes out for the blazes, however, as it is possible to lose your way by straying onto one of the intersecting trails.

In the first 0.4 mile, Massanutten/Tuscarora Trail is very mild-mannered and flat, but it gets serious about climbing to Shawl Gap. Over the next 2.0 miles, the trail gains about 1,200 feet as it switchbacks across the mountain. Throughout much of the climb, the trail is well graded and makes for pleasant walking, but as you near the gap, it becomes especially steep and rocky. At 2.4

An intrepid hiker scrambles for the views at Buzzard Rock.

miles, once you've surmounted this climb, the path arrives at a well-marked four-way intersection. The blue and orange blazes head south along the ridge; yellow blazes lead down the eastern face of the mountain; white blazes on the left turn north along the ridgeline and eventually to Buzzard Rock.

Turn left onto the white blazes of Buzzard Rock trail and continue climbing about 0.8 mile and 466 feet more (nope, Shawl Gap is not the top). Keep your eye out, however, as there are numerous perches from which you can peer out over Fort Valley to the west or to the east toward Shenandoah National Park. Many of these offer impressive vistas. Eventually, the climb will top out and you'll begin a descent to the cliffs of Buzzard Rock at 4.5 miles.

There's no mistaking the sheer rock faces that begin appearing on your left. Soon the route ambles along a knife's-edge ridge that is quite unusual for Virginia. Take time to explore the ridge; there are many excellent places to relax, have lunch, or get a terrific photo. In fact, if you're up to a short side trip, continue past the cliffs on the north side and walk down to a beautiful northward view of pastoral Virginia stretching toward Winchester. Of course, you'll have to climb back up again.

Once you've enjoyed the view, return on the white blazes and then take the orange and blue blazes down to Elizabeth Furnace at 9.0 miles. Be careful on the descent, however, as there is an unmarked trail that crosses the marked route. If you do get on it, however, never fear, as all roads lead to Elizabeth Furnace. Still, it's better to stay on the blazes.

DID YOU KNOW?

The cliffs of Buzzard Rock are sheer enough to attract local climbers. Be aware that they might be climbing beneath the trail and take care not to knock rocks down on them.

MORE INFORMATION

George Washington and Jefferson National Forests, Lee Ranger District (www .fs.usda.gov/main/gwj; 540-984-4101). Check online for announcements concerning trail conditions, road closures, prescribed burns, and other events that may affect your hike.

NEARBY

If you're looking for an easier way to reach Buzzard Rock, there is another trailhead off VA 619 (38° 56.264′ N, 78° 17.313′ W). An out-and-back trip to the rocks from this trailhead will total about 4.0 miles with about 700 feet of gain and loss.

The nearest settlements are Strasburg, Virginia (head west along VA 55), and Front Royal (head east along VA 55). Each offers all the establishments you would expect to find in a town along the interstate. There are number of big-box retail stores off I-66, Exit 6.

Location: Massanutten Mountain, George Washington
National Forest, VA
Rating: Moderate
Distance: 5.2 miles round-trip
Elevation Gain: 1,192 feet gain
Estimated Time: 2–4 hours
Maps: *Map G: Trails in the Massanutten Mountain—North Half,
Signal Knob to New Market Gap* (PATC)

**From this summit, you'll enjoy one-of-a-kind views of Fort Valley
and the north and central districts of Shenandoah National Park.**

DIRECTIONS

From I-66, Exit 13, head west on VA 55, 5.8 miles, through downtown Front
Royal to the junction with US 340. Turn left (south) onto US 340 and continue
23.2 miles, merging briefly with US 211 as you enter Luray. Turn left onto
North Hawksbill Street, then in 0.3 mile, take a right onto Mechanic Street,
which becomes Bixlers Ferry Road in 0.6 mile, then becomes VA 675 in 0.9
mile as it heads out of town. In 2.2 miles, after you cross the South Fork of the
Shenandoah River, take a left, then a quick right. You'll still be on VA 675, now
also VA 615. The road climbs into the mountains and tops out at Edith Gap,
which is the trailhead for Kennedy Peak, in 2.8 miles. A parking lot is on your
left, a hang-glider spot is on your right, and the trail is just across the road.
GPS coordinates: 38° 43.523′ N, 78° 30.582′ W.

TRAIL DESCRIPTION

The distinctively pyramidal shape of Kennedy Peak dominates the valley of
the South Fork of the Shenandoah River. With the exception of the last few
hundred yards beneath the summit, you'll be walking on orange-blazed Massanutten Trail for the entirety of this hike. Once you start hiking, you'll enjoy
about 1.5 miles of gentle walking as Massanutten Trail heads northeast along
the back of the ridgeline.

From the parking lot, look northward across VA 675 and spot the sign for
Kennedy Peak and the blazes. The trail is big and broad, and though it does
climb about 350 feet over this first stretch, you'll hardly notice. Ahead of you,

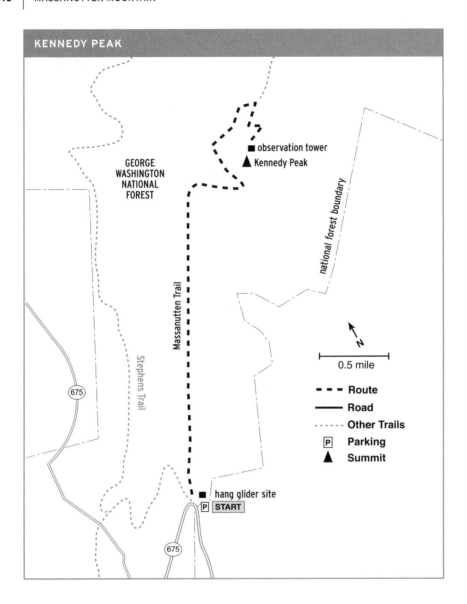

on the right, you should be able to spot Kennedy Peak itself. The trail dips down to a saddle at the mountain's shoulder, and you'll begin traversing rightward at 1.5 miles.

It's at this point that the trail begins to climb. The path becomes narrower and rockier, then switchbacks to the left across the face of the mountain at 1.8 miles, gradually working its way around to the northeastern side of the peak. Look for an unblazed spur trail on the left at 2.3 miles that leads to westward views of Fort Valley.

From its perch atop Kennedy Peak, the first CCC observation tower offers commanding views of the Shenandoah and Fort Valley.

Just beyond this unblazed spur, at 2.4 miles, a white-blazed spur trail intersects Massanutten Trail, which continues northward. Take the spur and begin a sharp climb southwest to reach the summit. Over the next 0.2 mile, the trail gains 185 feet to reach the shelter and the big eastward vistas of the summit. Take your time and enjoy your resting spot

When you're ready to return to your vehicle, you have only to retrace your steps, making sure to turn left onto the Massanutten Trail. Otherwise, the return to the trailhead is unproblematic (5.2/1,846).

DID YOU KNOW?

The observation tower atop Kennedy has stood there since it was built by the Civilian Conservation Corps (CCC) in the 1930s. Though it would build hundreds of such shelters throughout the nation, this was the first, since it stood in such close proximity to the first CCC camp, Camp Roosevelt, in Fort Valley. In the spring of 2014, the Potomac Appalachian Trail Club (PATC) and the U.S. Forest Service began renovating the tower, which had become dilapidated and dangerous.

MORE INFORMATION

George Washington and Jefferson National Forests, Lee Ranger District (www
.fs.usda.gov/main/gwj; 540-984-4101). Check online for announcements

concerning trail conditions, road closures, prescribed burns, and other events that may affect your hike.

NEARBY

If you're looking for a longer circuit hike that includes Kennedy Peak, consider walking farther north on Massanutten Trail, descending via Stephens Trail to Camp Roosevelt, and then climbing back to Edith Gap on Massanutten Trail. This more strenuous option will net you about 9 miles and 2,300 feet of climbing. Be sure to bring PATC's Map G along if you're planning to tackle this extended jaunt!

Luray, Virginia, is the nearest spot for you to grab supplies, or a quick bite to eat after the hike, though, of course, you'll also be passing through Front Royal on your way to and from the hike. If you're looking for more hiking in the area, the other trips in this section are all nearby. Elizabeth Furnace offers excellent vehicle camping facilities. Shenandoah National Park is just across the valley.

TRIP 32
DUNCAN KNOB

Location: Massanutten Mountain, George Washington National Forest, VA
Rating: Moderate
Distance: 3.5 miles, round-trip
Elevation Gain: 1,163 feet
Estimated Time: 2–3 hours
Maps: *Map G: Trails in the Massanutten Mountain—North Half, Signal Knob to New Market Gap* (PATC)

Scramble to reach an impressive vista of south Massanutten Mountain, the Blue Ridge Mountains, and Shenandoah Valley.

DIRECTIONS

From I-81, Exit 264, take US 211 east. In the town of New Market, turn left and follow US 11 briefly before turning right onto US 211, which soon climbs into the mountains. In 3.6 miles, at the top of the gap, turn left onto Crisman Hollow Road/Forest Development Road 274. Although the road turns to gravel, it is well maintained and suitable for cars. Pass signed trailheads for Massanutten Storybook Trail, Massanutten Trail, and Scothorn Gap Trail before reaching the Gap Creek trailhead, on the right, in 4.5 miles. *GPS coordinates:* 38° 42.549′ N, 78° 33.582′ W.

Note that Crisman Hollow Road is closed during winter. Be sure to check with the Forest Service before venturing out in the colder months. If you're determined to reach Duncan Knob even with the road closed, a longer hike can be started at US 211 in the south or VA 675 in the north.

TRAIL DESCRIPTION

The rocky top of Duncan Knob (2,803 feet) is one of the most dramatic perches in the region. To the south stretches Massanutten Mountain itself. In the east, the ridges of Shenandoah National Park are visible; in the west, the Alleghenies. In between are the valleys belonging to the forks of the Shenandoah River. Add to these glorious views the excitement of the final scramble to the summit, and you have an ideal short hike introducing you to the area. Be prepared to use your hands and be very cautious if the rocks are wet.

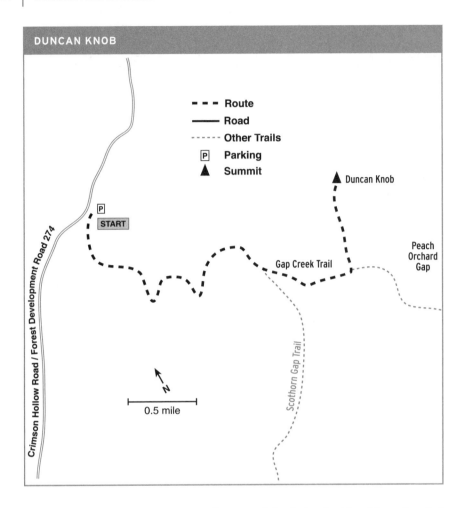

DUNCAN KNOB

- - - Route
—— Road
----- Other Trails
P Parking
▲ Summit

▲ Duncan Knob

Crimson Hollow Road / Forest Development Road 274

P
START

Gap Creek Trail

Peach
Orchard
Gap

Scothorn Gap Trail

N

0.5 mile

At the trailhead at Crisman Hollow Road, look for the blue blazes headed
southward away from the road. These mark Gap Creek Trail and lead initially
through a few impromptu campsites along Little Passage Creek. Cross over the
creek on a small bridge at 0.2 mile. The trail then gets down to business on its
1,171-foot climb to the top of the knob. Over the next mile, the trail switchbacks four times on a moderate grade as it ascends through the forest.

At 1.25 miles, the route arrives at a three-way intersection, where yellow-
blazed Scothorn Gap Trail traverses the forest to the southwest. Go straight
and keep following the blue blazes as they bring you to the mountain's shoulder. The soil becomes rather sandy as you near the top.

In another 0.25 mile, at Peach Orchard Gap, the trail clearly enters a saddle
atop the mountain. A large fire ring and a campsite on the right mark the spot.
Look to the left and you should see a white-blazed trail heading to the summit

The reward for scrambling up Duncan Knob is the gorgeous view southwards over the lower half of Massanutten Mountain and beyond to Shenandoah National Park.

of Duncan Knob. Follow this trail, which climbs moderately and brings you at last to the foot of the knob at 1.75 miles. To reach the summit, you'll need to scramble up this challenging boulder field.

As you begin making your way up the rocks, remember to bear left and upward. Keep your hands free, as you'll certainly need them to advance. Fortunately, the rocks are fairly stable, but if they are wet, this scramble can be a bit treacherous. When scrambling, always remember to have good holds with three points before you move the fourth. Though it's not an easy stretch, this part of the route is very short. Once you reach the summit, clamber out onto the rocky ledges, which make an ideal resting point to survey the route you've walked.

When you're ready, retrace your route back to Peach Orchard Gap. Take special care descending the rocks and take heed—you'll tend to veer too far to the right on the descent. Many hikers find themselves at the treeline and at a bit of loss concerning the location of the blazes. When you descend, hook to the left and spot the white blazes. If you reach the foot of the scramble and don't see the blazes, skirt around to the left. A good-sized cairn marks the trail. (If you become truly disoriented, take out your compass and walk a southwest bearing, staying on the shoulder of the mountain. Gap Creek Trail crosses your path in that direction and you're sure to find it.)

From Peach Orchard Gap, the walk down to your vehicle is a straightforward descent following blue-blazed Gap Creek Trail to Crisman Hollow Road.

DID YOU KNOW?

The origin of the American Indian word Massanutten is shrouded in the mists of history. Some claim that the word describes a basket, which American Indians believed the mountains, with their distinctive shape, resembled. Others have claimed that the word means "potato field" and that native inhabitants planted fields of sweet potatoes in the valleys. The Potomac Appalachian Trail Club (PATC) maintains an interesting archival note on the history of the Massanuttens at patc.us/history/archive/massntn.html.

MORE INFORMATION

George Washington and Jefferson National Forests, Lee Ranger District (www .fs.usda.gov/main/gwj; 540-984-4101). Check online for announcements concerning trail conditions, road closures, prescribed burns, and other events that may affect your hike.

NEARBY

If, after returning to your cars, you're ready for more, look across Crisman Hollow Road where the blue blazes continue past a forest gate. A 2.7-mile round trip (with about 900 feet of gain) will take you to Jawbone Gap, where another rock outcropping will permit you to gaze back at Duncan Knob. To reach this point, follow the blue blazes, first on moderately graded old forest roads, then on a steeper footpath. Look out for the sudden right-hand turn where the footpath leaves the road. At Jawbone Gap, you'll encounter a four-way intersection with the orange blazes of the Massanutten Trail leading away in two directions. Take the white blazes (left) about 0.2 miles to the vista. From there, it's an easy descent back to the cars.

If you're up for more than one hike in a weekend, consider combining the described route with a visit to Strickler Knob (Trip 34) while setting up a base-camp at Peach Orchard Gap or Duncan Hollow.

There are several restaurants where US 211 passes over Massanutten Mountain, and the little town of New Market has a number of restaurants, shops, and gas stations.

GRANDER THAN THE HIMALAYA

Three million years ago, the Appalachian Mountains were in their prime, rivaling the Himalaya in size. The story of the Shenandoah Valley is the story of all mountain ranges: it was born from tectonic shifts in the earth and worn down by time. Shenandoah is part of the Appalachian Range, which spans from Maine to Georgia. The range first formed during the Grenville orogeny, which created mountains that stretched from modern-day Texas to Quebec when tectonic plates collided 1 to 1.2 billion years ago. Some of the rocks created by the heat and pressure of this collision are still in Shenandoah today. Old Rag (Trip 21), Hogback Mountain, and Mary's Rock (Trip 14) have examples of these igneous and metamorphic rocks.

In Shenandoah, the Grenville orogeny's formations slowly succumbed to time, and its tall peaks wore away to smaller hills. About 500 million years ago, tectonic plates shifted again, this time moving apart. Rifts allowed lava to flow into valleys and eventually created an ocean. Some of these old lava flows are still visible in the shape of Shenandoah today—Big Meadows is located on one of them—and the layers of this rock look like staircases in some parts of the park; look for it near Stony Man (Trip 15), Bearfence, Loft Mountain (Trip 23), and Hightop (Trip 24). This basalt rock's unusual green color gave it its name: "greenstone."

When the plates that make up North America, Europe, and North Africa collided, ocean sediment vaulted skyward to become the Appalachian Mountains. Some of these sedimentary rocks can be seen in the park. Known together as the Chilhowee Group, geologists divided them into three formations to describe their sources more accurately: the Weverton Formation, with early river deposits; the Hampton Formation, with thick lagoon deposits; and the Erwin Formation, with quartz sand deposits. The Erwin Formation, with its quartzite cliffs and boulders, can be seen from some spots in southern Shenandoah, including Blackrock (Trip 28).

All of this shifting led to the creation of other mountains in the Shenandoah Valley. Massanutten Mountain, part of the Blue Ridge Range within the Appalachians, is a doubly-plunging synclinorium—or as non-geologists describe it, a mountain that has a downward fold with the youngest rock layers at the center. It also has two distinct sections divided by Market Gap: the northern part, marked by three parallel ridges that form Fort Valley and Little Fort Valley; and the southern section, which consists of ridges separated by gorges.

Eventually, the plates shifted again and time played its part with the mountains, moving into the map of the world that we recognize today.

TRIP 33
SIGNAL KNOB

Location: Massanutten Mountain, George Washington
National Forest, VA
Rating: Strenuous
Distance: 10.0 miles
Elevation Gain: 2,919 feet
Estimated Time: 5–6 hours
Maps: *Map G: Trails in the Massanutten Mountain—North Half,
Signal Knob to New Market Gap* (PATC)

**You'll feel much farther away from Washington, DC, much farther
than 90 minutes, as you climb for stunning views from Signal Knob.**

DIRECTIONS
From I-66, Exit 6 in Front Royal, turn left (south) onto US 340. After about
1.2 miles, turn right onto VA 55 and head west about 5 miles. Turn left onto
Fort Valley Road/VA 678 and enter the national forest. Drive 3.5 miles before
making a right turn into the Signal Knob parking area. *GPS coordinates:* 38°
56.102′ N, 78° 19.174′ W.

TRAIL DESCRIPTION
Signal Knob is a perfect hike for those seeking to try longer-mileage days.
With a few long, steady climbs, stretches of rock hopping, and a viewpoint
perfect for lunch, this trail has something for everyone. Massanutten Trail, the
71-mile path running along much of the mountain's ridgeline, cuts through
the Signal Knob parking lot. While most hikers do the trail counterclockwise,
our description goes clockwise, saving the better views for the end. To walk
this loop, start on Massanutten Trail, switch quickly to follow Tuscarora Trail,
and then rejoin Massanutten Trail for the final half.

In the parking lot, look south to spot the start of this loop. Just 40 feet
from the parking lot, the path arrives at the intersection with orange-blazed
Massanutten Trail. Turn left here, and start to follow the orange blazes. While
well blazed, this first stretch of trail was slightly eroded when Jen hiked it.
Keep an eye on your footing, and start making your way along the trail.
At 0.5 mile, the path arrives at a three-way intersection. Massanutten Trail
turns left here, but your route is straight ahead on blue-blazed Tuscarora

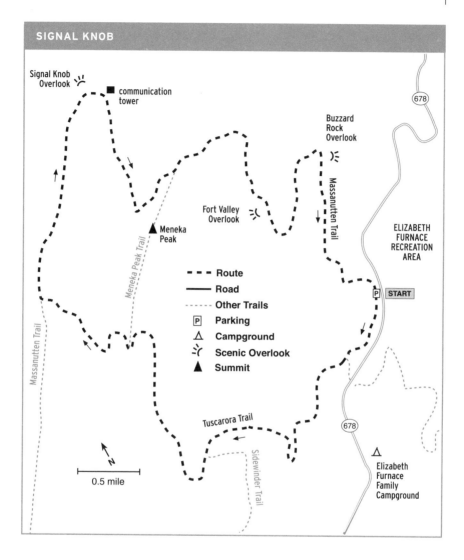

SIGNAL KNOB

Signal Knob
Overlook

■ communication
tower

678

Buzzard
Rock
Overlook

Massanutten Trail

Fort Valley
Overlook

▲ Meneka
Peak

Meneka Peak Trail

ELIZABETH
FURNACE
RECREATION
AREA

P START

Massanutten Trail

- - - Route
——— Road
······ Other Trails
P Parking
△ Campground
Scenic Overlook
▲ Summit

Tuscarora Trail

678

△
Elizabeth
Furnace
Family
Campground

Sidewinder Trail

N

0.5 mile

Trail. Keep following the blue blazes, and watch for a tricky hard left turn at 0.75 mile.

The trail passes over a stream and then arrives at another three-way intersection at 1.2 miles with a white-blazed connecter trail for Elizabeth Furnace to your left. Continue straight following the blue blazes up the trail.

As you climb, the trail begins to change, with tall trees yielding to mountain laurel, and eventually levels out for a bit. Pass another three-way intersection at 2.1 miles, this time with pink-blazed Sidewinder Trail. Continue on your blue-blazed path. The trail takes a quick hairpin turn to your right, promptly switchbacks left again, and then starts to get progressively rockier.

It's no wonder how Signal Knob got its name given its dramatic perch above the valley.

Tuscarora Trail takes another switchback, this time to the right, and views of the surrounding valley start to open up to your right at 2.6 miles. From this vantage point, it is clear just how far you've come.

But the climb isn't over yet. The trail continues its steady incline for another mile and then switchbacks to the left at 3.7 miles. The path gets rockier as it gets closer to the ridge, and at 3.9 miles it gains the top of the first climb at a three-way intersection with white-blazed Meneka Peak Trail. Continue to follow blue-blazed Tuscarora Trail; while not well marked at this point, your route is an obvious one and starts to descend the mountain.

(Meneka Peak Trail is an option for those seeking either to shorten the hike or to cut out the second climb. This white-blazed trail climbs for a bit but stays along the ridge. In 1.0 mile, you will arrive at an intersection with Massanutten Trail. To your left is Signal Knob, and to your right is your route back to the cars. Taking this option and skipping Signal Knob shortens the hike by 2.0 miles.)

Following the blue blazes, this steep and at times rocky trail loses some of the elevation it gained, dropping 500 feet in just over 0.5 mile. Cross Passage Creek on an easy rock hop, and arrive at an intersection with a fire road at 4.7 miles. Here, depart Tuscarora Trail and regain orange-blazed Massanutten Trail with a right turn. The orange-blazed fire road quickly starts recouping all the elevation you just lost at the descent. As you near the top of the fire road, around 5.6 miles, the trail starts to get steeper. At 5.9 miles, the fire road continues straight up the hill while the trail swings to the left to the Signal Knob overlook. An arrow points the way to the big view at 5.9 miles; follow the path as it swings around a campsite before the knob. (If you manage to miss this turn, don't fret. The fire road ends where Massanutten Trail continues its loop past the overlook. If you arrive at this junction, look to the left to spy Signal Knob.)

From here, you see the town of Strasburg, Virginia, and views of the northern Shenandoah Valley. It's a perfect spot to take a break and enjoy the scenery. You've arrived at the northern tip of the Massanutten Trail, the counterpart of Strickler Knob (Trip 34) to the south.

Once you're ready to start hiking again, continue to follow the orange blazes. The path quickly leads to a telecommunications tower at 6.0 miles, and then a plaque commemorating the hard work of the Massarock Volunteer Crew. The trail returns into the woods, becoming rocky at times and climbing for a bit longer. In 1.0 mile from the overlook, white-blazed Meneka Peak Trail comes in from the right. Go straight, following the orange blazes.

From here, the trail follows the ridge for a while and passes a number of campsites. At 7.75 miles, the treadway becomes steadily rockier and starts to encounter stretches of rock fields to hop across.

The trail gives you a bit of a break from the rocks as you arrive at the Fort Valley overlook and then swings slightly to the left at 8.2 miles. More rocky patches await you as you continue to work your way down the mountain. At 8.8 miles, the trail then takes a hard right hairpin turn around a campsite surrounded by several boulders. Keep your eye on the orange blazes at this point; many hikers have been known to miss this turn.

Once you successfully navigated this turn, look for a glimpse of Buzzard Rock (Trip 30) to your left. Look harder, and you may even see rock climbers tackling this popular climb.

From here, the trail continues to descend. Watch your footing—in places, the narrow trail is eroded, so go slowly through those spots. Cross a small stream, and follow the trail as it swings to the left at 9.6 miles. Continue to follow the path on its steady downhill, and arrive back at the parking lot.

DID YOU KNOW?

Both the Union and Confederate armies used Signal Knob as a key vantage point for the valley during the Civil War. The Confederates occupied it from 1862 to 1864; the Union won control of the peak by defeating the 61st Georgia Volunteer Infantry.

MORE INFORMATION

George Washington and Jefferson National Forests, Lee Ranger District (www .fs.usda.gov/main/gwj; 540-984-4101). Check online for announcements concerning trail conditions, road closures, prescribed burns, and other events that may affect your hike.

NEARBY

With 71-mile Massanutten Trail and 250-mile Tuscarora Trail intersecting in this area, you have multiple options for day hikes and longer treks. Buzzard Rock (Trip 30) sits directly across the valley from Signal Knob.

The town of Front Royal has multiple restaurants for hungry hikers, most of them along a quaint Main Street.

TRIP 34
STRICKLER KNOB

Location: Massanutten Mountain, George Washington
National Forest, VA
Rating: Strenuous
Distance: 10.0 miles round-trip
Elevation Gain: 2,215 feet gain
Estimated Time: 5–6 hours
Maps: *Map G: Trails in the Massanutten Mountain—North Half,
Signal Knob to New Market Gap* (PATC)

**Follow the rocky ridge of Middle Mountain to reach the dramatic
prominence of Strickler Knob and its commanding view southward.**

DIRECTIONS

From the junction of I-66 and I-81, head south on I-81 toward Roanoke. About
35 miles later, take exit 264 for US 211 and take a left onto West Old Cross
Street to pass under the interstate. You'll enter the town of New Market. Take a
left onto North Congress Street, and then take a right onto US 211, which will
head into the mountains. Reach the top of the pass. As you descend the eastern
side, look out for a trailhead parking lot on the right about 5.7 miles from New
Market. *GPS coordinates:* 38° 38.457′ N, 78° 35.389′ W.

TRAIL DESCRIPTION

When you're ready to begin, look north across VA 211 from the trailhead
parking lot. You should be able to spot a gate barring access to a grassy forest
road and a white blaze in the shape of a lowercase i, almost like an information
icon. You'll see this distinctive blaze along trails in the Massanuttens. These
particular white blazes mark Massanutten Connector Trail as it heads north to
rendezvous with orange-blazed Massanutten Trail.

At first, Massanutten Connector Trail follows a grassy old road grade, but
after 1.1 miles, it leaves this road on the left and becomes more of a footpath.
When there are few or no leaves on the trees, you should be able to look ahead
and make out the distinctive shape of Strickler Knob on your right. To your
left is the ridgeline of Waterfall Mountain. The route heads into the hollow
between these ridges. A few quick switchbacks bring you down to the junction
with the orange-blazed Massanutten Trail at 1.8 miles.

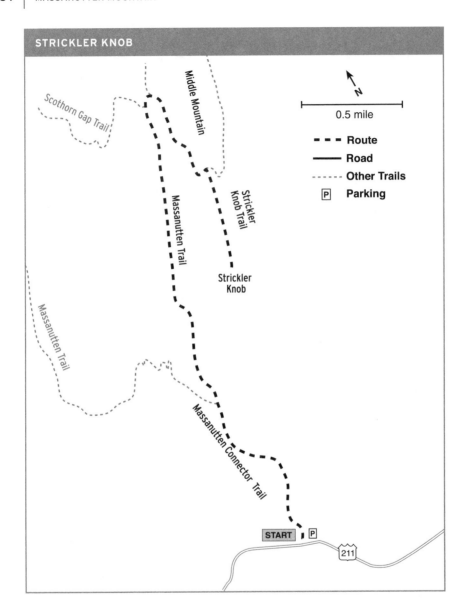

STRICKLER KNOB

Middle Mountain

Scothorn Gap Trail

Strickler Knob Trail

Massanutten Trail

Strickler Knob

Massanutten Trail

Massanutten Connector Trail

N

0.5 mile

- - - Route
—— Road
------ Other Trails
P   Parking

START P

211

Turning left would take you steeply up Waterfall Mountain. Your path is straight ahead. Begin a gentle but sustained climb up the hollow between the mountains. The trail takes you down to Big Run for a quick crossing, easily rock-hopped, before climbing again for some time on the east bank of the creek. It then descends for a second crossing of Big Run at 2.4 miles and climbs more determinedly on the west bank. The footing becomes rockier as you near

The rocky ledges of Strickler Knob overlook the farmland of Shenandoah Valley.

the top of the hollow. When you reach a dilapidated sign telling you that Scothorn Gap is about 0.5 mile ahead of you, the grade levels off.

At 3.6 miles, the trail reaches the four-way intersection in Scothorn Gap. Yellow blazes to the left head to Crisman Hollow Road; yellow blazes ahead lead to Duncan Knob (Trip 32). Your route turns right to follow the orange blazes of Massanutten Trail. Climb along this gently graded old road for about 0.6 miles, where it reaches the crest of Middle Mountain at 4.25 miles. A large stone cairn marks the unnamed trail that heads southward on this ridgeline to reach Strickler Knob in another 0.75 mile.

This trail has a peculiar existence, as it doesn't appear on official maps of the area and it is sometimes referred to as a bushwhack. When Michael last walked it for this book, however, it was blazed bright pink with fresh paint, and someone had obviously been working to maintain it. In fact, it was as well maintained as any trail in the area. If you find that the trail is in less-than-ideal condition, just remember that you have only to follow the ridgeline south to reach the knob. There is no ascending or descending to speak of.

The path, however, is rather rocky, so be prepared for fractured ground as you make your way to the knob. Once you draw near your destination, a few rock obstacles require you to use your hands to advance, but they should not test your resolve. Summiting Strickler Knob at 5.0 miles requires some additional scrambling but rewards you with magnificent views of the southern

Shenandoahs to the east, the south Massanutten ridges straight ahead, and the mountains of West Virginia in the west.

When you've taken in this scene, return along the pink blazes to rejoin Massanutten Trail. Descend to Scothorn Gap, then follow Massanutten and Massanutten Connector trails back to US 211 and your vehicle.

DID YOU KNOW?

The orange blazes of Massanutten Trail represent one of the major arteries of the region, tracing a 71-mile loop around this distinctive series of ridgelines. In the north, Massanutten Trail shares footway with Tuscarora Trail, which allows you to join up with the Appalachian Trail in Shenandoah National Park. Opportunities for exploration abound.

MORE INFORMATION

George Washington and Jefferson National Forests, Lee Ranger District (www .fs.usda.gov/main/gwj; 540-984-4101). Check online for announcements concerning trail conditions, road closures, prescribed burns, and other events that may affect your hike.

NEARBY

If you're looking for a shorter hike to Strickler Knob, park at the Scothorn Gap Trailhead on Crisman Hollow Road. Follow the yellow blazes about 1.4 miles in the forest to the four-way intersection described above. Stay straight on orange-blazed Massanutten Trail to follow the above guide to the cairn atop Middle Mountain. Your round-trip to Strickler Knob and back from this direction should be about 6.0 miles.

If you're up for more than one hike in a weekend, consider combining the described route with a visit to Duncan Knob (Trip 32) while setting up a base camp at Peach Orchard Gap, Duncan Hollow, or along Crisman Hollow Road.

If you're in need of post-hike refreshment, look no farther than US 211, New Market, or perhaps Front Royal on the way into town.

6

GREAT NORTH MOUNTAIN AND THE RAMSEYS DRAFT WILDERNESS

BEYOND THE FOOT OF MASSANUTTEN MOUNTAIN, across the North Fork of the Shenandoah River, beyond the towns of Strasburg, Woodstock, and Edinberg, another ridge-and-valley system, typical of the Appalachians, rises to the northwest. Great North Mountain is 50 miles long with a highpoint of 3,293 feet, but like many of its Appalachian cousins it lacks a single, defined summit. In the south, part of the ridge forms the border between Virginia and West Virginia. In the north, VA/WV 55 crosses the ridge. Between and around these two points, much of the mountain itself is protected by the George Washington National Forest as part of its Lee Ranger District. The mountain's height and prominence over the valley give it views over the Shenandoah River as well as west into the Allegheny Mountains of West Virginia. Three hikes described in this section are on Great North Mountain: Big Schloss (Trip 35), Tibbet Knob (Trip 36), and Halfmoon Mountain (Trip 37)

Also along Virginia's western state border, largely west of Shenandoah National Park's southernmost district, is the 6,518-acre Ramseys Draft Wilderness, one of 23 Wildernesses protected by the George Washington and Jefferson National Forests. Managed by means that preserve the true "untrammeled" spirit of the land, Wildernesses like this one make for more primitive experiences for those who recreate in them. The Ramseys Draft Wilderness is traversed by the 26.2-mile Wild Oak National Recreation Trail, a popular backpacking loop that this book uses, with the addition of a gorge walk, to make a route worthy of a day hike (Trip 38).

TRIP 35
BIG SCHLOSS

Location: Great North Mountain, George Washington
National Forest, VA and WV
Rating: Moderate
Distance: 4.4 miles round-trip
Elevation Gain: 1,297 feet gain
Estimated Time: 3–4 hours
Maps: *Map F: Great North Mountain—North Half of George
Washington National Forest, Lee Ranger District—Virginia and
West Virginia* (PATC)

**On the border between Virginia and West Virginia, climb to a
spectacular view of Trout Run Valley from the dramatic cliffs of
Big Schloss.**

DIRECTIONS

From I-81, Exit 283, follow VA 42 west 5.3 miles. Take a right onto VA 768/
Union Church Road, which quickly becomes VA 623/Back Road. About 0.25
mile farther along, take a right onto VA 675/Wolf Gap Road and follow it for
6.3 miles to the state line with West Virginia. As the road crests the ridge on
the border, turn right into the Wolf Gap Recreation Area, where there is a
parking lot for day-hikers, as well as restrooms. *GPS coordinates:* 38° 55.463′
N, 78° 41.359′ W.

TRAIL DESCRIPTION

From the parking lot, walk through the Wolf Gap Recreation Area and locate
the orange blazes of Mill Mountain Trail on the north side of the campground.
(If you crossed VA 675 instead, you'd find the trail to Tibbet Knob [Trip 36].)
The trail here is broad and well worn and proceeds north along Great North
Mountain, essentially following the border between Virginia and West Virginia. Over the next 0.8 mile, the trail gains about 650 feet, switching back
periodically as it climbs the westward face of the mountain.

If the day is clear, you'll know when you've crested the mountain: This high
point commands impressive views of the Virginia Blue Ridge to the east and
Trout Run Valley to the west. Your route continues north, however, descending gradually as the trail winds its way past numerous viewpoints amid a

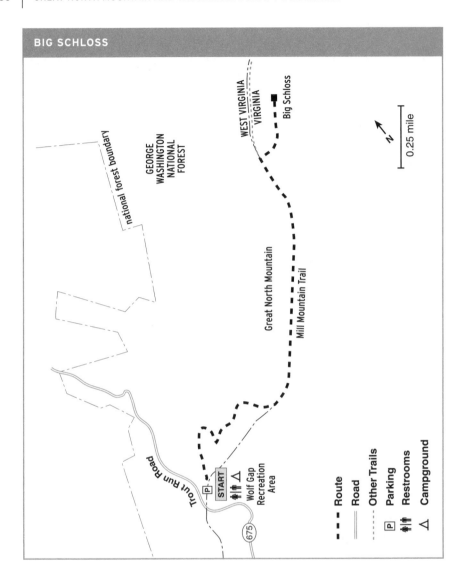

BIG SCHLOSS

Big Schloss

WEST VIRGINIA
VIRGINIA

GEORGE
WASHINGTON
NATIONAL
FOREST

national forest boundary

Great North Mountain

Mill Mountain Trail

0.25 mile

START

P

Wolf Gap
Recreation
Area

Trout Run Road

675

- Route
Road
Other Trails
P Parking
Restrooms
Campground

number of rock formations. For a ridge in the Mid-Atlantic, this line is sharply defined and views will open out, often on both sides simultaneously, as you head toward Big Schloss.

At 1.6 miles, Mill Mountain Trail eventually reaches a broad ridgeback with a few improvised campsites just south of Big Schloss itself. From this point, the trail climbs gently and, at 1.9 miles, arrives at a white-blazed spur trail on the right, where your route leaves Mill Mountain Trail. The white-blazed spur leads toward the Schloss, at first climbing steeply and ruggedly. The trail soon levels out as you approach the cliffs at 2.2 miles.

There are few more iconic views of the Shenandoah Valley than those from Big Schloss.

A little wooden bridge takes you over a particularly wide fissure to reach the best views. Take time to explore this striking feature, as viewpoints open out on all sides. For an especially lovely vista, stand at the very head of the

A wooden bridge spans a fissure and provides hikers with easy access to the cliffs.

cliffs, where Trout Run Valley is displayed incomparably beneath you. You'll be glad you brought your camera for this hike.

When you've enjoyed a break, soaking up these airy views, return the way you came to reach your vehicle at Wolf Gap.

DID YOU KNOW?

Until the Civil War, West Virginia and Virginia were united politically. When Virginia voted to secede from the Union on April 17, 1861, the delegates from the area that would become West Virginia voted 30 to 17 to remain a part of the United States. In 1863, West Virginia joined the Union as a new state. Initially, delegates had planned to name the state Kanawha (after a river), but cooler heads prevailed, and the name of West Virginia stuck.

MORE INFORMATION

George Washington and Jefferson National Forests, Lee Ranger District (www .fs.usda.gov/main/gwj; 540-984-4101). Check online for announcements concerning trail conditions, road closures, prescribed burns, and other events that may affect your hike.

NEARBY

Trout Run Valley offers hikers numerous opportunities to get out and explore. The route to Tibbet Knob (Trip 36) also leaves from the Wolf Gap Recreation Area. Halfmoon Mountain (Trip 37), also nearby, has very fine views of the valley. The Wolf Gap and Trout Run recreation areas both offer vehicle camping, and for those seeking a backcountry challenge, *AMC's Best Backpacking in the Mid-Atlantic* offers a 27-mile loop that circumnavigates the valley and ties together all of these sights. Finally, the Tuscarora Trail passes through the area on its journey from the Shenandoah to the AT near Harrisburg, Pennsylvania.

The nearest towns are Wardensville, West Virginia, to the west, or Woodstock, Virginia, to the east.

THE TUSCARORA TRAIL

One of the great footpaths of the region, the Tuscarora Trail is often wilder than more frequently walked counterparts like the Appalachian Trail, offering hikers greater opportunities for solitude. The trail stretches 250 miles from Hogback Overlook in Shenandoah National Park to Blue Mountain, west of Harrisburg, Pennsylvania. As it traces this arc from the south to the north, it passes through four states—Virginia, West Virginia, Maryland, and Pennsylvania—and eventually joins up with the Appalachian Trail at its northern terminus.

This junction isn't happenstance: in the 1960s, members of the Potomac Appalachian Trail Club became concerned that development and disputes over land rights in northern Virginia and near Harpers Ferry, West Virginia, would mean that the Appalachian Trail could be closed to future hikers. Club members began scouting and building an alternate route, which took hikers through wilder lands to the west. Old-timers know the southern section of the trail as "Big Blue," for its blue blazes. In 1995, the entire length of the Tuscarora Trail was opened after more than three decades of work.

The Tuscarora Trail takes its name from an American Indian tribe of Iroquois descent who lived in North Carolina. In the early eighteenth century, the Tuscarora clashed with European settlers, reportedly due to the settlers' taking Tuscarora children as slaves. Beginning in 1714, the survivors of this conflict began migrating north to return to their ancestral lands in Pennsylvania and New York. This migration took 90 years, and the path these refugees followed was referred to as the "Tuscarora Path." Descendants of these Tuscarora still live near Niagara Falls, New York.

The modern trail doesn't follow the exact path of these displaced people, as the Tuscarora would have preferred to pass through valleys instead of following ridgelines; however, as you walk the trails of Shenandoah Valley, don't be surprised to see the name Tuscarora attached to many places. The refugees lingered along their journey, and these place names are evidence of their passage.

You'll find yourself on the Tuscarora Trail if you walk Overall Run (Trip 11), the Buzzard Rock hike (Trip 30), the Signal Knob hike (Trip 33), or several of the trips in the area of Great North Mountain (Trips 35, 36, and 37). To learn more about the Tuscarora Trail, see *The Tuscarora Trail: A Guide to the South Half in West Virginia and Virginia* (Vienna: Potomac Appalachian Trail Club, 2013).

TRIP 36
TIBBET KNOB

Location: Great North Mountain, George Washington
National Forest, VA and WV
Rating: Easy
Distance: 3.1 miles round-trip
Elevation Gain: 1,001 feet
Estimated Time: 2–4 hours
Maps: *Map F: Great North Mountain—North Half of George
Washington National Forest, Lee Ranger District—Virginia and
West Virginia* (PATC)

**Summit Tibbet Knob and enjoy a spectacular view of Trout Run
Valley from this crag high above the Virginia–West Virginia border.**

DIRECTIONS

From I-81, Exit 283, follow VA 42 west 5.3 miles. Take a right onto VA 768/
Union Church Road, which quickly becomes VA 623/Back Road. About 0.25
mile farther along, take a right onto VA 675/Wolf Gap Road and follow it for
6.3 miles to the state line with West Virginia. As the road crests the ridge on
the border, turn right into the Wolf Gap Recreation Area, where there is a
parking lot for day-hikers, as well as restrooms. *GPS coordinates:* 38° 55.463′
N, 78° 41.359′ W.

TRAIL DESCRIPTION

From the parking lot, cross VA 675 and spot the sign for Tibbet Knob. (If
you walk through the campground instead you'll reach the trailhead for Big
Schloss [Trip 35].) The orange-blazed trail passes a primitive campsite on the
right, then in about 0.2 mile the trail begins a steady climb. Though it is not
steep, this grade leads you up to your first view of the Massanutten ridges and
Blue Ridge Mountains eastward, on your left at 0.5 mile. At this point the trail
follows a fairly typical Virginia ridge. Looking ahead you can see a knob that
the trail will round before climbing Tibbet Knob itself.

The trail descends briefly and shortly, and then evens out. The footing is
rather rocky, so take care. As the trail winds around the knob you glimpsed
a while back, it passes through a forested area. Eventually the trail begins
to climb a bit, and you reach obscured views to the left and the right. Pass a
switchback and start climbing more aggressively to the ridgeline.

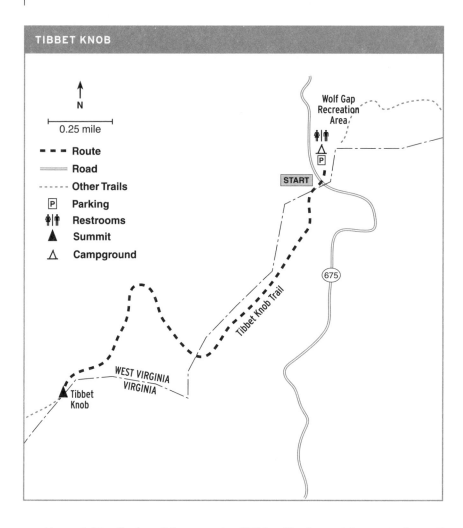

About 0.25 mile shy of the summit of Tibbet Knob, a quick turn in the trail leads across to the first stretch of rocky terrain considered Class 3 in the Yosemite Decimal System, which means that you'll periodically need your hands to advance but ropes are not required. If you use trekking poles, affix them to your pack as they are more encumbrances than aids when scrambling. Make sure that you always have three points in firm contact with rock before moving a fourth. The two stretches of Class 3 ground on this hike are not especially troublesome, however; just remember to be sure of your footing and balance before you advance.

The first scramble is no more than 50 or 60 feet long. After that, cross over relatively even ground. The second stretch of Class 3 terrain, and the steeper of the two, comes very near the summit at 1.5 miles.

On a clear day Tibbet Knob offers incomparable views of Trout Run Valley.

Just beyond the second bit of scrambling the trail passes through some thick woods and then emerges on top of Tibbet Knob (2,930 feet). The rocky outcropping offers a beautiful 180-degree view to the west, including Big Schloss in the north and Devil's Hole Mountain in the northwest.

Savor this amazing view and perhaps enjoy your lunch. When the time comes to return, merely turn back and retrace your steps to Wolf Gap and your waiting vehicle.

DID YOU KNOW?

Standing atop Tibbet Knob, you're approaching the western boundary of the ridge-and-valley system that typifies Virginia and the Shenandoah Valley. Westward, the ridges you can see are more properly referred to as the Alleghenies.

MORE INFORMATION

George Washington and Jefferson National Forests, Lee Ranger District (www .fs.usda.gov/main/gwj; 540-984-4101). Check online for announcements concerning trail conditions, road closures, prescribed burns, and other events that may affect your hike.

NEARBY

Trout Run Valley offers hikers numerous opportunities to get out and explore. The route to Big Schloss (Trip 35) also leaves from the Wolf Gap Recreation Area. Halfmoon Mountain (Trip 37), also nearby, has very fine views of the valley. The Wolf Gap and Trout Run recreation areas both offer vehicle camping, and for those seeking a backcountry challenge, *AMC's Best Backpacking in the Mid-Atlantic* offers a 27-mile loop that circumnavigates the valley and ties together all of these sights. Finally, the Tuscarora Trail passes through the area on its journey from the Shenandoah to the AT near Harrisburg, Pennsylvania.

When it's time to return to civilization, head either to Wardensville, West Virginia, or to Woodstock, Virginia, for an array of local businesses.

TRIP 37
HALFMOON MOUNTAIN

Location: Great North Mountain, George Washington
National Forest, WV
Rating: Strenuous
Distance: 8.9 miles, round-trip
Elevation Gain: 2,469 feet gain
Estimated Time: 4–6 hours
Maps: *Map F: Great North Mountain—North Half of George Washington
National Forest, Lee Ranger District—Virginia and West Virginia* (PATC)

**Climb high to enjoy an eagle's eye of Trout Run Valley from the
north, taking in Big Schloss and Tibbet Knob.**

DIRECTIONS

From I-81, Exit 296 near Strasburg, head west on US 48/VA 55/WV 55 for
about 19.9 miles over the mountains into Wardensville. In town, turn left onto
Trout Run Valley Road, which you'll follow south for about 6.0 miles. On the
left, spot the turnoff for Bucktail Trail. Bear right at the circle and look for the
sign for the trail on the right. Parking is abundant. *GPS coordinates:* 39° 0.834′
N, 78° 39.827′ W.

TRAIL DESCRIPTION

The trickiest part of this hike is certainly the beginning. From the sign marking the start of Bucktail Trail, walk into the woods a few yards on an orange-
blazed forest road. The trail broadens into a clearing, but follow the blazes,
which lead left. Keep your eyes peeled for the pink-blazed footpath on your
right at 0.2 mile: this is Bucktail Cutoff Trail, which heads east along the foot
of Halfmoon Mountain for about 2.5 miles.

After the right turn onto Bucktail Cutoff Trail, it climbs gently (about 500
feet) to the knees of the mountain but then weaves its way along the undula-
tions of the hollows, periodically dropping down slightly to cross little creeks,
all of which are easily hoppable. In this way, the trail makes its way east before
entering some slightly more open country as it descends to Halfmoon Run.
There is a bit of space between blazes here, but you should be able to sniff out
the trail easily enough.

The old forest road grade reenters the woods and heads upstream along
Halfmoon Run on the ride. Hike along this idyllic little creek for a spell before

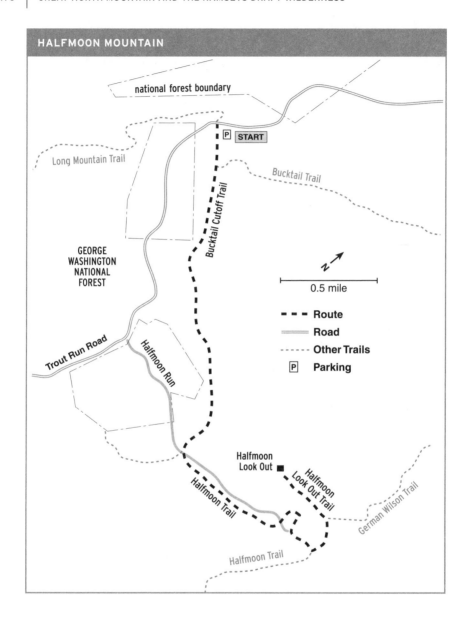

HALFMOON MOUNTAIN

national forest boundary

Long Mountain Trail

P START

Bucktail Trail

Bucktail Cutoff Trail

GEORGE
WASHINGTON
NATIONAL
FOREST

N

0.5 mile

- - - Route
═══ Road
····· Other Trails
P Parking

Trout Run Road

Halfmoon Run

Halfmoon
Look Out ■

Halfmoon
Look Out Trail

Halfmoon Trail

German Wilson Trail

Halfmoon Trail

Bucktail Cutoff Trail ends at yellow-blazed Halfmoon Trail at 2.5 miles. The intersection of these two trails is signposted by a good-sized backcountry campsite on the right.

If you followed the yellow blazes over the run and down the mountain (to the right), they would take you to another parking lot on Trout Run Road. Instead, follow the yellow blazes to the left and begin climbing about 700 feet over the next 1.0 mile. Though this is certainly the most strenuous section of the trip, the trail is quite well graded and a pleasure to walk.

Halfmoon Mountain offers another fine view of Trout Run Valley, Big Schloss, and Tibbet Knob—this time from the north.

Once you arrive at the saddle between Halfmoon Mountain and Mill Mountain at 3.7 miles, pause to catch your breath at the three-way intersection with white-blazed Halfmoon Look Out Trail. Halfmoon Look Out Trail on the right leads to Tuscarora Trail; instead head left and follow Halfmoon Look Out Trail's white blazes toward the summit of Halfmoon Mountain. The trail here is very flat, if rocky. Pass the pink blazes of German Wilson Trail on the right, and continue to follow the white blazes as they take you out on the promontory of the mountain.

You've almost reached your objective when the trail bends sharply to the right at 4.4 miles, just shy of a well-placed campsite on the mountain's nose. The last stretch of this trail is quite steep and rocky, but this more difficult section is mercifully short. At the summit, look for the ruins of the old fire tower and take advantage of a fine vista, one of the best in the valley. Away to the south, on a clear day, you can spot Big Schloss and Tibbet Knob; on the right, Long Mountain marches away to the south. Take your time and explore past the foundations, as there are a number of views farther along the ridgeline.

When you're ready to return, retrace your route carefully along Halfmoon Look Out Trail (white), Halfmoon Trail (yellow), Bucktail Cutoff Trail (pink), and finally Bucktail Trail (orange). Obviously, there are a number of turns here before you reach your vehicle.

DID YOU KNOW?

Fire towers like the one that once stood atop Halfmoon Mountain were manned through the twentieth century to give rangers a heads-up concerning any forest fires. If you're in the mood to spend the night on the high and narrow ridge, you'll find a number of small campsites past the stone ruins of the tower's tumbled-down foundation.

MORE INFORMATION

George Washington and Jefferson National Forests, Lee Ranger District (www .fs.usda.gov/main/gwj; 540-984-4101). Check online for announcements concerning trail conditions, road closures, prescribed burns, and other events that may affect your hike.

NEARBY

If you wished to shorten this route, consider parking at the trailhead for the Halfmoon Trail, also on Trout Run Valley Road.

Trout Run Valley offers hikers numerous opportunities to get out and explore. The routes to Big Schloss (Trip 35) and Tibbet Knob (Trip 36) both leave from the Wolf Gap Recreation Area. The Wolf Gap and Trout Run recreation areas both offer vehicle camping, and for those seeking a backcountry challenge, *AMC's Best Backpacking in the Mid-Atlantic* offers a 27-mile loop that circumnavigates the valley and ties together all of these sights. Finally, the Tuscarora Trail passes through the area on its journey from the Shenandoah to the AT near Harrisburg, Pennsylvania.

The nearest towns are Wardensville, West Virginia, to the west, or Woodstock, Virginia, to the east.

THE APPALACHIAN TRAIL IN VIRGINIA

Of the 2,180 miles the Appalachian Trail (AT) covers on its route from Georgia to Maine, about one-quarter passes through Virginia. The majority of those approximately 550 miles follow the state's ridge-and-valley topography through the Shenandoah Valley. As you study a map, you can trace the AT's line along the state's backbone, from Damascus, Virginia, to Harpers Ferry, West Virginia.

Within Virginia, the greatest American thru-hike can be divided into four sections. In southwest Virginia, the state's most remote section of the AT, the trail passes through some of the state's highlights, including the Grayson Highlands and Mount Rogers (the highest point in Virginia). In spring, when the rhododendron are blooming, few hiking destinations can rival the open balds of this area, where hikers can gaze south to the mountains of North Carolina and Tennessee. Damascus, Virginia, is perhaps the Platonic ideal of what a trail town should be. Though it is not, properly speaking, within the Shenandoah Valley, all hikers in the region should book the time to explore the trail in this distant and beautiful area.

Between the Grayson Highlands and Shenandoah National Park, the AT generally follows the Blue Ridge Parkway through the central portion of the state. Though the hiking is tougher in this section, with a number of big climbs, there are many superb vantage points, including Tinker Cliffs (Trip 46), Dragon's Tooth (Trip 48), and Three Ridges (Trip 50). All hikers will want a photo of themselves dangling their legs from McAfee Knob (Trip 47), one of the greatest outlooks along the entire AT.

For the next 104 or so miles, the AT stays up high in Shenandoah National Park, following Skyline Drive through this exceptionally beautiful mountainscape. Some of the park's most memorable highlights are either on the AT itself, or a short hop, skip, and jump away, so day-hikers will often find themselves using the AT to make interesting loops. Trips in this book that follow portions of the AT in the park include Jeremy's Run (Trip 13), Mary's Rock (Trip 14), Jones Run and Doyles River (Trip 25), Riprap Hollow (Trip 29), and many others.

After leaving Shenandoah National Park, the AT heads north through hilly piedmont terrain, eventually following the West Virginia border to Loudoun Heights and Harpers Ferry (Trips 1 and 2) before crossing the Potomac into Maryland. The stretch of trail near Raven Rocks (Trip 3), just south of Snickers Gap, is infamously nicknamed the "Roller Coaster" for its series of what a thru-hiker would call "pointless ups and downs," or PUDs.

TRIP 38
NORTH RIVER GORGE AND WILD OAK TRAIL

Location: George Washington National Forest, VA
Rating: Moderate
Distance: 11.5-mile loop
Elevation Gain: 2,096 feet
Estimated Time: 4–7 hours
Maps: *Trails Illustrated: Staunton/Shenandoah Mountain,*
George Washington Forest, Map 791 (National Geographic).

Combining gentle hiking along the scenic North River Gorge with a ridge walk along the Wild Oak Trail, this route offers the best of both worlds and a fine opportunity to explore terrain on the western edge of the Shenandoah Valley.

DIRECTIONS

Getting to the trailhead of the North River Gorge Trail can be a bit of an odyssey. From I-81, Exit 240, head west on VA 257 for about 3.3 miles. In the little town of Bridgewater, turn left (south) onto VA 42/N Main Street. Follow this road 3.7 miles, then turn right onto VA 747. This road shares its number with VA 613 for a spell but continue to follow VA 747. In the village of Mount Solon, about 3.5 miles from VA 42, turn right onto VA 731, drive 1.0 mile, then turn left onto VA 730. In 3.6 miles, now within the national forest, turn right onto VA 718. In 1.0 mile, turn left onto FR 95, and see a sign for the Wild Oak Trail.

You're almost there. Drive 3.1 miles on FR 95 (passing the Todd Lake Recreation Area), then continue straight on Leading Ridge Road—the road turns to gravel, but it is fairly well maintained and accessible to cars. About 1.3 miles later, turn left onto FR 425. About 1.0 mile farther, arrive at the North River Campground on your left. Pass the campground, cross a little bridge, and park in the bay on your left, which is wide enough to hold several cars. *GPS coordinates:* 38° 20.290′ N, 79° 12.384′ W.

TRAIL DESCRIPTION

From the parking bay, you should be able to immediately spot North River Gorge Trail leading into the forest. The trail is blazed purple, a color that can be somewhat difficult to spot, but fortunately the trail follows the creek and is not difficult to follow. It begins by passing the campground on the left, but then veers

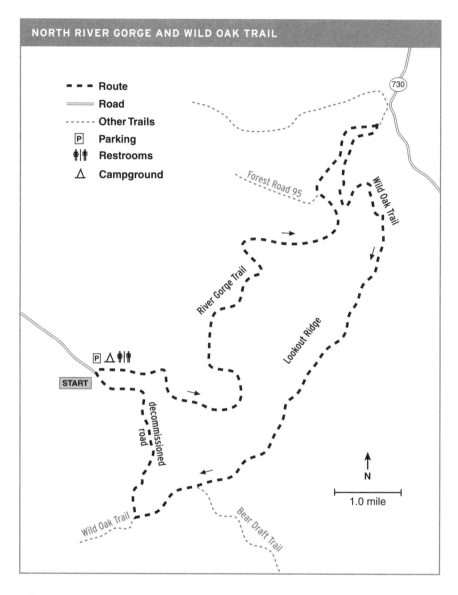

off deeper into the woods. Over the next 4.5 miles, enjoy the very gentle walking as the trail crosses and recrosses the stream, visiting a number of striking rocky gorges. Be careful crossing the stream, however; though the water is usually not especially high, the rocks have algae growing on them and can be quite slippery. If the water is high, these crossings can become problematic. It's always best to be prudent in such situations and not cross anything above your knees.

North River Gorge Trail intersects with white-blazed Wild Oak National Recreation Trail at 4.5 miles. Although you will be taking a hard right to begin

Hikers enjoy a break at an overlook of North River Gorge.

the climb of Lookout Mountain, first continue left on the white blazes to reach a bridge spanning the North River. In spring, this is often a beautiful creek, and there are a number of swimming holes downstream, making it a fine spot for a break.

Return to the intersection of North River Gorge Trail and Wild Oak Trail, continue ahead on the white blazes of Wild Oak Trail, and start the stout climb to this ridgeline, now on your left; the path gains about 1,800 feet over the next 4.8 miles. Fortunately, the ascent is broken up by a spur trail on the right that takes you down, over a short rocky grade, to a cliff overlooking the gorge. After enjoying this view, continue the climb, largely on a new and well-maintained stretch of trail that keeps the mountain on your left, actually bypassing the summit (2,860 feet) but offering you a few good views of the Alleghenies.

The stretch ends when Wild Oak Trail brings you at last to the ridgeline at 9.3 miles. A sign there commemorates the creation of this new trail, and there is another trail (sign: "513") leading east off the mountain. Continue southwest, following the ridgeline and the white blazes. A little later, the path reaches the intersection with Bear Draft Trail, heading down the mountain, to the east (left). This trail once also went west (right), but that section has been decommissioned and is quite overgrown.

Continue southwest (straight ahead) on Wild Oak Trail. At last, you will reach an intersection with a disused forest road on your right at 9.6 miles (*GPS coordinates:* 38° 19.384′ N, 79° 12.046′ W). Follow this road as it descends gently over the next 2.0 miles. It winds to the north and the west, bringing you almost directly to the bay where you parked your vehicle. Turn right at the gate when you reach the road, and you should see the bay.

DID YOU KNOW?

Wild Oak National Recreation Trail is the great artery through this portion of the forest, tracing a 26.2–mile loop around the valley of the North River, and crossing it twice. Though this area is on the very edge of the Shenandoah Valley (and thus not treated extensively in this book), there is great deal of excellent hiking to be had here, either along Wild Oak Trail itself or nearby in the Ramseys Draft Wilderness. See *AMC's Best Backpacking in the Mid-Atlantic* for a description of a backpacking loop that includes this path.

MORE INFORMATION

George Washington and Jefferson National Forests, North River Ranger District (www.fs.usda.gov/main/gwj; 540-432-0187). Check online for announcements concerning trail conditions, road closures, prescribed burns, and other events that may affect your hike. There is also a host at the North River Campground who will have up-to-date information about the nearby trails. Remember: Motorized equipment and mechanical transport are not allowed in the Ramseys Draft Wilderness; group sizes here are limited to ten people. For more information on designated Wildernesses, visit wilderness.net.

NEARBY

Although this hike is on the western periphery of the area covered in this book, you're really not too far from the southern district of the Shenandoah or hikes such as Mount Pleasant (Trip 45) or Cold Mountain (Trip 44). Nearby Ramseys Draft also makes a fine hike, and of course Wild Oak Trail offers great opportunities for exploration.

Harrisonburg is the nearest good-sized town, and you'll be able to find the full range of businesses there.

7

JEFFERSON NATIONAL FOREST AND THE BLUE RIDGE MOUNTAINS

ON ITS SOUTH SIDE—BEYOND THE REACHES OF THE SHENANDOAH RIVER— the Shenandoah Valley stretches geologically and culturally into the James River and Roanoke valleys. Like the rest of the Shenandoah area, the valley here is bounded to the east by the Blue Ridge Mountains and the northern Virginia highlands and to the west by ridge-and-valley formations.

Combined administratively with George Washington National Forest in 1995, Jefferson National Forest encompasses 709,596 acres, 690,106 of which are in Virginia. The four districts of Jefferson National Forest stretch mostly south of the Shenandoah Valley and the George Washington National Forest districts: Glenwood & Pedlar Ranger Districts, south of I-64 and east of I-81 (co-managed with George Washington National Forest); Eastern Divide Ranger District, west of I-81 and stretching nearly from I-64 in the north southward across I-77; the Mount Rogers National Recreation Area just southwest of that; and the Clinch Ranger District, along Virginia's westernmost border with Kentucky. Most of the hikes in this chapter fall within the Glenwood & Pedlar Ranger Districts (Trips 39, 40, 43, 44, 45, 49, and 50) and the Eastern Divide Ranger District (Trips 46, 47, and 48).

Two hikes (Trips 41 and 42) are located east of I-81, about 20 miles northwest of Roanoke, within Peaks of Otter Recreation Area, which is managed by the National Park Service. Located in the Blue Ridge Mountains along the Blue

Ridge Parkway, the area is rich with things to do and see. A lodge and visitor center are located at milepost 86 on the Blue Ridge Parkway. A campground on Sharp Top Mountain offers sites by reservation and on a first-come, first-served basis. Six trails cross the recreation area itself; another three National Scenic Trails are within an eight-mile radius. Abbot Lake is open for fishing (with a valid permit), and two historical buildings offer a chance to look back at life here in the mid-1800s.

TRIP 39
SPY ROCK

Location: Glenwood & Pedlar Ranger Districts, George Washington and Jefferson National Forests, VA
Rating: Moderate
Distance: 3.2 miles
Elevation Gain: 1,223 feet
Estimated Time: 1–2 hours
Maps: *Trails Illustrated: Lexington/Blue Ridge Mountains, George Washington and Jefferson National Forests, Map 789* (National Geographic)

An unassuming walk along a fire road leads you to one of the better views in the area. Time this hike for spring, when the rhododendron are blooming.

DIRECTIONS
From I-81/I-64, Exit 205, take VA 606 east toward Raphine for 1.5 miles. Turn left onto US 11 N/North Lee Highway, and then make a quick right onto VA 56 E/Tye River Turnpike. Follow VA 56 east for 8.8 miles, and turn right onto Fish Hatchery Road/VA 690. Pass the hatchery, and follow the signs for hiker parking in 0.5 mile. *GPS coordinates:* 37° 50.515′ N, 79° 7.876′ W.

TRAIL DESCRIPTION
This long, steady climb along a fire road eventually brings you to the Appalachian Trail (AT) and then to Spy Rock itself. The bonus after enjoying the great views: the way back is all downhill.

From the parking lot, cross over the dirt road and aim for a yellow gate that marks entry to a fire road. (When we hiked this route, the path was helpfully labeled with a green street sign for Spy Rock Road.) Start heading up the fire road, which is blazed sporadically with blue blazes. The road starts out rather open but eventually gets more tree cover, lending some welcome shade. Overall, the road is easy to follow, with the exception of one tricky left-hand turn near a rather oddly shaped tree. To make sure you take it, just stay to the left and keep an eye out for blue blazes.

The trail passes a red gate, then intersects the AT at 1.0 mile. Turn left onto the AT, and keep climbing up the trail, passing a wooden gate. The climb culminates with a sign that points the way to Spy Rock at 1.4 miles. Turn right

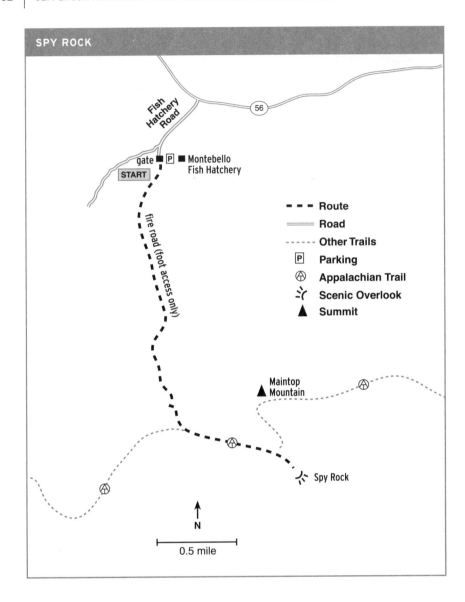

SPY ROCK

onto this spur trail from the AT, and pass several (dry) campsites before arriving at the base of Spy Rock.

Getting up to Spy Rock requires a bit of rock scrambling. Walk a short distance to the right, which leads to the tricky climb; take it slow as you navigate the rock. While the scramble can be daunting, it is the more obvious and least impactful route to the top.

The scramble is worth it. The top of Spy Rock (3,877 feet) has 360-degree views of the area, giving you a good look at the famous Religious Range, which includes the Priest, Little Priest, the Friar, the Little Friar, and the Cardinal.

Commanding views of the countryside await you at the top of Spy Rock.

After enjoying the views, retrace your steps back down the AT and the fire road to your vehicle.

DID YOU KNOW?

The 360-degree views may have contributed to Spy Rock's name. It's rumored that Confederate soldiers used Spy Rock as a base to monitor Union troop movements in the valley below.

MORE INFORMATION

George Washington and Jefferson National Forests, Glenwood & Pedlar Ranger Districts (www.fs.usda.gov/main/gwj; 540-291-2188). Check online for announcements concerning trail conditions, road closures, prescribed burns, and other events that may affect your hike.

NEARBY

This hike serves as an excellent base to explore the area. Hikers up for a challenge can tackle nearby Three Ridges (Trip 50), or check out the famous Crabtree Falls (Trip 40).

The town of Roseland has food if you're looking for a meal in the Blue Ridge area.

TRIP 40
CRABTREE FALLS

Location: Glenwood & Pedlar Ranger Districts, George Washington and Jefferson National Forests, VA
Rating: Moderate
Distance: 2.8 miles, round-trip
Elevation Gain: 1,642 feet
Estimated Time: 1–2 hours
Maps: *Trails Illustrated: Lexington/Blue Ridge Mountains, George Washington and Jefferson National Forests, Map 789* (National Geographic)

A steep climb rewards you with near-constant views of one of Virginia's prettiest waterfalls.

DIRECTIONS
From I-81/I-64, Exit 205, take VA 606 east toward Raphine for 1.5 miles. Turn left onto US 11 N/North Lee Highway, and then make a quick right onto VA 56 E/Tye River Turnpike. Follow VA 56 east for 11.8 miles and look for the Crabtree Falls parking lot on your right. Day-use fees apply. *GPS coordinates: 37° 51.122′ N, 79° 4.655′ W.*

TRAIL DESCRIPTION
Crabtree Falls is often listed as a "must-see" hike for anyone traveling the Blue Ridge Parkway. It's a hike that invites lingering with its multiple overlooks and great views of the falls. With five major cascades and falling a total distance of 1,200 feet, Crabtree Falls is the highest vertical-drop cascading waterfall east of the Mississippi River. It is well worth the short hike.

Despite its elevation gain, the trail itself is an easy one to follow—well maintained and well marked with guardrails and stairs to help with the steeper portions. You may find yourself idling away the day here as you wander up and down the trail, enjoying the views of the falls and the surrounding valley.

The trail starts off as a paved one and brings you quickly to the bottom of the lower falls at just 0.1 mile. It's a short distance for a great payoff, but even better views await you at the top. To continue the journey, keep following the trail, which now turns to dirt, swings to the right, and starts to switchback up

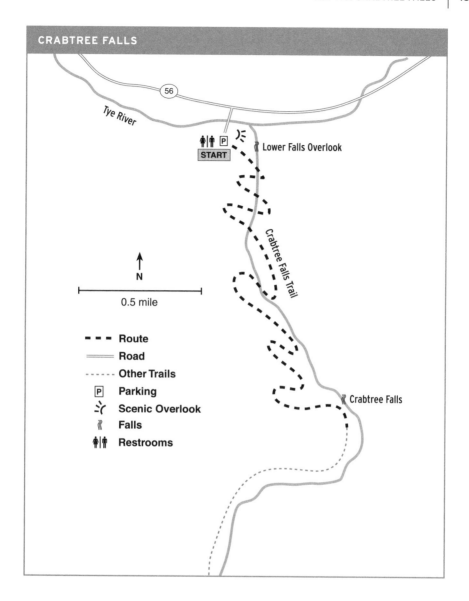

CRABTREE FALLS

56

Tye River

START

Lower Falls Overlook

Crabtree Falls Trail

N

0.5 mile

- - - Route
=== Road
----- Other Trails
P Parking
Scenic Overlook
Falls
Restrooms

Crabtree Falls

the mountain. Numerous overlooks dot the trail and extend into the falls, giving you multiple opportunities to pause for pictures.

About 0.5 mile into the hike, pass a rock formation that may tempt rock climbers to scramble up the cave and navigate the chimney. It's another good spot for a short break, and a chance to enjoy the views below.

At about 1.4 miles, arrive at the top of the falls. Cross a small wooden bridge to an overlook that gives views of the valley and the Blue Ridge Mountains.

The lower cascade of Crabtree Falls is a short walk from the parking lot; hike to the upper falls to see the big vertical drop in person. (Photo courtesy J David MacLuskie)

Hikers are strongly cautioned, however, against climbing onto the slippery rocks. More than twenty people have fallen to their deaths while scrambling along these rocks.

At this point, turn around, cross back over the footbridge, and follow the trail back to your vehicle.

DID YOU KNOW?

Crabtree Falls has had its 15 minutes of fame. *The Waltons*—the popular 1970s television show about a family living in rural Virginia—often referred to the falls as a Sunday outing for the family. But its fame is in name only; the falls were never shown on the program during its nine-year run.

MORE INFORMATION

George Washington and Jefferson National Forests, Glenwood & Pedlar Ranger Districts (www.fs.usda.gov/main/gwj; 540-291-2188). Check online for announcements concerning trail conditions, road closures, prescribed burns, and other events that may affect your hike.

NEARBY

If you're looking for a slightly longer day, turn left after the footbridge at the top of the falls and follow a trail that takes you along Crabtree Stream. The trail flattens out if you decide to take this route and eventually leads you to the upper parking area in about 1.0 mile from the overlook. To return to your vehicle from this point, turn around and retrace your steps back to the car. This results in a hike of about 4.8 miles.

Crabtree Falls serves as an excellent base to explore the area. If you are up for a challenge, you can hike nearby Three Ridges (Trip 50); Spy Rock (Trip 39) is a good counterpart to Crabtree Falls, with a short distance but mighty views.

The town of Roseland has food if you're looking for a meal in the Blue Ridge area.

TRIP 41
SHARP TOP

Location: Peaks of Otter Recreation Area, Blue Ridge Parkway, VA
Rating: Moderate
Distance: 3.3 miles round-trip
Elevation Gain: 1,461 feet
Estimated Time: 2–4 hours
Maps: *Trails Illustrated: Lexington/Blue Ridge Mountains,*
George Washington and Jefferson National Forests, Map 789
(National Geographic)

**This popular out-and-back offers spectacular 360-degree views of
the surrounding Blue Ridge and Virginia piedmont.**

DIRECTIONS

From I-81, Exit 167 (north of Roanoke), follow US 11 toward Buchanan for 1.5
miles. In town, take a very sharp left onto VA 43 South/Parkway Drive. The
road passes an industrial area then climbs along a narrow, twisty road for 4.8
miles until VA 43 joins the Blue Ridge Parkway. Head north on the Blue Ridge
Parkway/VA 43 for 5.0 miles. The Peaks of Otter Recreation Area Visitors
Center is on the left; for better hiker parking, turn right onto Peaks Road/VA
43. In another few hundred feet, make a right at the traffic triangle onto Sheep
Creek Road. A parking lot on your left is in another few hundred feet, near
an old building. This is the trailhead for Sharp Top itself. *GPS coordinates: 37°
26.593' N, 79° 36.557' W.*

TRAIL DESCRIPTION

Once believed to be Virginia's highest mountain, Sharp Top dominates the
surrounding landscape. The climb up Sharp Top is a demanding one, but it is
quite short—just 1.6 miles with 1,300 feet of gain—and the rewards more than
merit the effort involved.

From the parking lot, look for the placard detailing a bit of history about the
mountain. Your route, the unblazed trail, begins climbing from here. The big,
broad, and well-maintained route is easy to follow, though it is not marked. It
crosses a little paved road (used by a bus that takes non-hikers to a trailhead
just beneath Sharp Top's summit). Beyond the road, the trail transitions to a
footpath, becomes steeper, and switchbacks a couple of times.

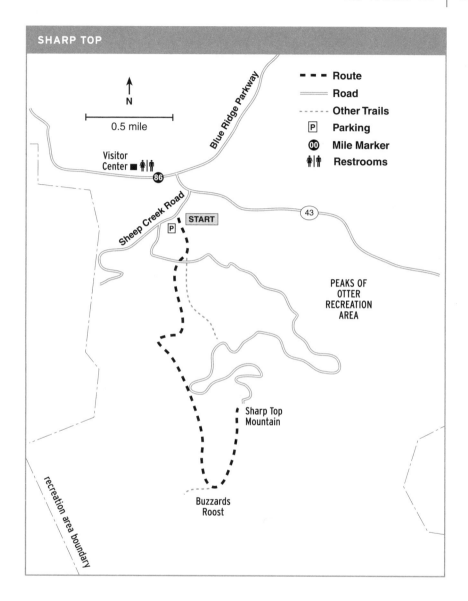

SHARP TOP

N

0.5 mile

- - - Route
—— Road
----- Other Trails
P Parking
00 Mile Marker
♦♦ Restrooms

Blue Ridge Parkway

Visitor
Center ■ ♦♦
86

Sheep Creek Road

START
P

43

PEAKS OF
OTTER
RECREATION
AREA

Sharp Top
Mountain

Buzzards
Roost

recreation area boundary

Eventually, the path traverses a slope with the mountain on your left. You can almost look up to see Sharp Top's summit. At 1.25 miles, the trail reaches the saddle on the mountain's left. The sign says you have 1,600 feet to go—fortunately, that's trail distance, not vertical feet! Turning right will take you to Buzzards Roost (this route describes a visit after you summit); turn left instead. The climb here remains steep, but there are well-maintained stone staircases for you, some with metal handrails. Cut through two rocky gaps and pass the spur trail on the right leading to the bus trailhead. Keep climbing. Very soon,

From Sharp Top's built-up summit, dramatic views of the Blue Ridge await.

the path arrives at a shelter atop the mountain. A stone staircase winds around the rocky summit to bring you to the very top at 1.6 miles (3,862 feet), where the huge view of the Blue Ridge opens out around you. The broader, wooded peak across the lake is Flat Rock, also in the Peaks of Otter area (Trip 42.)

After enjoying this view, return down to the saddle. At the intersection with the side trail, head straight for the side trip to Buzzards Roost. The spur trail is only a few hundred feet long and is basically flat. Of course, it is much less frequently visited than the Sharp Top summit. A scrambling move or two brings you to a nice view that is similar, if somewhat less dramatic, than that from Sharp Top itself at 2.0 miles. From Buzzards Roost, you can also wrangle a good view back to Sharp Top, which will emphasize why visitors in past centuries thought this this mountain was higher than it is.

From the saddle, descend the trail to your waiting vehicles.

DID YOU KNOW?

During the Colonial period, most settlers regarded Sharp Top as the highest peak in Virginia. Illustrating the difficulties of early surveying, this estimate was, in fact, nowhere near accurate. Even nearby Flat Rock and Apple Orchard Mountain are higher, and of course Mount Rogers (the state's true highpoint) is almost 2,000 feet higher! None of these peaks is nearly as dramatic in prominence as Sharp Top, however, so the locals may be forgiven their error. When the Washington Monument was dedicated, a stone was sent from Sharp Top, inscribed "From Otter's Summit, Virginia's Loftiest Peak, To Crown a Monument to Virginia's Noblest Son."

MORE INFORMATION

National Park Service, Peaks of Otter Recreation Area (nps.gov/blri; 828-271-4779). Stop in at the visitor center on the Blue Ridge Parkway/VA 43 for more information about the area.

NEARBY

Flat Top (Trip 42) is the natural companion hike for Sharp Top. There are a number of other fine hikes in nearby Jefferson National Forest, including Apple Orchard Falls (Trip 43), Cold Mountain (Trip 44), Mount Pleasant (Trip 45), and the Devil's Marbleyard (Trip 49). A little farther south, near Roanoke, is the cluster of trips including McAfee Knob (Trip 47), Tinker Cliffs (Trip 48), and Dragon's Tooth (Trip 48).

For civilization, Roanoke is the nearest city to the south, while Lexington is the nearest city to the north, both along the I-81 corridor.

TRIP 42
FLAT TOP

Location: Peaks of Otter Recreation Area, Blue Ridge Parkway, VA
Rating: Moderate
Distance: 3.7 miles out-and-back
Elevation Gain: 1,667 feet gain
Estimated Time: 2–4 hours
Maps: *Trails Illustrated: Lexington/Blue Ridge Mountains,*
George Washington and Jefferson National Forests, Map 789
(National Geographic)

**Catch nice views from a peak less traveled—and taller—than its
cousin, Sharp Top.**

DIRECTIONS

From I-81, Exit 167 (north of Roanoke), follow US 11 toward Buchanan for
1.5 miles. In town, take a very sharp left onto VA 43 South/Parkway Drive.
The road passes an industrial area then climbs along a narrow, twisty road for
4.8 miles until VA 43 joins the Blue Ridge Parkway. Head north on the Blue
Ridge Parkway/VA 43 for 5.0 miles. The Peaks of Otter Recreation Area Visitors Center is on the left; for better hiker parking, turn right onto Peaks Road/
VA 43. In 0.8 mile, turn left into a picnic area and cross Little Stony Creek. You
should see a sign for Flat Top straight ahead. Park here. *GPS coordinates: 37°
26.538′ N, 79° 35.846′ W.*

TRAIL DESCRIPTION

The hike to Flat Top's summit is a pure and demanding climb—1,600 feet
over 1.8 miles. While the view isn't quite as grand as the one you'll see
from neighboring Sharp Top (Trip 41), you're more likely to have this trail
to yourself.

Starting from the trailhead parking lot, look to the right. The trail, which is
not blazed but is never difficult to follow, heads to the right out of the parking
lot, following a flat grade. It soon veers to the left and gets to business, following the mountain to its summit.

Though blissfully short, the next part of the trail is a relentless climb. There
are few switchbacks and the best that can be said is that, from time to time,
the grade goes easy on you. Near the ridgeline, the trail bears left across the

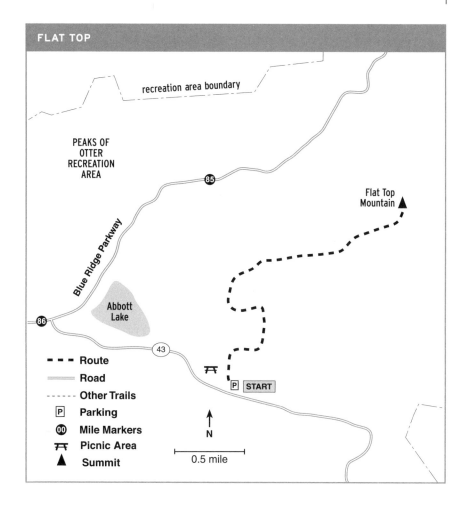

FLAT TOP

recreation area boundary

PEAKS OF
OTTER
RECREATION
AREA

85

Flat Top
Mountain ▲

Blue Ridge Parkway

Abbott
Lake

86

43

🏕 Picnic

P START

- - - Route
═══ Road
----- Other Trails
P Parking
⓪⓪ Mile Markers
🏕 Picnic Area
▲ Summit

↑
N

0.5 mile

mountain's shoulder for about 0.5 miles. At last you've crested the ridgeline. But there's still more climbing to be done, albeit at a much gentler grade.

Hike along the ridgeline, climbing, though comparatively gently. The trail reaches a rocky outcropping to the left (west) onto the ridgeline. This is not the summit, but scramble out on the slabs for a fine view of the mountains to the west. Continue on the trail for just a few feet more to reach the sign marking the summit of Flat Top at 1.8 miles. Past this sign is a well-worn path to the right that takes you, in no time at all, to an inverse L shape in the rock.

The view from these slabs is so fine that you may feel like you're on top of an Adirondack peak once you've scrambled out to see it. Pause to take it all in, and perhaps enjoy a lunch from this dreamy, eastward vista.

When the time has come, retrace your steps, descending all the way back to your vehicle at the Peaks Road picnic area.

The summit of Flat Top is slabby and open, which makes for great views.

DID YOU KNOW?

From the summit of Flat Top, you can see the town of Bedford, Virginia, which World War II buffs may recognize as the town that lost more soldiers, per capita, in the war than any other city in the United States. Twenty-three soldiers from this town lost their lives, including nineteen fatalities during the invasion of Normandy. In 2001, President George W. Bush dedicated the National D-Day Memorial here.

MORE INFORMATION

National Park Service, Peaks of Otter Recreation Area (nps.gov/blri; 828-271-4779). Stop in at the visitor center on the Blue Ridge Parkway/VA 43 for more information about the area.

NEARBY

Of course, if you've not yet hiked Sharp Top (Trip 41), then you should definitely do so during your visit. There are a number of other fine hikes in nearby Jefferson National Forest, including Apple Orchard Falls (Trip 43), Cold Mountain (Trip 44), Mount Pleasant (Trip 45), and the Devil's Marbleyard (Trip 49). A little farther south, near Roanoke, is the cluster of trips including McAfee Knob (Trip 47), Tinker Cliffs (Trip 46), and Dragon's Tooth (Trip 48).

INVASIVE SPECIES IN VIRGINIA

Invasive species—nonnative plants, animals, and diseases that harm both the environment and the economy—are a serious problem in Virginia and the rest of the United States. Virginia's Department of Conservation and Recreation estimates that invasive species cost the state $1 billion and the nation upward of $120 billion annually. These species often spread quickly and aggressively, destroying native species, disrupting fragile ecosystems, harming crops, and spreading disease.

Hikers and other outdoorspeople have a deep and abiding interest in doing their part to prevent invasive species from attacking the environment we love and enjoy. Not only can invasive plants take over forests and trails, destroying cherished native species, but some can cause direct harm to hikers. Anyone who has ever visited the South and been bitten by a fire ant or seen the damage caused by wild hogs can understand why hikers should be committed to keeping these troublesome pests from the Shenandoah Valley. A number of species are of immediate concern:

- **Emerald Ash Borer:** This wood-boring beetle was accidentally imported from Asia and has caused the deaths of more than 40 million ash trees.
- **Hemlock Woolly Adelgid:** The small, aphid-like insect first established itself near Richmond, Virginia, and has spread from Maine to Georgia. These insects have decimated one of the few remaining stands of old-growth hemlocks in the Shenandoah Valley near Ramseys Draft.
- **Kudzu:** Introduced from Japan and China in the early twentieth century, this climbing, semi-woody vine is common throughout the eastern half of the United States. When left to its own devices, kudzu can overwhelm native species, choking them under its leaves and vines.
- **Gypsy Moth:** From Virginia northward, the gypsy moth has exacted a terrible toll on hardwood forests, defoliating millions of acres since it was introduced in the late nineteenth century.
- **Fire Ant:** Fortunately, these biting pests are confined to the area around Tidewater, Virginia; a quarantine is in place to keep them from spreading through the state.

Although controlling infestations of invasive species is a monumental undertaking, you can do a great deal to help prevent the spread of these pests so that the places we love can remain natural and unaffected.

- Know what troublesome invasive plant species look like and avoid traveling through them.
- If you do travel through an infestation, try to remove all seeds from your clothes and person before you continue.
- Clean equipment such as boots, tents, and clothing between trips, and when you leave one area for another.
- Do not transport firewood. Instead, gather or buy it locally.

TRIP 43
APPLE ORCHARD FALLS

Location: Glenwood & Pedlar Ranger Districts, George Washington and Jefferson National Forests, VA
Rating: Moderate
Distance: 6.7 miles round-trip
Elevation Gain: 2,438 feet
Estimated Time: 3–5 hours
Maps: *Trails Illustrated: Lexington/Blue Ridge Mountains, George Washington and Jefferson National Forests, Map 789* (National Geographic)

This hike, past the 200-foot cascade of Apple Orchard Falls, is justifiably one of the most popular in Jefferson National Forest.

DIRECTIONS

From I-81, Exit 168, take VA 614 east, following the signs for Arcadia. About 3.3 miles later, take a left onto North Creek Road. At first the road is paved, but just as you pass the established campsite on the left at about 2.8 miles, continue straight onto a single gravel lane. The road is not too rough, however, and is suitable for cars. A few miles later, you'll arrive at a circular parking lot, which is the trailhead for both Apple Orchard Falls and Cornelius Creek trails. *GPS coordinates: 37° 31.780′ N, 79° 33.189′ W.*

TRAIL DESCRIPTION

On a warm summer's day, catch the very striking Apple Orchard Falls and then stroll down the beautiful and verdant Cornelius Creek, which also offers an especially inviting swimming hole or two.

At the trailhead, orient yourself by looking to up the trails and away from the road. The trail to the left is Apple Orchard Falls Trail, while the one coming more directly down the mountain, to the right, is Cornelius Creek Trail. Both are blazed blue. Enter the forest following Apple Orchard Falls Trail and soon come upon a fork in the trail. Follow the sign and bear right as the trail climbs gently, at times riding up high to the right of the creek. Eventually, at 1.7 miles, you'll arrive at two bridges over the creek. The lower one leads to another trailhead, so cross the creek at the higher bridge, then continue to follow the blue blazes as the trail climbs more steeply and winds its way between boulders.

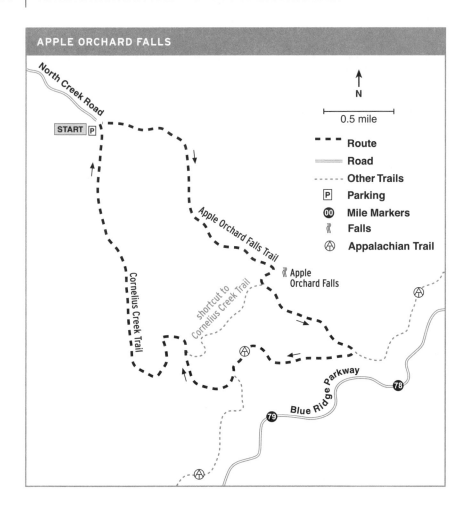

At last, the path reaches a boardwalk that takes you directly beneath the falls at 1.9 miles. Don't be surprised if, like many visitors, you gasp in surprise at the verticality and beauty of these falls, especially on a nice spring day, when they are full of water. They seem to come as if from nowhere.

Beyond the falls, the trail continues to climb via wooden stairs and the occasional switchback. Stay alert here; it's not hard to miss one of the path's sharp left-hand turns, though you won't go very far. The trail passes by an idyllic spot just above the falls where the creek tumbles over a boulder, then climbs more sedately along the left of the stream. It arrives at and crosses an old grassy forest road at 2.3 miles.

(If you're looking for a shortcut, consider following the road grade to the right here. This will bring you to Cornelius Creek Trail, without walking along the Appalachian Trail [AT].)

A hiker pauses to admire the beauty of Apple Orchard Falls on a spring morning.

The trail then switchbacks slowly and steadily for about 0.5 mile, gaining about 500 vertical feet before it intersects with the AT; turn right. The AT, through this stretch, follows fairly gentle rolling terrain along the shoulder of the Blue Ridge.

At 3.8 miles, turn right onto Cornelius Creek Trail and begin your descent toward the trailhead, first through a forest footpath. After you cross the old forest road, which you also crossed on your ascent, bear left, and walk down the old road grade. At 5.0 miles, the route brings you to Cornelius Creek itself. The trail bears to the right and follows a lovely creekside stretch. Keep your eye out for attractive places to pause for a rest and soak your feet—there's at least one pool suitable for swimming where the creek cascades over an 8-to-10-foot rock wall.

In the lower reaches of the creek, the trail leaps over the water a few times, both by bridge and by crossings, which are easy to rock-hop. Before long, Cornelius Creek's valley widens out and brings you back to the trailhead and your waiting vehicle.

DID YOU KNOW?

Apple Orchard Falls takes its name from the mountain it drains. Standing at 4,244 feet elevation, Apple Orchard Mountain is one of the most prominent peaks in Virginia. Its summit is bald, and the radar post atop the mountain makes it easy to spot. To reach the summit, follow the route as described to the intersection of Apple Orchard Falls Trail and the AT. Instead of turning right (south) onto the AT, turn left (north). The peak is about 1.5 miles from the junction.

MORE INFORMATION

George Washington and Jefferson National Forests, Glenwood & Pedlar Ranger Districts (www.fs.usda.gov/main/gwj; 540-291-2188). Check online for announcements concerning trail conditions, road closures, prescribed burns, and other events that may affect your hike.

NEARBY

Of course, where the AT runs, there is always more hiking to be had. The Devil's Marbleyard (Trip 49) is the closest hike described in this book. If you head farther south, Tinker Cliffs (Trip 46), McAfee Knob (Trip 47), and Dragon's Tooth (Trip 48) are all great options. Farther north, Mount Pleasant (Trip 45) and Cold Mountain (Trip 44) are well worth a visit.

Natural Bridge, Virginia, is a popular destination for tourists seeking to visit the cave, so you're likely to find the familiar array of services there. Looking for an even bigger town? Lexington, Virginia, is the best bet.

TRIP 44
COLD MOUNTAIN

Location: Glenwood & Pedlar Ranger Districts, George Washington and Jefferson National Forests, VA
Rating: Moderate
Distance: 6.1 miles round-trip
Elevation Gain: 1,586 feet
Estimated Time: 5–6 hours
Maps: *Trails Illustrated: Lexington/Blue Ridge Mountains, George Washington and Jefferson National Forests, Map 789* (National Geographic).

Cold Mountain's alpine meadows and balds are not especially large, but they are an interesting change of pace from the Mid-Atlantic's more expected ridgelines and forests.

DIRECTIONS

From I-81, Exit 188A, drive east on US 60. Climb over the mountains and pass the Blue Ridge Parkway, and 12.5 miles from the interstate, take a left onto VA 634 and drive about 1.6 miles before turning right onto Wiggins Spring Road/ VA 755. This road soon becomes a rather rough gravel road that, while accessible to cars, requires that you drive slowly and carefully. When you spot the Appalachian Trail, you've reached Hog Camp Gap, 2.7 miles from the intersection with VA 634. Park here. There are also a few spots a few hundred yards up the road. *GPS coordinates:* 37° 45.578′ N, 79° 11.680′ W.

A 0.3-mile road walk (described below) connects the terminus of the trail to this parking lot.

TRAIL DESCRIPTION

As you wander across the bald fields of Cold Mountain (4,020 feet), sometimes also referred to as Cole Mountain, you might imagine yourself strolling through the alpine meadows of New Hampshire, Colorado, Alaska, or Switzerland. Take special care to stay on the path in these areas; alpine vegetation is particularly fragile. The climb to these meadows is not especially steep, but the views at the top are well worth the easy grade, and the unusual ecosystem at the top makes for a singular Mid-Atlantic hike.

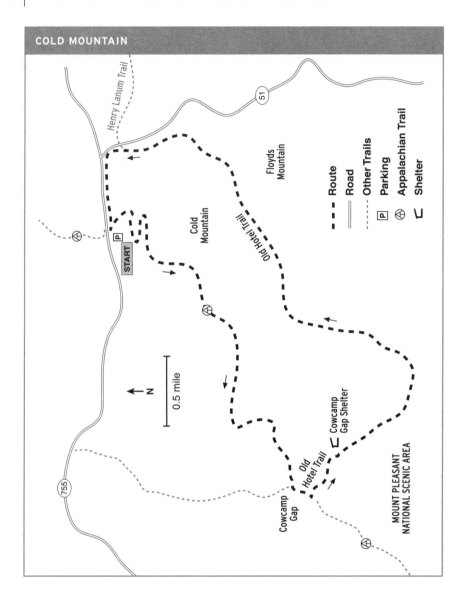

COLD MOUNTAIN

From Wiggins Spring Road and the parking lot, head south on the Appalachian Trail (AT) and begin a moderate and gentle switchbacked climb of about 500 feet over the next 0.9 mile to reach the open areas atop Cold Mountain. As the trail opens out, note the signs warning against camping. In spring, wildflowers bloom in these open balds. Any time of the year, expect to see wide-open views to the east, west, and south as you traverse the gently rolling meadows for the next 0.25 mile. The white blazes of the AT are marked on posts.

The open balds of Cold Mountain are a rare pleasure in the heavily forested Mid-Atlantic, especially if the wildflowers are in bloom.

If you want a very short trip, you can simply walk back to your vehicle from here, but the remainder of the trail also takes you past some attractive, if more typically Mid-Atlantic, scenery.

The forest closes about you as you descend the AT about 600 feet over 1.25 miles to Cowcamp Gap, where the white blazes meet the blue blazes of Hotel Trail. A short trail to the right leads to an obscured view. Pause for a break here, then turn left to follow Hotel Trail as it rounds the eastern face of Cold Mountain. Once you arrive at a creek, a spur trail on the left takes you quickly to the AT's Cowcamp Gap Shelter. If you happen to be low on water, this is a good place to stop and fill up.

Continue to follow the blue blazes as Hotel Trail continues its descent. It bottoms out eventually, then over the next mile or so it covers some rolling terrain that ultimately gains another 550 feet. The grade evens out, and the route enters some open meadows where camping is allowed at 4.5 miles. This popular site, with its wide-open fields, also makes a great spot for a picnic or a breather.

When you're ready, continue to follow the trail as it traverses the meadows and enters the woods. The remainder of the loop is gentle as Hotel Trail draws near a streambed on the right, follows a sandy jeep trail, and passes through a copse of dead trees. At last, the trail bears to the right and arrives at the Mount Pleasant Trailhead at 5.8 miles. To return to your vehicle, take a left onto the road and walk about 0.3 mile to reach the trailhead from which you started.

DID YOU KNOW?

The origin of balds such as those on Cold Mountain is a bit of a topographic mystery. While peaks in the North—such as Mount Washington or the high peaks of the Adirondacks—are devoid of vegetation due to the combined effect of latitude and elevation, peaks in the South are not technically alpine peaks because of the warmer climate. In some cases, such as with Cold Mountain, one peak will develop a bald while another peak of similar elevation will not (you might contrast Cold Mountain with nearby Mount Pleasant). Most experts tend to believe that balds of this sort developed due to the habits of grazing animals. In some cases, the National Park Service and the Forest Service have continued to allow animals to graze these areas to maintain their open characteristics.

If you enjoy Cold Mountain, you should plan a trip to the Grayson Highlands, farther south in Virginia. See *AMC's Best Backpacking in the Mid-Atlantic* for a description of these beautiful highlands.

MORE INFORMATION

George Washington and Jefferson National Forests, Glenwood & Pedlar Ranger Districts (www.fs.usda.gov/main/gwj; 540-291-2188). Check online for announcements concerning trail conditions, road closures, prescribed burns, and other events that may affect your hike.

NEARBY

The Mount Pleasant loop (Trip 45) is the natural companion to Cold Mountain. If you're after still more miles, consider visiting Apple Orchard Falls (Trip 43) or the unique boulder field of the Devil's Marbleyard (Trip 49), both of which are also near Lexington.

Food, lodging, shopping and more may be found in Lexington. Nearby Natural Bridge, Virginia, is also popular destination for tourists seeking to visit the cave.

Location: Glenwood & Pedlar Ranger Districts, George Washington and Jefferson National Forests, VA
Rating: Moderate
Distance: 6.5 miles
Elevation Gain: 1,781 feet
Estimated Time: 3–5 hours
Maps: *Trails Illustrated: Lexington/Blue Ridge Mountains, George Washington and Jefferson National Forests, Map 789* (National Geographic).

Treasure the expansive view of the Blue Ridge Mountains from Mount Pleasant's westward vista.

DIRECTIONS

From I-81, Exit 188A, drive east on US 60. Climb over the mountains and pass the Blue Ridge Parkway. At 12.5 miles from the interstate, take a left onto VA 634 and drive about 1.6 miles before turning right onto Wiggins Spring Road/ VA 755. This road soon becomes a rough gravel road that, while accessible to cars, requires that you drive slowly and carefully. When you spot the Appalachian Trail, you've reached Hog Camp Gap, 2.7 miles from the intersection with VA 634. Park here. There are also a few spots a few hundred yards up the road. *GPS coordinates: 37° 45.578′ N, 79° 11.680′ W.*

TRAIL DESCRIPTION

Given the stunning views from Mount Pleasant and the relative ease of reaching its summit, this hike may well offer one of the best payoffs in the Shenandoah Valley. From the parking lot, where the Appalachian Trail crosses Wiggins Spring Road, walk east along the road. It bears to the right at a sign for Mount Pleasant. On your right, pass the trailhead for Hotel Trail (the Cold Mountain loop, Trip 44, passes through this point). Just ahead are the dual trailheads for Henry Lanum Trail. The leftward trail is your return route. Bear right.

For the next 1.2 miles, Henry Lanum Trail descends very gently along a nearly flat road grade. It begins to wind through a few hollows, crossing a few creeks. The second creek is your only easy-to-reach, reliable water source on the trail, so make sure you have plenty of water.

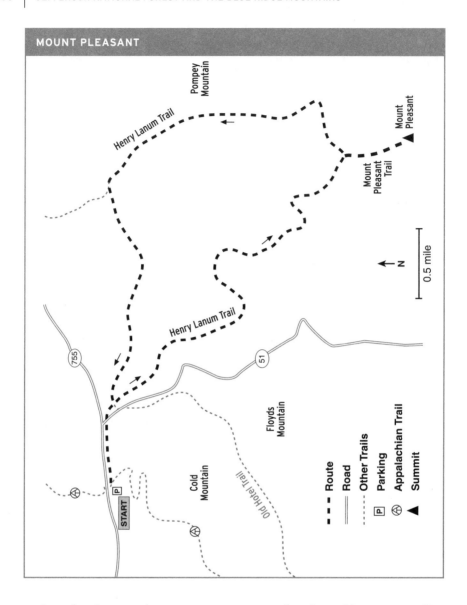

Just after the second stream crossing at 1.6 miles, the trail begins ascending to the gap between Mount Pleasant and Pompey Mountain, gaining approximately 500 feet of elevation over 0.9 mile. Though the climb is not especially steep, it is steady. The trail reaches a T intersection in the gap. To the left, the trail departs toward Pompey Mountain and the end of the route. For now, turn right and continue your climb to the summit of Mount Pleasant.

As you begin the remaining 300 vertical feet of climbing, pass a sign to the left indicating another water source; reaching it requires a bit of a descent

The sunset from Mount Pleasant may be among the best sights in the Shenandoah Valley.

down into the eastward-facing hollow. The remaining climb is a bit stiffer than earlier sections of the trail, featuring a few rocky stretches, but you'll soon come to a second T intersection at 3.0 miles. On the left is an eastward vista; to the right, ahead, is a more dramatic westward view. Visit the latter first.

To reach the westward vista, make your way for about 0.1 mile along the ridgeline until you reach a campsite just beneath the rocks of the vista. A simple scrambling move brings you to the rocky outcropping of the westward vista, where you'll be able to drink in the view of the Blue Ridge and Cold Mountain, and even scope out the route you've walked. As you explore these exposed rocks, do be careful. There are rattlesnakes in the area, and they are fond of sunning themselves on the warm slabs.

Return to the second T intersection, and follow the trail ahead to take in the eastward view over the piedmont—also very pretty but less dramatic. Return to the second T intersection, and turn right to head back to the gap between the mountains. From the gap and the first T intersection you encountered, continue straight. The trail climbs about 300 feet, fairly moderately, to the broad back of Pompey Mountain at 4.6 miles. Keep an eye out for this otherwise unremarkable summit. A small, unmarked track leads to the right to reach a rocky outcropping that offers a view.

Back on main trail, the route descends about 400 feet, then climbs about 200 feet more—all over 0.8 mile—before beginning its final descent toward the trailhead. The path, however, is gentle and pleasant walking and the forest itself is beautiful and lush.

When you arrive at the Mount Pleasant trailhead, walk up the road to your waiting vehicle.

DID YOU KNOW?

The trail you'll follow was formerly known as Mount Pleasant/Pompey Mountain Trail, but it was a renamed to honor Henry Lanum, an especially dedicated member of the local Appalachian Trail club.

MORE INFORMATION

George Washington and Jefferson National Forests, Glenwood & Pedlar Ranger Districts (www.fs.usda.gov/main/gwj; 540-291-2188). Check online for announcements concerning trail conditions, road closures, prescribed burns, and other events that may affect your hike.

NEARBY

A short road walk connects the Hog Camp Gap parking lot and the Wiggins Spring Trailhead, from which the route to Cold Mountain (Trip 44) departs.

Also in the vicinity you'll find the Apple Orchard Falls hike (Trip 43) and the Devil's Marbleyard out-and-back (Trip 49). Three Ridges (Trip 50), Spy Rock (Trip 39), Sharp Top (Trip 41), and Flat Top (Trip 42) are not far, either.

If you're looking for post-hike refreshment, Lexington is nearby and offers a wide range of restaurants and businesses.

TRIP 46
TINKER CLIFFS

Location: Eastern Divide Ranger District, Jefferson National Forest, VA
Rating: Strenuous
Distance: 7.2 miles
Elevation Gain: 2,632 feet
Estimated Time: 3–4 hours
Maps: *Appalachian Trail Guide to Central Virginia* (Appalachian Trail Conservancy)

On this challenging and rewarding hike, find out how Scorched Earth Gap got its name and climb to Tinker Cliffs, the first of the three jewels in Virginia's Triple Crown.

DIRECTIONS

From I-81, Exit 141, turn north onto VA 419. In 0.5 mile, turn right (north) onto Route 311. Drive 6.7 miles then turn right onto VA 779/VA 698, and then make a quick right onto VA 779. Follow this for 8.3 miles to the trailhead, which will be on the right. *GPS coordinates:* 37° 27.439′ N, 80° 1.058′ W.

TRAIL DESCRIPTION

Whether you're speaking literally or figuratively, it's a hike to get up to Tinker Cliffs, but it is a hike worth tackling. As you make your way uphill to the first point in the state's Triple Crown (McAfee Knob [Trip 47] and Dragon's Tooth [Trip 48] are the other two), you can comfort yourself knowing that the return route is (mostly) downhill. From the parking area, look for the start of yellow-blazed Andy Layne Trail and start following it into the woods. For most of the hike, you'll be walking through land owned by the Roanoke Cement Company. Hikers must stay on the trail as they make their way up to Tinker Cliffs.

The trail passes through a stile at 0.6 mile and then in relatively quick succession goes over a bridge, passes a second stile, and then crosses a second bridge. Just past the second bridge, the trail seems to split, but both routes quickly meet again. Now the trail gets down to business and start to climb up the mountain.

At 1.1 mile, the route passes a metal gate on its climb, going uphill steeply, and then just slightly eases its grade at 2.1 miles as it begins a series of long switchbacks to Scorched Earth Gap. This col got its name thanks to the creative

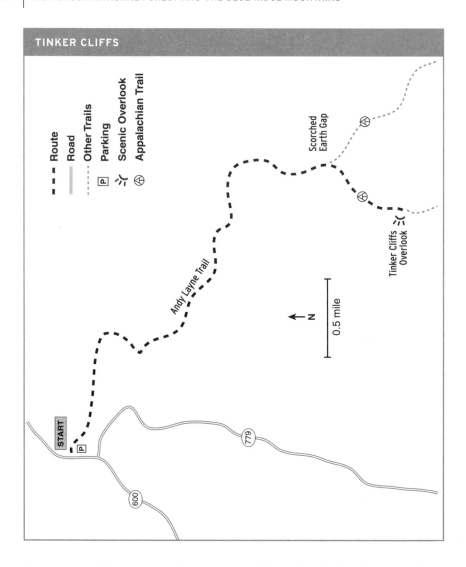

TINKER CLIFFS

Route

Road

Other Trails

P Parking

Scenic Overlook

Appalachian Trail

Scorched Earth Gap

Tinker Cliffs Overlook

Andy Layne Trail

N

0.5 mile

START

779

600

language used by a woman during a 1982 hike. It's said that the ground was "smoking" due to her string of epithets hurled at the hike leader, who took the group on a "bushwhack" down Tinker Mountain.

While the climb is steep, the trail is wide and well maintained thanks to the efforts of the Roanoke Appalachian Trail Club; however, watch for social trails that try to cut off the switchbacks. Keep following the main trail, and eventually arrive at Andy Layne Trail's intersection with the Appalachian Trail (AT) at 2.9 miles.

Turn right to start following the white-blazed AT as it continues to make its way farther up the mountain. The trail starts to switchback again, this time

Multiple overlooks dot Tinker Cliffs, giving you a chance to find your own viewing spot.

among large rock formations, which give you a taste of what you're about to see. Watch for some tricky turns as you navigate this last bit—just keep an eye out for the white blazes. Soon, the trail swings to the left and leads to the first of several overlooks from Tinker Cliffs. The rocks on which you stand are nearly 450 million years old. On a clear day, look to the south to see McAfee Knob. Below is Catawba Valley, and North Mountain is the next ridge.

After soaking in the views, retrace your steps along the AT to Andy Layne Trail and to your car.

DID YOU KNOW?

Scorched Earth Gap isn't the only creative name given to sights along this trail. The valley below Tinker Cliffs also contains the Murder Hole, a cave system that is one of the few in Virginia to have a sinkhole entrance. This entrance is known as Daylight Cave. From here, people can crawl into Fatman's Squeeze or Screw Hole to descend even farther into the cave system.

MORE INFORMATION

Jefferson National Forest, Eastern Divide Ranger District (www.fs.usda.gov/main/gwj; 540-552-4641). Check online for announcements concerning trail conditions, road closures, prescribed burns, and other events that may affect your hike.

NEARBY

Make a weekend of it by exploring the two other hikes that make up the famous Triple Crown: McAfee Knob (Trip 47) and Dragon's Tooth (Trip 48). For an extended day hike, you can continue past Tinker Cliffs to McAfee Knob, making it an epic outing. *AMC's Best Backpacking in the Mid-Atlantic* describes the Triple Crown in a single route. Drive north on I-81 to reach the other trips in this section.

Restaurants in the Roanoke area are well known to thru-hikers and connoisseurs alike. Just ask where you can find the fried chicken.

TRIP 47
MCAFEE KNOB

Location: Jefferson National Forest, VA
Rating: Moderate
Distance: 7.7 miles
Elevation Gain: 2,460 feet
Estimated Time: 3–4 hours
Maps: *Appalachian Trail Guide to Central Virginia* (Appalachian Trail Conservancy)

There's a good reason why this spot is famous: A pleasant hike coupled with a striking rock outcropping makes for a good day and good pictures. Plus, standing on McAfee Knob can make you feel like you are on top of the world!

DIRECTIONS
From I-81, Exit 141, take VA 419 north for 0.4 mile then turn right onto VA 311. Drive 5.6 miles and look for the McAfee parking lot on the left. *GPS coordinates: 37° 22.820′ N, 80° 5.414′ W.*

TRAIL DESCRIPTION
A steady uphill and one of the best views in the area make McAfee Knob one of the famous jewel in Virginia's Triple Crown (Tinker Cliffs [Trip 46] and Dragon's Tooth [Trip 48] are the other two). There's a reason why this spot is the most photographed site along the Appalachian Trail (AT): The dramatic rock outcropping cantilevers into the valley, allowing adventurous hikers to sit and feel like they are floating.

From the parking area, cross VA 311 and start heading up the white-blazed AT. The trail quickly climbs the ridge and arrives at an information kiosk. Continue along the AT, which continues to climb but at a mild pace. Eventually, the trail pulls farther away from VA 311, losing the sounds of traffic and gaining a peaceful atmosphere.

Go over the first of six bridges—the bridges are numbered, but note that there is no bridge #2 and the numbers jump from #1 to #3—and make your way along the trail, which dips down as it passes the Johns Spring Shelter at 1.0 mile. The trail climbs again, and continues to maintain a steady uphill grade—with

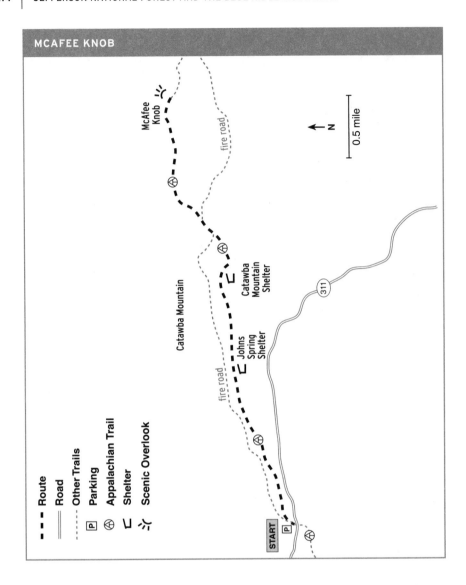

MCAFEE KNOB

Route

Road

Other Trails

Parking

Appalachian Trail

Shelter

Scenic Overlook

McAfee Knob

fire road

Catawba Mountain

Catawba Mountain Shelter

Johns Spring Shelter

fire road

START

311

N

0.5 mile

a few steep pitches—as it makes its way past the Catawba Mountain Shelter at 2.25 miles. The trail bears to the left after passing a large campsite.

Continue along the AT, which crosses over a fire road at 2.6 miles and then a power-line clearing at 3.1 miles. From here, the trail starts to get a little rockier and flattens out a bit as you near the top of the climb. The route swings to the left at 3.6 miles and brings you toward the intersection with McAfee Knob Spur Trail in another 0.3 miles. Incredible views are just a few steps away. To your right, McAfee Knob juts out into the valley. Brave hikers sit on the edge,

Many hikers have had their photograph taken in this very pose while sitting on McAfee Knob's famous outcropping. This picture was captured at dawn. (Photograph courtesy Karan [B.A.])

but be cautious if you do the same. From the Knob, an expansive view stretches to the Catawba Valley below and North Mountain beyond. Look for Tinker Cliffs (Trip 46) to the west.

It will be hard to tear yourself away from the views. If possible, try to time your hike for sunrise, when the light is at its best. But any time is a good time to hike to this famous panorama. When you're ready to resume your hike, simply retrace your steps back down the AT and to your vehicle.

DID YOU KNOW?

McAfee Knob is a milestone of sorts for thru-hikers. The northbounders emerge from the long green tunnel they've been in since Mount Rogers, and then hit Dragon's Tooth (Trip 48), first before making their way to the town of Catawba. Here they fuel up with a hearty meal, and start the climb to McAfee Knob. The area is packed with day-hikers, many of whom are curious about hiking the Appalachian Trail. Most hikers aim to get to McAfee Knob for sunrise or sunset, and one thru-hiker remembers seeing an amazing sunset that set the horizon on fire. From there, they head to Tinker Cliffs and then continue their journey north. This is just one of the many reasons why this area is known as the Triple Crown.

MORE INFORMATION

Jefferson National Forest, Eastern Divide Ranger District (www.fs.usda.gov/main/gwj; 540-552-4641). Check online for announcements concerning trail conditions, road closures, prescribed burns, and other events that may affect your hike.

NEARBY

Make a weekend of it by exploring the two other hikes that make up the famous Triple Crown—Tinker Cliffs (Trip 46) and Dragon's Tooth (Trip 48). For an extended day hike, you can continue past Tinker Cliffs to McAfee Knob, making it an epic outing. *AMC's Best Backpacking in the Mid-Atlantic* describes the Triple Crown in a single route. Drive north on I-81 to reach the other trips in this section.

Restaurants in the Roanoke area are well known to thru-hikers and connoisseurs alike. Just ask where you can find the fried chicken.

TRIP 48
DRAGON'S TOOTH

Location: Jefferson National Forest, VA
Rating: Moderate
Distance: 4.7 miles
Elevation Gain: 1,720 feet
Estimated Time: 3–4 hours
Maps: *Appalachian Trail Guide to Central Virginia* (Appalachian Trail Conservancy)

A rock scramble leads you to one of the more striking rock formations you'll see—jagged rocks that tower over the valley and provide good views from the base or the top.

DIRECTIONS
From I-81, Exit 141, take VA 419 north for 0.4 mile then turn right onto VA 311. Drive 9.5 miles to the trailhead on the right. *GPS coordinates:* 37° 22.739′ N, 80° 9.336′ W.

TRAIL DESCRIPTION
Dragon's Tooth makes up the final third of Virginia's Triple Crown (Tinker Cliffs [Trip 46] and MacAfee Knob [Trip 47] are the other two), and it is an adventure to get there. An easy walk through the woods yields to rock scrambling as you make your way up Cove Mountain; Dragon's Tooth, however, offers the route's most impressive sights.

From the parking area, head toward the information kiosk and start to follow blue-blazed Dragon's Tooth Trail. It's a relatively flat walk for the start of the hike. Cross two small footbridges, and in 0.3 mile arrive at the intersection with Boy Scout Connector Trail. Bear to the right to continue following blue blazes.

The trail—a wide and well maintained one—starts to make a steady climb uphill toward Lost Spectacles Gap. Arrive at the intersection with the Appalachian Trail (AT) at 1.6 miles, and make a right to continue heading toward Dragon's Tooth. From here, it is less than a mile to the top—but it gets a little interesting! The AT starts to get a bit rockier, climbing rock steps and making you do a bit of rock hopping. As you draw closer to the top, the rock hopping

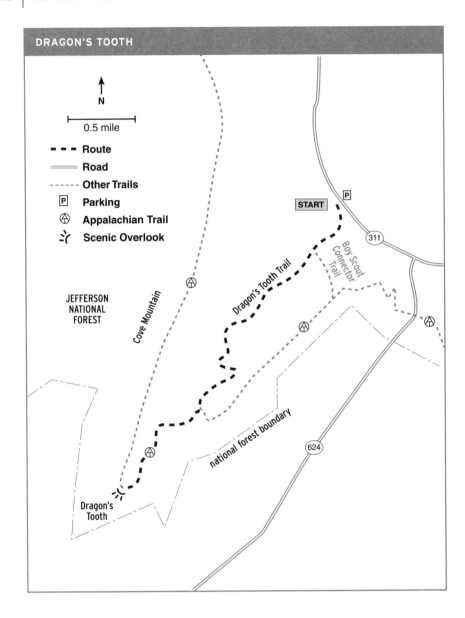

yields to more rock scrambling; stone steps help you climb up, and there are two sets of iron bar steps to give you a boost. For some hikers, these scrambles may seem daunting, but taking it slow and looking for obvious steps will help you advance. (These rocks, however, can be slippery when wet. Use extra caution.) Also, keep an eye on the blazing; at times, the trail can be a bit tricky to follow, but just look for the white blazes to make sure you stay on track.

Gaining the top at 2.3 miles also brings you to the intersection with blue-blazed Dragon's Tooth Trail. Turn left to follow this trail. Pass a few overlooks

Rock scramblers rejoice when seeing the dramatic Dragon's Tooth.

before arriving at the main attraction: Dragon's Tooth. Several rock spires (formed from Tuscarora quartzite) are clustered here, the tallest of which stands nearly 35 feet.

Good views of the surrounding valley can be found around the base of Dragon's Tooth. For the intrepid, it is possible to climb up the Tooth—just circle around the base and look for a crevice—but this is a tricky climb that requires a bit of confidence and skill.

After exploring the Tooth, retrace your steps back along the spur trail and follow the AT back down the rock scramble. For some, going down may be a little harder. Once again, take your times with the rocks, and arrive at the intersection with Dragon's Tooth Trail. Turn left to retrace your steps back along the blue-blazed trail to the parking lot.

DID YOU KNOW?

South of the Eastern Divide Ranger District and extending to the North Carolina border is the Mount Rogers National Recreation Area, also part of Jefferson National Forest. Though it's far south of the geographic boundaries of the Shenandoah Valley, it's a notable site for recreation in the larger Great Appalachian Valley, of which Shenandoah is one part.

The 200,000-acre parcel was designated by the Secretary of Agriculture in 1966 as a haven for recreation. Five hundred miles of hiking and multiuse trails crisscross the area, including sections of the Appalachian Trail, the Virginia Creeper Trail, and the Virginia Highland Horse Trail. Though the Mount Rogers National Recreation Area welcomes more than 1 million visitors every year, this outdoor playground has places that still feel wild: four designated Wilderness Areas are within its boundaries and the 5,000-acre Crest Zone offers rugged ascents of peaks stretching above 4,000 feet in elevation. Virginia's two highest peaks, Mount Rogers and Whitetop Mountain, are also here.

MORE INFORMATION

Jefferson National Forest, Eastern Divide Ranger District (www.fs.usda.gov/main/gwj, 540-552-4641). Check online for announcements concerning trail conditions, road closures, prescribed burns, and other events that may affect your hike.

NEARBY

Make a weekend of it by exploring the two other hikes that make up the famous Triple Crown—Tinker Cliffs (Trip 46) and MacAfee Knob (Trip 47). *AMC's Best Backpacking in the Mid-Atlantic* describes the Triple Crown in a single route. Drive north on I-81 to reach the other trips in this section.

Restaurants in the Roanoke area are well known to thru-hikers and connoisseurs alike. Just ask where you can find the fried chicken.

TRIP 49
DEVIL'S MARBLEYARD

Location: Glenwood & Pedlar Ranger Districts, George Washington and Jefferson National Forests, VA
Rating: Moderate
Distance: 3.2 miles round-trip
Elevation Gain: 1,073 feet
Estimated Time: 2–3 hours
Maps: *Trails Illustrated: Lexington/Blue Ridge Mountains, George Washington and Jefferson National Forests, Map 789* (National Geographic).

Very atypical for Virginia, these giant marble boulders look like they've been imported from the Andes or the Himalaya.

DIRECTIONS

From I-81, Exit 180A, take US 11 south for 2.3 miles. In Natural Bridge, Virginia, take a left (east) onto VA 689. In just over 1.0 mile, turn right onto VA 608 then take an immediate left onto VA 130. In 2.0 miles, turn right onto VA 759. Cross over the James River. On the south bank, pass the signs for Gunter Ridge and other Jefferson National Forest attractions. After 3.1 miles, take a left onto VA 781/Petites Gap Road. You'll reach the parking lot for Belfast Trail about 1.2 miles later on the left. The parking lot is rather small, and there are a few pull-out spots nearby, but be sure to get your vehicle's tires off the road, as there have been reports of poorly parked vehicles being towed. *GPS coordinates:* 37° 34.270′ N, 79° 29.501′ W.

TRAIL DESCRIPTION

You'll hardly believe your eyes as you emerge from the forest to scramble up this gigantic boulder field, filled with marble rocks sometimes as large as cars or buses.

From the parking lot, cross a bridge over Belfast Creek to begin hiking in on blue-blazed Belfast Trail. Initially, the trail is wide, flat, and sandy. Pass by the stone foundations and ruins of an old summer camp, intersect and cross over Glenwood Horse Trail, cross a creek or two, and then intersect once again with the horse trail at 0.2 mile.

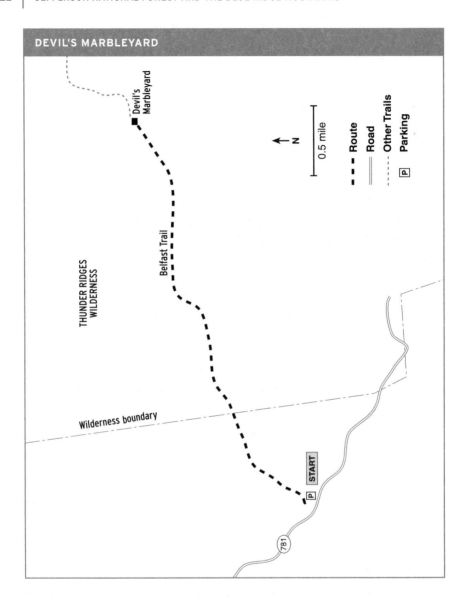

DEVIL'S MARBLEYARD

Here, Belfast Trail turns right and begins climbing more steeply and rug-gedly as it follows the creek up the valley, giving you occasion to rock-hop across the creek a few more times. The trail bends right and begins tackling a longer, steep grade. Between the trees around 1.4 miles, you should be able to glimpse the boulder field. The trail runs along the right edge of the field, climbing steeply (and sometimes wetly) on rugged trail. There are many access points from which you can reach the boulder field all along its length. Do so, and scramble to your heart's content, but be careful: As you will no doubt

The scramble up this boulder field is an epic and invigorating undertaking.

quickly recognize, the marbleyard is a place where injuries can definitely occur. Be sure of your footing and take your time.

If you time it right, visiting the marbleyard at sunset can be a spectacular sight, as the boulder field has plenty of western exposure and the marble takes on a brilliant glow in the setting sun.

Once you've had your fill of scrambling, descend the way you came via Belfast Trail to your waiting vehicle.

DID YOU KNOW?

The Devil's Marbleyard is a striking feature that is perfectly visible in satellite images. How did it form? Long ago—hundreds of millions of years—the Marbleyard was once a white-sand beach infested with worms that burrowed through the sand. If you look closely, you can still see striations in the rock that are the remnants of these tracks. Over time, the sand was buried and compressed into rock, which lay hidden for millennia. When the rock was then exposed, ice did the work of breaking the surface into the boulder field we see today.

MORE INFORMATION

George Washington and Jefferson National Forests, Glenwood & Pedlar Ranger Districts (www.fs.usda.gov/main/gwj; 540-291-2188). Check online for announcements concerning trail conditions, road closures, prescribed burns, and other events that may affect your hike.

NEARBY

If you're looking for a longer and more ambitious hike centered on the Devil's Marbleyard, consider climbing past the marbleyard. Just shy of the Appalachian Trail, Belfast Trail encounters a three-way intersection. By turning left, you can descend via Gunter Ridge Trail and return to your vehicles by Glenwood Horse Trail. Definitely do bring your map along and do consider this variation a challenging one, as the loop will total around 10–11 miles.

If you've thoroughly explored the Devil's Marbleyard, consider driving a little farther south to hike Apple Orchard Falls (Trip 43). The Cold Mountain and Mount Pleasant trips (Trip 44 and Trip 45) are also nearby, as is the cluster of hikes near Roanoke (Trips 46–48).

To the north, Lexington offers the best nearby choice of local businesses, while Roanoke is your best bet to the south.

TRIP 50
THREE RIDGES

Location: Glenwood & Pedlar Ranger Districts, George Washington and Jefferson National Forests, VA
Rating: Strenuous
Distance: 13.2 miles
Elevation Gain: 4,914 feet
Estimated Time: 6–7 hours
Maps: *Trails Illustrated: Lexington/Blue Ridge Mountains, George Washington and Jefferson National Forests, Map 789* (National Geographic)

Climb—and then climb some more—for this epic hike filled with great views and even some waterfalls.

DIRECTIONS
From I-81/I-64, Exit 205, take VA 606 east toward Raphine for 1.5 miles. Turn left onto US 11 N/North Lee Highway, and then make a quick right onto VA 56 E/Tye River Turnpike. Follow VA 56 east for 16.6 miles, and look for the parking lot on the right. *GPS coordinates: 37° 50.297′ N, 79° 1.392′ W.*

TRAIL DESCRIPTION
Make no mistake. This hike is one of the more challenging routes in the area, starting off with a 5.3-mile climb. However, it rewards those who persevere with vista after vista.

Starting from the parking lot, cross VA 56 and look for the white blaze that marks the Appalachian Trail (AT). For most of the day, you will be following those white blazes. Follow the trail over a suspension bridge that spans the River Tye. After crossing the bridge, get ready to start climbing.

The trail meanders up through the trees and eventually leads to an intersection with Mau-Har Trail at 1.9 miles. Continue straight to follow the AT as it gives you a slight respite from climbing and dips down around the mountain. Cross a small stream, and keep an eye on the white blazes. Through the trees, the Harpers Creek Shelter emerges, and side trails lead off to various campsites. Keep following the white blazes, and arrive at an intersection with a spur trail to the shelter. Turn right to continue on the AT.

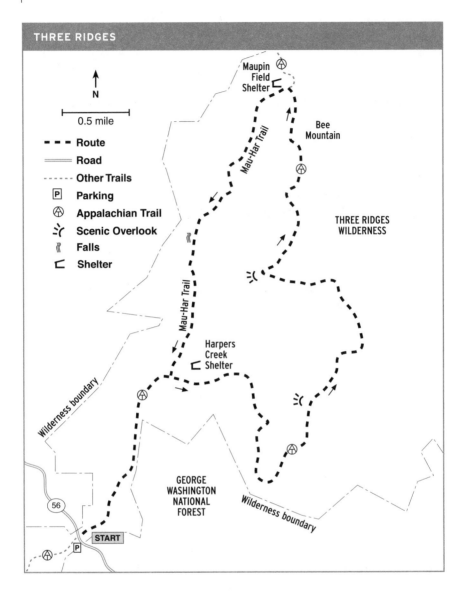

The AT continues its climb up the mountain, which is somewhat steep at times. Overall, the path is well blazed and obvious, but some turns are tight as the trail switchbacks up the mountain, and a few may give you cause to take a quick pause. Just keep an eye on the white blazes and continue up the trail. Roughly 3.5 miles into the hike, views of the valley start to come into sight, giving welcome spots for a break. As the trail progresses up the mountain, more views pop into sight, and at 4.2 miles Chimney Rock prompts a quick rock scramble to spy even better views.

A hiker makes his way along one of the easier stretches of this trail.

Still, the trail continues to climb, finally reaching its peak—and accompanying view—5.3 miles into the hike. The next 3.3 miles are gentler, passing one more great view at 6.2 miles and making one last mild climb over Bee Mountain. At 8.6 miles, the trail arrives at the Maupin Field Shelter; look for an information board and wooden post marking a left turn off the AT to the shelter itself. To the left of the shelter is a sign marking blue-blazed Mau-Har Trail, your return route.

At first, Mau-Har Trail leads with a gentle descent through the trees. A few stream crossings require some quick rock hopping, and the trail becomes rocky and starts to descend more steeply. The path follows the left bank of Campbell Creek; when flowing well, the creek has some enjoyable waterworks to admire. The trail gets rockier, with some large boulders to navigate. Keep an eye out for a tricky turn; the trail seems to go right at one point but actually continues over the rocks. A partially hidden blue blaze to the left signals that you are on the correct path.

All the rock hopping leads to another treat: At 9.6 miles, a short spur trail to the right (sign: "Waterfalls") leads to a small campsite, a swimming hole, and some cascades.

After the waterfalls, the trail becomes less rocky but leads to one last climb for the day. The trail levels out and then starts a gentle downhill before arriving at another intersection with the AT at 11.3 miles; you passed this point earlier in the day. Turn right onto the AT and retrace your steps back downhill to your car.

DID YOU KNOW?

"Blue blazing" is the term that AT thru-hikers use for opting to take some of the side trails (typically marked with blue blazes, like Mau-Har Trail), rather than staying on the white-blazed route for the entire journey.

MORE INFORMATION

George Washington and Jefferson National Forests, Glenwood & Pedlar Ranger Districts (www.fs.usda.gov/main/gwj; 540-291-2188). Check online for announcements concerning trail conditions, road closures, prescribed burns, and other events that may affect your hike.

NEARBY

This hike serves as an excellent base to explore the area. If you're looking for an easier day, head to Spy Rock (Trip 39) or check out the famous Crabtree Falls (Trip 40).

The town of Roseland has food if you're looking for a meal in the Blue Ridge area.

APPENDIX: INFORMATION AND RESOURCES

Bull Run Mountains Conservancy
17405 Beverley Mill Drive
P.O. Box 210
Broad Run, VA 20137
703-753-2631
info@brmconservancy.org
brmconservancy.org

Harpers Ferry National Historical Park
171 Shoreline Drive
P.O. Box 65
Harpers Ferry, WV 25425
304-535-6029
nps.gov/hafe

George Washington and Jefferson National Forests
5162 Valleypointe Parkway
Roanoke, VA 24019
888-265-0019 (toll free); 540-265-5100
www.fs.usda.gov/gwj/

Eastern Divide Ranger District
Counties: Bland, Botetourt, Craig, Giles, Monroe (WV), Montgomery, Pulaski, Roanoke, Smyth, Tazewell, and Wythe
110 Southpark Drive
Blacksburg, VA 24060
540-552-4641

Glenwood & Pedlar Ranger Districts
Counties: Amherst, Augusta, Bedford, Botetourt, Nelson, and Rockbridge
27 Ranger Lane
Natural Bridge Station, VA 24579
540-291-2188

Lee Ranger District
Counties: Frederick, Hampshire (WV), Hardy (WV), Page, Rockingham, Shenandoah, and Warren
95 Railroad Avenue
Edinburg, VA 22824
540-984-4101

North River Ranger District
Counties: Augusta, Highland, Pendleton (WV), and Rockingham
401 Oakwood Drive
Harrisonburg, VA 22801
866-904-0240 (toll free); 540-432-0187 (local)

Peaks of Otter Recreation Area
Blue Ridge Parkway Headquarters
Milepost 384, Ashville NC
199 Hemphill Knob Road
Asheville, NC 28803-8686
828-271-4779 (headquarters); 828-298-0398 (information)
nps.gov/blri

Peaks of Otter Visitor Center
Blue Ridge Parkway Milepost 85.9

Shenandoah National Park
3655 Highway 211 East
Luray, VA 22835
540-999-3500 (information); 800-732-0911 (emergency); 877-444-6777 (campground reservations)
nps.gov/shen; recreation.gov (campground reservations)

Shenandoah River State Park
350 Daughter of Stars Drive
Bentonville, VA 22610
540-622-6840; 800-933-7275 (reservations)
shenandoahriver@dcr.virginia.gov
www.dcr.virginia.gov/state-parks/shenandoah-river.shtml;
reserveamerica.com (reservations)

Sky Meadows State Park
11012 Edmonds Lane
Delaplane, VA 20144
540-592-3556; 800-933-7275 (reservations)
skymeadows@dcr.virginia.gov
www.dcr.virginia.gov/state-parks/sky-meadows.shtml;
reserveamerica.com (reservations)

OTHER RESOURCES

AMC Washington, D.C., Chapter
AMCDC@amc-dc.org
amc-dc.org

Appalachian Trail Conservancy, Mid-Atlantic Regional Office
4 East First Street
Boiling Springs, PA 17007
717-258-5771; 888-287-8673 (store)
atc-maro@appalachiantrail.org;
incident@appalachiantrail.org (incident report)
appalachiantrail.org; atctrailstore.org

Potomac Appalachian Trail Club
118 Park Street, S.E.
Vienna, VA 22180-4609
703-242-0315
patc.net

INDEX

ABOUT THE AUTHORS

JENNIFER ADACH'S first camping trip was in 2004, and she was quickly bitten by the bug to get outdoors and to hike as much and as far as she could. Over the years, she's become an accomplished hiker and backpacker, and is now one of the co-organizers of the DC UL Backpacking group. She has thru-hiked Sweden's Kungsleden trail and the John Muir Trail, and has logged several thousand miles on trails throughout the Mid-Atlantic area. At home, she's addicted to testing out new recipes and reading the latest in nonfiction. Jennifer grew up on Long Island, and now resides in Old Town Alexandria.

MICHAEL R. MARTIN is a lifelong backpacker and outdoorsman. He grew up on the trails in Texas, Arkansas, New Mexico, and Colorado, and points farther west; more recently, he has piled on several thousand miles (and a few hundred nights) in the Mid-Atlantic. His more exotic trips have taken him to Sweden, France, Nepal, Peru, and Iceland, where he completed a north-south crossing of the island—his most ambitious trip to date. Author of *AMC's Best Backpacking in the Mid-Atlantic*, he also leads, organizes, and teaches for the DC UL Backpacking group. When he's not on the trail, or plotting new ways to sneak away and get on the trail, he's often writing, learning how to make his camera work, or trying to limber up his rusty video-gaming skills. His more permanent dwelling is Old Town Alexandria.

BE OUTDOORS

Since 1876, the Appalachian Mountain Club has channeled your enthusiasm for the outdoors into everything we do and everywhere we work to protect. We're inspired by people exploring the natural world and deepening their appreciation of it.

With AMC chapters from Maine to Washington, D.C., including groups in Boston, New York City, and Philadelphia, you can enjoy activities like hiking, paddling, cycling, and skiing, and learn new outdoor skills. We offer advice, guidebooks, maps, and unique eco-lodges and huts to inspire your next outing.

Your visits, purchases, and donations also support conservation advocacy and research, youth programming, and caring for more than 1,800 miles of trails.

Join us!
outdoors.org/join

ABOUT AMC IN THE MID-ATLANTIC

EACH YEAR, THE APPALACHIAN MOUNTAIN CLUB'S WASHINGTON, D.C., Delaware Valley, New York-North Jersey, and Mohawk Hudson chapters offer thousands of outdoor activities including hiking, backpacking, bicycling, paddling, and climbing trips, as well as social, family, and young member programs. Members also maintain local trails, lead outdoor skills workshops, and promote stewardship of the region's natural resources. AMC manages Mohican Outdoor Center in the Delaware Water Gap National Recreation Area, a four season, self-service destination for hiking, paddling, skiing, snowshoeing and camping, a short distance from the Appalachian Trail in New Jersey.

AMC is a leader of the Highlands Coalition, which works to secure funding for land conservation funding in the four-state Highlands region of Connecticut, New York, New Jersey, and Pennsylvania. AMC also monitors energy development proposals across that impact public lands. It is leading the effort to establish the 100-mile Pennsylvania Highlands Trail Network. AMC staff and volunteers maintain 1,800 miles of trails throughout the Northeastern and Mid-Atlantic states, including portions of the Appalachian Trail in Pennsylvania, Connecticut, Massachusetts, New Hampshire, and Maine.

To learn more about AMC's work in the Mid-Atlantic, visit outdoors.org.

AMC BOOK UPDATES

AT AMC BOOKS, WE KEEP OUR GUIDEBOOKS AS UP-TO-DATE as possible to help you plan safe and enjoyable adventures. After publishing a book, if we learn that trails have been relocated, or that route or contact information has changed, we will post an update online. Before you hit the trail, check outdoors.org/bookupdates.

While hiking, if you notice discrepancies with the trip description or map, or if you find any other errors in the book, please submit them by email to amcbookupdates@outdoors.org or by letter to Books Editor, c/o AMC, 10 City Square, Boston, MA 02129. We will verify all submissions and post key updates each month. We are dedicated to making AMC Books a recognized leader in outdoor publishing. Thank you for your participation.

AMC's Best Day Hikes near Washington, D.C., 2nd Edition

Beth Homicz and Annie Eddy

Discover 50 of the best hikes that can be completed in less than a day in and around the nation's capital, including Maryland and Virginia—from wilderness experiences to close-to-home immersions in nature, with an increased focus on Annapolis and Baltimore.

$18.95 • 978-1-62842-037-1

Quiet Water Mid-Atlantic

Rachel Cooper

Discover 60 spectacular trips on 64 of the best flatwater ponds, lakes, and rivers for paddlers of all skill levels in New Jersey, eastern Pennsylvania, Delaware, Maryland, Virginia, and Washington, D.C. This title—brand new to the trusted Quiet Water series—features an at-a-glance trip planner, driving directions and GPS coordinates for parking, and turn-by-turn descriptions of the trip routes, with maps included.

$19.95 • 978-1-62842-087-6

AMC's Mountain Skills Manual

Christian Bisson and Jamie Hannon

This comprehensive guide tackles the essential skills every outdoor lover should master. Beginners will learn the basics, covering gear, navigation, safety, and stewardship. More experienced readers can hone backpacking skills, including trip planning, efficient packing, and advanced wilderness ethics. All readers will set new goals, perfect their pace, and gain the tools to plan and enjoy their next outdoor adventure.

$21.95 • 978-1-62842-025-8

Blazing Ahead

Jeffrey H. Ryan

The Appalachian Trail is one of America's most revered resources, but few know the story behind its creation. The proposal could have died in the pages of a journal had it not been for Benton MacKaye and Myron Avery. *Blazing Ahead* tells the true but little-known story of a shared vision, the rivalry it bred, and the legacy of the trailblazers behind one of the nation's greatest treasures.

$18.95 • 978-1-62842-063-0

Find these and other AMC titles, in print and e-book formats, available from booksellers, outdoor retailers, or directly from AMC at **outdoors.org/amcstore** or **800-262-4455.**